Textual Construction of the Female Body

A Critical Discourse Approach

Lesley Jeffries

© Lesley Jeffries 2007

First published 2007 by
PALGRAVE MACMILLAN
Houndmills, Basingstoke, Hampshire RG21 6XS and
175 Fifth Avenue, New York, N.Y. 10010
Companies and representatives throughout the world

PALGRAVE MACMILLAN is the global academic imprint of the Palgrave
Macmillan division of St. Martin's Press, LLC and of Palgrave Macmillan Ltd.
Macmillan® is a registered trademark in the United States, United Kingdom
and other countries. Palgrave is a registered trademark in the European
Union and other countries.

ISBN-13: 978–0–333–91451–9
ISBN-10: 0–333–91451–1

This book is printed on paper suitable for recycling and made from fully
managed and sustained forest sources. Logging, pulping and manufacturing
processes are expected to conform to the environmental regulations of the
country of origin.

A catalogue record for this book is available from the British Library.

A catalog record for this book is available from the Library of Congress.

10 9 8 7 6 5 4 3 2 1
16 15 14 13 12 11 10 09 08 07

Printed and bound in Great Britain by
Antony Rowe Ltd, Chippenham and Eastbourne

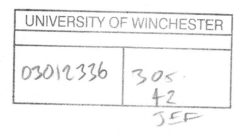

Contents

Acknowledgements

I would like to thank my colleagues, students, friends and family who have had to put up with this book for more years than is fair. Like them, I had intermittent doubts about it ever being finished, and I am very grateful that they helped me to continue to believe in it. I would like to thank Dan McIntyre particularly for reading the script at a late stage and improving it enormously, despite his misgivings about the subject-matter! The remaining problems are, of course, my responsibility. I am also grateful to the University of Huddersfield for a period of sabbatical leave when most of the research for this book was carried out, as well as a more recent period of leave when the writing finally got done.

Thanks also to the team at Palgrave Macmillan, which was still just called Macmillan when this project started out, and to the series of editors who have passed the baton one to another, and who continued to support this project when they really wanted me to write textbooks. My current editor, Jill Lake, is especially to be thanked for her support.

Finally, may I thank my immediate family for their patience and support. Dave, Sam and Ella have put up with the usual consequences of a family member finishing a book, and they have been great.

LESLEY JEFFRIES

Preface: Code and Body – an Intervention

This book deals with two issues that are very important to me; the question of how women live their lives physically, and the way in which language both constrains us and enables us to live fuller lives. As a preamble to the main business of the book, I would like to draw these two strands together in an exercise inspired by Rob Pope's intervention techniques (Pope 1995) in which the re-writing of an extract from a feminist theory text about the body explores the similarities between the lived and constructed body on the one hand, and the material or experienced language and its core system on the other.

The extract is taken from J. Butler's *Bodies that Matter* (1993) as reprinted in Price and Shildrick (1994: 240):

Certain formulations of the radical constructivist position appear almost compulsively to produce a moment of recurrent exasperation, for it seems that when the constructivist is construed as a linguistic idealist, the constructivist refutes the reality of bodies, the relevance of science, the alleged facts of birth, aging, illness, and death. The critic might also suspect the constructivist of a certain somatophobia and seek assurances that this abstracted theorist will admit that there are, minimally, sexually differentiated parts, activities, capacities, hormonal and chromosomal differences that can be conceded without reference to 'construction'. Although at this moment I want to offer an absolute reassurance to my interlocutor, some anxiety prevails. To 'concede' the undeniability of 'sex' or its 'materiality' is always to concede some version of 'sex', some formation of 'materiality'. Is the discourse in and through which that concession occurs – and yes, that concession invariably does occur – not itself formative of the very phenomenon that it concedes? To claim that discourse is formative is not to claim that it originates, causes, or exhaustively composes that which it concedes; rather, it is to claim that there is no reference to a pure body which is not at the same time a further formation of that body. In this sense, the linguistic capacity to refer to sexed bodies is not denied, but the very meaning of 'referentiality' is altered. In philosophical terms, the constative claim is always to some degree performative.

The following is an intervention in the above passage, with the radical constructivist's role being given to the integrationist linguist, for whom there is no linguistic meaning without context and with the role of the body being taken by language:

> Certain formulations of the radical integrationist position appear almost compulsively to produce a moment of recurrent exasperation, for it seems that when the integrationist is construed as a linguistic idealist, the integrationist refutes the reality of language, the relevance of linguistic description, the alleged facts of word classes, morphology, syntax and semantics. The critic might also suspect the integrationist of a certain code-phobia and seek assurances that this abstracted theorist will admit that there are, minimally, linguistically differentiated categories, processes, meanings that can be conceded without reference to 'construction'. Although at this moment I want to offer an absolute reassurance to my interlocutor, some anxiety prevails. To 'concede' the undeniability of 'code' or its description is always to concede some version of the 'code', some version of its description. Is the discourse in and through which that concession occurs – and yes, that concession does invariably occur – not itself formative of the very phenomenon that it concedes? To claim that discourse is formative is not to claim that it originates, causes, or exhaustively composes that which it concedes; rather it is to claim that there is no reference to a pure code which is not at the same time a further formation of that code. In this sense, the linguistic capacity to refer to structures and categories of language is not denied, but the very meaning of 'referentiality' is altered. In philosophical terms, the constative claim is always to some degree performative.

What this passage achieves in relation to both the perceptions of the female body and theories of language, is to argue that the continuous construction and reinforcement of perceptions of both gender and language do not mean that there is no such thing as either gender or language, except in context. Thus, the reality of the lived female experience in a female body may only be perceived through social constructions, but it is nevertheless real. Likewise with language, there is a core of what is recognizably linguistic which is only accessible through our everyday experience of it, but is nonetheless relatively stable and can be described separately from its context.

We may accept the material nature of the body much more readily than that of language, but we can see a kind of linguistic code as being equivalent to the body, rather than the acoustic or graphic properties of language practice although the very tangibility or concreteness of language might incline us to accept its materiality in the other sense. However, I would argue that Western culture is just as wedded to the 'existence' of something we call language as to the existence and separateness of our bodies.

In both cases, theorists have been labouring for a while now to demonstrate that what we understand by 'the body' or 'the language' is very largely dictated by norms and conventions that belong not to the nature of the body/language itself, but to the context in which they find themselves. Feminist theory has moved away from seeing the mind and body as distinct and separable, with feminist aims being to rise above the corporeal, through the revalidating of the female form where the body was a kind of 'given', to the current position where the essential fluidity and constructed nature of the body allows the mind–body union to have a range of different relationships depending on context. Judith Butler's view in the extract above is that this perception of the interdependency of mind (that is, cultural and personal constructions) and body (including the materiality of sex) does not deny the existence of the body itself, but constantly reviews and revises the ways in which the idea of the body can be accessed, without any possibility of accessing 'directly' the thing itself, independently of discourse.

As for the codedness of language, linguists have been moving inexorably away from Saussurean notions of code ever since his ideas were so widely taken up in the early part of the twentieth century. The reasons for this are clear: every time a linguist comes up with a 'rule' – even the variable rules that sociolinguistics came up with in the 1970s and 1980s – there is someone waiting to show that this rule is not watertight. On the one hand, this process means that many inventive and insightful models have developed in response to the challenges of exceptions to proposed rules. On the other hand, there has been a growing awareness that there is much in the everyday use of language that depends not on some definitive system, but on the fluidities and leakages of context.

I use the words *fluidity* and *leakages* deliberately here, because the female form, which has given so much trouble to patriarchy over the last century, has often been seen as troublesome precisely because of its untidy boundaries, its ability to grow another form within it, the processes of menstruation and lactation that link the inner body to the outside world.

The problems associated with the code, I would argue, are closely analogous to those of the female form. Whilst it would be neat and controllable to have a finite code that defined the language human beings use, it is neither the situation we find ourselves in, nor a seriously desirable situation. Just as the 'leakages' of the female form are often associated both with literal creativity (motherhood) and metaphorical creativity (art), so the creativities of language (whether artistic, political or social) are dependent on the essential existence of the code and at the same time could not exist without the contextual flexibility of the code. And in both cases, I would argue, to lose the essential – the body of the mother or the coded core of language – would be to lose the whole. To repeat myself (and Butler) somewhat, the recognition of these existences is not direct or unmediated. It can only happen through discourse, which may be theorized discourse in an academic context, but may just as well be everyday discourse too.

Where does that leave the feminist/linguist who wishes to describe what she sees around her? I think it leaves her using the tools available to her, from theories that seem to her to model best the fluctuating body/mind complex or code/contextual meaning complex. It leaves the human being who has a female form dealing on an everyday basis with the realities of that body and the speaker/hearer of a language likewise dealing with the language and needing enough commonality of understanding (that is, code) for her to climb out of the purely contextual and start to make contact with other users. Theorists, surely, have to start from these positions too?

That is not to say that description is all there is to do. Feminists assess the current state of the female body in order to improve the position of women. Linguists ought to (and some do) work towards a better understanding of how human beings communicate in order to improve communication.

LESLEY JEFFRIES

1
Studying the Language of the Female Body: Some Context

Theories and practices

What the reader will find in this book is a critical study of the language of texts taken from women's magazines in 2000. These texts are all in some direct way connected with the female body, and include texts concerning everything from fashion to plastic surgery, but exclude articles on furniture, holiday destinations and other similar texts not referring to the body. Later in the chapter we will see how the data were chosen, but here it is important to emphasize that the motivation for choosing these data was to try and avoid the 'trap' of choosing an easy target, such as pornographic texts or tabloid newspaper representations of women, which are known to continue certain representational practices that demean women and treat them as sexual and/or domestic objects (see Lanis 1995).

This study, then, had as its hypothesis the idea that although things have changed greatly since I was a small girl in the 1950s and 1960s, nevertheless, the magazines which many (most?) girls and women read at formative points in their lives may still influence the reader's perception of her body. Though the hypothesis was that some of this potential influence would still reflect patriarchal and thus, from a feminist standpoint, unacceptable, images of women's bodies, I had no specific ideas about how such ideologies would be embedded linguistically, or indeed precisely what they would turn out to be.

The impetus behind this research came from two directions. One was the desire to investigate how far feminist movements had succeeded in influencing the public construction of the female form, potentially giving women a less patriarchal view of their bodies. The other was the wish to try out and develop the methods and ideas of Critical Discourse

Analysis on a larger body of data than has recently been attempted by a qualitative study.[1] The two sets of theories, which are complementary, will be discussed in this chapter and in the conclusion, though the main business of the book is to engage with a fairly large amount of data and try to answer some basic questions about the nature of the representation of women's bodies in the early twenty-first century.

Most of the book, then, is taken up with analysis of data and interpretation of these results. These activities in themselves are not, of course, irrelevant to the development and understanding of theories of language and identity, and such impacts will be discussed as they occur. More important here, though, is to see firstly what happens when we try to apply Critical Discourse Analysis in a systematic way to a large body of texts and, secondly, what representations of the female body were being put forward in mainstream women's and girls' magazines at this time.

Critical discourse analysis

Critical Discourse Analysis (labelled CDA from here on) has been around for a number of years now, and like any long-lived practice, it has spawned a great many offshoots, both in terms of the theoretical background it draws on and in terms of the textual analysis that is considered to be central to its practice. A recent survey of CDA work (Wodak 2002: 3) summarizes this eclecticism of methodology:

> Small qualitative case studies can be found as well as large data corpora, drawn from fieldwork and ethnographic research.

Wodak also emphasizes the theoretical and descriptive range of CDA, but stresses that 'three concepts figure indispensably in all CDA: the concept of power, the concept of history and the concept of ideology' (Wodak 2002: 3). The way in which these three concepts relate to the current work are as follows. The research reported on here takes as its premise that women and girls who read mainstream magazines are at least potentially vulnerable to influence from the representations they find there. This is because the ubiquity of these mass media and the repetitive messages that they disseminate may be read as the ideology of those who have the power to decide what is fashionable, acceptable, normal, ideal and so on. The individual reader may, indeed, be capable of resisting, to some extent, these messages, but it should not be assumed that readers are necessarily able to be fully and consistently resistant, or that they want to be. In many cases, I would argue that readers are likely to be reading from multiple viewpoints at any one time (Jeffries

2001) and thus may be both vulnerable to and also resistant to the ideologies embodied in the texts they encounter. This approach, though deriving from CDA, reflects feminist views about the constructed nature and performativity of gender:

> Influenced by Foucault, Judith Butler asserts that discourse is constitutive of the phenomena that it regulates and constrains (1993: 2). Her theories elaborate Sedgwick's notion of performativity and the idea that identities do not pre-exist but are performed in a highly regulated fashion. In fact identities are constructed iteratively through what are deemed to be processes of citation – a literal copying of the performances of others with the same identity. Rather as a judge cites case law to enforce his power, a citational performance of gender asserts the authority of this text as legitimate. (Butler 1993: 225)
>
> (Morrish 2002: 178)

The role of magazines, then, as we will see in the analysis in this book, is to provide women and girls with just the exemplars they need to cite in their own lived experiences.

As for history, the work represented here is contextualized in two ways. Firstly, it considers the representation of the female body at the turn of the millennium and in what is sometimes called a 'postfeminist' Western cultural context (see Terry and Schiappa 1999). The consideration of what effect the various forms of feminism have had on these representations is probably outside the scope of this study, though I hope that the findings reported here will contribute to that debate. Secondly, this study also occurs at a point in the development of CDA when the considerations of mediation (see Jäger 2002) and contextual definition (see van Dijk 2002) have all but erased the detailed text analytical origins of the discipline, and it proposes a particular kind of return to analysis, drawing upon the traditions of CDA, but, I hope, enhancing some of its methodological features so that others may take up and develop them

Finally, the relation of this work to ideology is probably already quite clear and reflects Fairclough's view that one of the inequities of power is reflected in an 'unequal capacity to control how texts are produced, distributed and consumed ... in particular sociocultural contexts' (Fairclough 1995: 1). We will assume, in general terms, that the reader of women's magazines will 'normally' be women themselves. The cultural imperative for women to look good remains strong and readers will therefore often be in a relatively weak position in relation to the producers of the various ideologically-laden messages about the female body, since they offer advice about the best way to improve looks and attractiveness. Such ideologies may not be homogenous, and they may not all be obviously patriarchal, but they are clearly handed down by a powerful media and, being naturalized, some of them are very difficult or even impossible to conceive of as anything other than absolute. Some such ideologies, which seem even to this researcher to be perfectly natural and good, will be investigated in later chapters.

Widdowson (1996, 1998) and Toolan (1997) have been among the people who have attacked CDA both for its theoretical and its methodological flaws. The fact that the previous sentence contains a presupposition embedded in the nominal group ('its theoretical and its methodological flaws') may alert the critical reader to the fact that I would tend to agree with this criticism. There are indeed problems with CDA, and yet I cannot bring myself to throw out the baby with the bathwater,[2] since I think that the insights which CDA brings to text analysis have helped many of us clarify the model of language that we wish to work with, and the methods that we may use.

Let us consider, first of all, the theoretical problems that CDA's critics have raised. I will use Widdowson's (1998) review article as the focal point of this discussion, because he summarises many of the important issues there. In this article, Widdowson criticizes the theory of CDA as being:

> the reaffirmation of the familiar Whorfian notion of linguistic determinism, but applied not only to cognition in respect of the language code, but in respect to its use in communication as well. (Widdowson 1998: 139)

Though he doesn't say so explicitly, Widdowson implies that a strongly Whorfian take on the relationship between language and social cognition is now unacceptable (cf. the negative connotations of 'determinism'). And he goes on to suggest that CDA proponents have extended this view beyond the 'code' to include the use of language too – both langue *and* parole in Saussurean terms. There is an implicature[3] here, for me anyway, that if it is ridiculous to suggest that the code is conceptually dominant, it's even crazier to suggest that the practice of language use, which by definition freely shrugs off the rigours of the code, could also be part of the conspiracy to trap speakers into certain ways of thinking.

Whilst the strong version of Whorf is not accepted by many linguists these days, there is also no appetite for rejecting it altogether. It is generally accepted that language can – and does – have some effect on the perceptions of the speakers of that language, both through the systematic aspects of the langue and also through parole:

> The range of materials relevant to providing an adequate theoretical account of linguistic relativity is daunting. An account has to deal with both the underlying processes upon which all language and thought relations are necessarily built and with the shaping role of discourse as it is implemented in social institutions and cultural traditions. (Lucy 1997: 308)

Lucy surveys the research into linguistic relativity and concludes that more, and particularly more empirical work needs to be done. What he does not do is to contest the notion that there is some influence from language to thought, though the nature of this relationship is still not fully understood. The assumption in the current work is that the everyday repetition of ideology in discourse is indeed likely to have an effect on the perceptions of women in relation to their bodies. The question remains to what extent, under what conditions and how do the answers to those questions affect our understanding of, and theoretical model for, language.[4]

Widdowson summarizes the theory of language espoused by Kress as:

> The theory of language suggested here, then, is a theory of semiotic change in language as brought about by its use. (Widdowson 1998: 138)

He then goes on to criticize Kress for failing to demonstrate *how* such change takes place. But he doesn't mention that there are enormous difficulties in such a demonstration; that CDA, like any scientific practice, will need to take some theoretical premises for granted; and that there is a place in the process for textual analysis which will reveal a range of more-or-less 'hidden' and more-or-less politically motivated ideologies in texts or bodies of texts.

If Widdowson is overreliant on a distinction between langue and parole, then Toolan (1996) goes too far the other way, it seems to me, in rejecting the notion of code entirely. As one of a group of people calling themselves 'integrationalists', who suggest that *all* meaning is *only* contextual, he puts forward a criticism of code-based models of language by describing the position of Lyons, who Toolan quotes as arguing that:

> despite their undoubted importance, a full account of these contextual features is impossible in practice, 'and perhaps also in principle', and [he] notes that such considerations cast doubt on the possibility of ever being able to construct a complete theory of the meaning of utterances. (Toolan 1996: 6)

I have argued elsewhere (Jeffries 2000) that Lyons is right to take this view, and

> that if we try in any one model to take into account the full complexity of the communicative situation, we will fail to adequately explain anything. This does not mean that models should not focus on different aspects of the context as well as the text, as indeed they do, but that it is often counter-productive, and anyway theoretically nonsensical to aim for a fully integrated or comprehensive theory. (Jeffries 2000: 5–6)

This is not only of practical, but also of theoretical significance. Like many other linguists, I take the langue–parole / competence–performance / code–inferencing distinctions to be partial models of what is going on in language, but at the same time I am conscious that there is no clear division between these somewhat idealized categories. In fact, rather than categories, it would be helpful to see them as reference points, on analogy with the cardinal vowels which have served phoneticians so well for many years. What we have, then, is not a fixed set of self-referential items and structures which are variously used and abused when real people speak and write real language. Instead, we have a slowly-evolving, but flexible, set of items and structures which vary across time, space and context, and whose evolution can indeed be affected by the kind of usage which steps outside the 'norms', especially if such variation is repeatedly reinforced in a particular body of texts.

This model, from prototype theory as developed from Katz and Postal (1964) and by Rosch (1973, 1978) has so far been used largely in relation to features of the langue, including semantic systems such as colour terms which were explored in a famous study by Berlin and Kay (1969). More recently, MacLaury (1991: 71) concludes that types of categorization in human language are more varied still, but include some aspects of prototypicality, and Croft and Cruse (2004) argues that even proto-type theory is too simplistic and needs to be enhanced by Barsalou's model of 'frames'. In the current context, we may conclude that the perceptions of female bodies may be both relatively stable and langue-like on the one hand and also subject to change over time, influenced by both technological and social change and by the discourse that reflects and constructs these changes.

These ideas are not new. And to that extent Widdowson is right to suggest that the CDA adherents have been guilty of ignoring some of the debates in other sub-disciplines of linguistics such as socio-linguistics, psycholinguistics, discourse analysis, literary theory and, one might add to Widdowson's list, pragmatics. I am drawing most here on the uses which sociolinguistics has made of variation theory, though the insights of pragmatics and Conversation Analysis into the patterning of what was once thought unpatterned, is another analogy. Despite these *de facto* omissions by CDA in communicating with other areas of the discipline, it seems to me that one could hold an entirely coherent theory of language based on a flexible code and its use, even though modelling it is somewhat more difficult than modelling the two-category theories (for example langue and parole or competence and performance) we were accustomed to rely upon throughout the twentieth century.

Levinson (1983) demonstrates this view of the mutability of the langue/parole boundary in discussing conversational implicature:

> the notion of conversational implicature offers a way out, for it allows one to claim that natural language expressions do tend to have simple, stable, and unitary senses ... but that this stable semantic core often has an unstable, context-specific pragmatic overlay – namely a set of implicatures. (Levinson 1983: 99)

Another criticism of CDA rests on the notion that there is a methodological circularity in its search for 'ideology', which is rooted in the pre-existing socio-political motivation for CDA's very existence. Widdowson, rightly, points out that even with the contextualized usage of language included, there is a tendency for CDA to read meanings from texts as though they were embedded in the linguistic material itself, despite many assertions to the contrary. He continues:

> If these discursive practices have not been adequately taken into account, the textual analyses are correspondingly inadequate,

precisely because they are dissociated from the contextual conditions which lend them pragmatic significance. This admission would seem to invalidate the whole critical operation. (142–3)

I would disagree that concentrating on the texts themselves necessarily invalidates the analysis of those texts. The reason for this is that I take seriously the axiom that all discourse is ideologically saturated, as does Kress (1996). It is also worth reiterating Schulz's (1990) argument that though further empirical work may be needed to prove the effect on readers, we can nevertheless conclude something about the attitudes of society by what that society has encoded in its discourses.

We may, nevertheless, accept Widdowson's criticisms of the CDA exponents as wanting to 'have their cake and eat it' in that they wish to both espouse the 'all discourse is ideological' view and at the same time to suggest that their task and aim in their work is to 'expose' ideologies which in some sense pervert the meanings that would be carried by a more 'neutral' version of the same text. Widdowson is right to point out that the techniques developed by CDA to expose right wing ideological infiltration:

can, of course, be taken up to further *any* cause, right wing as well as left, evil as well as good. They are the familiar tactics of polemic and propaganda, and they have a long history in human affairs. (Widdowson 1998: 150)

He is not so neutral in describing what those techniques are as I would like to be ('the procedures of ideological exposure by expedient analysis which characterise the practices of CDA' Widdowson 1998: 150), but nevertheless it does seem to be vital that we start to acknowledge that the Left is not the only group with 'truth' in its sights, and that indeed, there may be an infinite range of ideologies, some of which we may not want to evaluate on these lines at all, which can be exposed by textual analysis. In this connection, literary stylistic analysis can be enriched by the same techniques and procedures used by CDA, to demonstrate the text's ideologies, with no (evaluative) criticism, except possibly evaluations of aesthetics and literary worth, intended at all. This approach underlies, among other works, Simpson (1993), and, in my opinion, greatly strengthens the credibility of the techniques of CDA and the stylistics that is influenced by it.

As well as criticizing the theory of CDA, Widdowson also attacks the methods and practices represented in the key texts of the sub-discipline.

He correctly points out the circularity that is evident in the rather small pieces of 'analysis' which are included to illustrate the CDA 'manifestoes' of Fairclough, Fowler and Kress. He picks on Fairclough, for example, in the following way:

> What strikes a particular reader, even one as astute as Fairclough, is hardly conclusive evidence of how ideological significance is written covertly into texts.

He is right, of course, to criticise the evident interpretative positivism (see Simpson 1993: 111*ff*), in such examples though wrong in his conclusions, that the whole enterprise is thereby doomed. Very many such examples are the kinds of illustrative examples included in text-books which are not expected to be anything other than convenient for making one's point.[5] However, the main protagonists of CDA, and Fair-clough in particular, have not spent much time discussing or exploring the methodological principles of CDA. The only attempt to set out a methodology that I am aware of is in Fowler's (1991) investigation of news reporting, and this appears to be a simple set of tools for the non-specialist to use. The methodological problems of CDA could be seen as analogous to those explored by early sociolinguists, such as the apparently insurmountable problem of the observer's paradox and the problem of acquiring recordings of casual speech when the tape recorder created an inevitable formality. Such problems could have led to the whole development of sociolinguistics being abandoned, if it had not been for Labov and others like him who used their ingenuity to step around the difficulties and develop methods that were rigorous and replicable. However, the focus on objectivity and methodological principles has not been the overriding concern of CDA practitioners.

But here, perhaps, is where we come up against the real difficulty that Widdowson sees with the CDA enterprise; it does not claim to be objective, though like other stylisticians, CDA practitioners in fact often demonstrate their independence from the data, or at least show that whilst they may have a political impetus for doing the research, it is nevertheless plain to all that their findings are accurate. Having a general hypothesis that the data in this study is likely to reproduce certain culturally dominant views of the female body and then testing this hypothesis against the data is no less objective than hypothesizing about the nature of Shakespeare's style and then testing this against his plays. The relative objectivity of stylistics of this latter sort has also been questioned in the recent past (see Mackay 1996 and 1999; Short *et al.* 1998), but there is a consensus that it is possible to build rigour and replicability into such studies, so that while scientific levels of objectivity (which are also not absolute) are not achievable, we can demonstrate a reasonable level of independence in literary stylistics. I would add that CDA is very similar to stylistics in that it uses textual evidence to support certain interpretative conclusions. The difference is that the interpretations will normally be ideological in one and literary or affective in another, though it would be possible, of course, to look at ideology in literature too.

If we were to make explicit what Widdowson calls 'the essential instability of language and the necessary indeterminacy of all meaning', and to build it into our model of language more clearly, perhaps the practice of critical discourse analysis would not be seen as so far in rigour from any other branch of linguistics. Indeed, in Wodak (2002: 16), Meyer points out this inevitable circularity in the hermeneutic model of interpretation that underlies almost all linguistic analysis, and yet is accepted, with all its difficulties, as a reasonable methodology:

> As for the methods and procedures used for the analysis of discourses, CDA generally sees its procedure as a hermeneutic process, although this characteristic is not completely evident in the position taken by the various authors. Compared to the (causal) explanations of the natural sciences, hermeneutics can be understood as the method of grasping and producing meaning relations. The hermeneutic circle – which implies that the meaning of one part can only be understood in the context of the whole, but that this in turn is only accessible from its component parts – indicates the problem of intelligibility of hermeneutic interpretation. Therefore hermeneutic interpretation in particular urgently requires detailed documentation.

Where this work stands, then, in relation to CDA and its detractors, is as an example of how one might bring as much rigour into the process of qualitative textual analysis as possible, whilst not abandoning the motivated impetus behind CDA, and whilst acknowledging the presence of an inevitable circularity in the hermeneutic approach.

Hallidayan functionalism

This inevitable circularity of the process of analysing texts is also evident in the Hallidayan processes that are normally favoured by CDA practitioners. The descriptive tools, in the form of categories and labels that arise from a Hallidayan approach, tend to be intermediate categories, based on formal features, but only interpretable in context and not tied purely to their form, nor indeed to the kinds of meaning that are susceptible to testing. These features, and some which are proposed in this book, will be discussed in more detail in the next section.

Here, I would like to consider the more general nature of the tools adopted by CDA, to try and see how they fit with other aspects of a linguistic approach to textual meaning. The popular tools that CDA practitioners have used over the years include analysis of nominalization, transitivity, modality and to some extent the creation of semantic presuppositions. This list does not amount to a comprehensive account of meaning, nor is it made clear by those using these techniques why they have been chosen specifically or what has been ignored as less helpful to the project in hand. It is also interesting to note that although these seem to be Hallidayan categories on the whole, there is some influence from transformational grammar evident in analyses by CDA practitioners (see Fowler 1991: 76–80).

In relation to Halliday's metafunctions, transitivity and nominalization have often been seen as ideational in effect, since they are particular ways of presenting certain information textually. Modality and presuppositional meaning is often characterized more as interpersonal in its function, as it introduces authorial opinion and this can be seen as personal intervention in the message of the text in a fairly straightforward way.

However, I would like to suggest that what CDA is doing with texts questions the division between ideational and interpersonal, since the thrust of its claim is that the construction of texts in particular ways by an author (or authors) may influence the reader in specific ways, by the manipulation, either consciously or unconsciously, of texts to produce naturalized ideologies. This looks as much like something happening between the people involved (author, narrator, reader, audience, etc.) as something that is to do with the presentation of ideas by subterfuge. Fairclough (1995: 6) expresses this view as follows:

> Texts are social spaces in which two fundamental social processes simultaneously occur: cognition and representation of the world, and social interaction. A multifunctional view of text is therefore essential. I have followed systemic linguistics [Halliday 1978] in assuming that language in texts always simultaneously functions ideationally in the representation of experience and the

world, interpersonally in constituting social interaction between participants in discourse and textually in tying parts of a text together into a coherent whole (a text, precisely) and tying texts to situational contexts.

When a research project, like the one reported here, focuses largely on a body of textual data, it may simply be investigating more thoroughly the ideational process, though some of the interpretation of the analysis will question the interpersonal context, and consider the effects suggested by the context of production and reception of these magazines. As Fairclough (1995: 9) says:

> But there is a danger here of throwing out the baby with the bathwater, by abandoning textual analysis in favour of analysis of audience reception ... Textual analysis is therefore an important part, if only a part, of the picture, and must be defended against its critics.

'Traditional' tools of analysis in CDA

This section heading is potentially misleading, because there is no single 'tradition' of CDA, and certainly no agreed set of analytical tools that 'should' be used in this practice. There is a tendency to draw upon a systemic-functional approach in most cases, because of the inbuilt social or contextual aspects of this theory of language. However, there are certain systems that are more favoured by CDA researchers than others, and these almost always include nominalization, transitivity and modality.

One of only a few attempts to list some of the tools that might be used by critical linguists is in Chapter 5 of Fowler (1991), which is entitled 'Analytical Tools: Critical Linguistics'. Here, Fowler explains and illustrates the use of transitivity, syntactic transformations, in particular the agentless passive, lexical structure, modality and speech acts. Fowler (1991: 89) does not claim that this list is comprehensive:

> This chapter has provided *some explanatory notes*, and illustrations, of *some aspects* of linguistic structure which *my experience has shown* to be quite often involved in the construction of representations, in signifying beliefs and values when writers are reporting or commenting on the world. (My italics)

This reluctance to claim that the list is complete, coupled with the rather shaky grounds given for choosing the structures (from 'experience') have helped to give CDA its critics and, unfortunately, with the possible exception of Simpson (1993) who is using CDA in a new, stylistic way, there is no real attempt elsewhere to construct a rationale for the tools to be used, nor a comprehensive set of such tools.

In some senses this is understandable, since CDA, like stylistics more generally, is dependent on the developments in theory and practice from linguistics and has not so far developed its own general theory of language, though this has been mooted by some as one of its ultimate aims (Fairclough 1995: 10, referring to Kress 1993). The tools of analysis are also problematic for CDA analysts in some ways, as van Leeuwen (1996) points out:

> There is no neat fit between sociological and linguistic categories, and if Critical Discourse Analysis . . . ties itself in too closely to specific linguistic operations or categories, many relevant instances of agency might be overlooked. One cannot, it seems, have it both ways with language. Either theory and method are formally neat and semantically messy, or they are semantically neat but formally messy. Linguists tend toward preserving the unity of formal categories. I shall here attempt the opposite approach, hoping to provide a set of relevant categories for investigating the respresentation of social actors in discourse. (van Leeuwen 1996: 33)

In this project, one of the aims has been to identify systems which are similar to transitivity and modality, but are not as well-recognized as them. What these other systems have in common with the 'traditional' tools of CDA is that they reflect van Leeuwen's comments and are simultaneously formal and functional at the level at which the naturalization of ideology and hegemony may work. They each seem to depend on a standard form–function relationship (such as modal verbs for modality) but also have other manners of delivery so that the style of the text performs certain meaningful functions. We will see more of these functions later in the chapter (pp. 16–17), but here I will explain a little more what is meant by this particular level of functionality in texts.

If we take modality as a classic case of this kind of textual function, we can note that there is a typical, or core, form, which delivers certain kinds of modality in English; the modal auxiliary. Thus, the epistemic uncertainty of a speaker might be introduced by a modal verb as in *Susan might come to the party,* and the speaker's view or opinions as to what is desirable may equally well be delivered by a modal verb as in *Susan*

<u>*should*</u> *come to the party*. Note that with the right context (including intonation), these meanings can be reassigned in reverse:

> Susan might come to the ↘↗ party, if only to please her ↘ mother.
> Susan ↘ should come to the party, all things being ↘↗ equal.[6]

Although the range of meaning of modals, and their assignment to the different modal verbs, is quite complex, nevertheless, if we restrict ourselves to this formal indicator of modality, the picture looks quite straightforward, with certain forms delivering particular meanings. However, the full range of modal meaning, in itself very difficult to define, can in fact be delivered by an open-ended range of forms, including modal adverbs (*probably, hopefully*), modal adjectives (*possible, likely*) and lexical verbs (*imagine, think*) and at the other extreme, modal intonation (rising tone on statements) and body language (shrug, eyebrow lift).

The result of this vagueness of the boundaries of a formal category in relation to a meaning that is so significant in relation to power and ideology is that we are obliged to analyse texts using the provisional set of categories, without ever arriving at a discovery procedure that will ensure that we can capture all modal forms. The lack of straight-forward mapping of meaning onto form, then, is one of the factors that militate against any *purely* objective analysis, since a case may have to be made for the analysis offered, rather than being an automated procedure.

A slightly different situation is found when we consider transitivity. It is probably fair to say that transitivity is tied closely to the choice of verb in a clause, and this choice has consequences for the number and type of participants. It might seem, therefore, that the formal basis of transitivity is assured and clear. The lack of form-meaning match in this case, however, is a result of the mismatch between the number of possible syntactic positions in the clause (five in total: SPOCA) and the number of identifiably different participant roles which may cluster around the verbal element. Thus, the grammatical subject may be an agent, an actor, an instrument, or even a goal, as we can see from the examples below:

> *John* used the hammer to knock in the nail.
> *John* knocked the nail in.
> *The hammer* knocked the nail in.
> *The nail* was knocked in.

It is therefore not possible on purely formal grounds to identify the semantic roles of all noun phrases associated with the main verb in a clause. This means that analysis on the basis of transitivity relations relies on the analyst's understanding of the verbal meaning as well as the surface structure, leading to the kind of circularity that hampers much linguistic analysis when it attempts to be completely formal in nature.

We have seen two examples here of how the form and meaning of English sentences are not mapped onto each other in a simple one-to-one manner. This is not a sign of inadequacy but one of the necessary complexities in human language that make it possible to be creative, as well as being manipulative. The other tools of analysis used in this study are equally complex and just as rich in meaning as these examples (see pp. 16–17).

Critical stylistics

The approach taken here is to set aside for now the question of the influence (or otherwise) of texts on readers, and to take it for granted first of all that all texts present ideologies (as propositions, assumptions or implications) and secondly that, as a result of this, the analysis of meanings as created by texts in particular ways (that is, stylistics) is fundamental to CDA. The fact that some ideologies are more manipulative and/or undesirable than others should not blind us to the fact that the technical means of achieving meaning are similar, whether we wish to criticise that meaning or simply wish to analyse that way of achieving a particular effect.

The remainder of this section will discuss and exemplify the main analytical tools that are used in discussing the texts analysed in this book. As explained above, they are Hallidayan in the sense that they take a basically functional approach, so that the meanings and the way that they are delivered textually are both incorporated into the analysis throughout. The potential problem with this, of course, occurs if you try to demonstrate a complete lack of circularity in the investigation, and yet I hope to have argued convincingly above (and elsewhere – Jeffries 2000) that this aim is neither realistic not necessary as long as certain key principles are in place.

This research was carried out in the context of an expectation that certain key perceptions of women's bodies are likely to be ubiquitous in texts that clearly denigrate or demean women's bodies (such as the 'page 3' type text in tabloid newspapers, or the new male magazines that are proliferating at the moment). I can also make an educated guess that texts ostensibly written *for* women, such as women's magazines, will do a little 'better' ideologically, but perhaps not so well as we might expect. This does not, however, give even a linguist with a fair amount of linguistic experience a clue as to what kinds of features will carry ideologies – nor to what extent they will be politically correct or otherwise. There may also be ideologies naturalized in the data which are unexpected, or hard to critique, so not all of the analysis is expected to produce shock or horror.

The kind of study that I embarked upon here, then, is analogous to many respectable linguistic enterprises, including for example the sociolinguistics of the 1970s and 1980s, where there is a hypothesis, a set of data and a set of analytical tools based on a theory of language which can be (and will be) disputed by others, and which inevitably will take for granted some basic premises about the nature of language. I hope to show that the socio-political underpinnings of this study are no more dangerous or biased (nor less so) than those in the great sociolinguistics studies of, for example, class dialects in Norwich (Trudgill, 1974) or youth dialects in New York (Labov 2006) or Belfast (Milroy 1980).

I often make the case to students that whilst researchers have every right to try and establish what differences (presupposing there are some) there are between males' and females' (or different racial groups') brain processes, that, nevertheless, we need to be aware that people do research because they feel that it will get to some important 'truth' (sociologically and/or politically), or are paid by people with these views. I would not necessarily disagree with the findings of such research, though I may find it offensive, suspecting as I do that there is a right-wing agenda which is either behind such studies, or would anyway be well-served by convenient biological differences between genders or races. It is important to make clear the fundamental assumptions underlying a piece of research, to make the methodology and results as clear as possible, and to make the basis of any interpretation of those results. Other researchers are then free to take issue with any (or all) of these factors, but at least the debate – and resulting human knowledge – will make progress. Objectivity, as real scientists know, is relative. What we need instead is clarity – of goals, of methods and of conclusions.

Analytical categories

The last section gave a sense of what the collected tools of analysis in this study were attempting to bring to the practice of CDA, which is a rationale for the kind of feature that is being analysed. With the exception of the first two categories below (genre and rhetoric), which are more global in their reach, the tools of analysis used here are aimed at finding out what the text is *doing* ideationally – and thus ideologically – in certain key ways. I have therefore analysed the data in terms of the 'textual-ideational' features listed below. Their main formal realizations are listed beside the function label:

- **Naming**: choice of nominals, nominalization, construction of noun phrases.
- **Describing**: choice of adjectives, positioning of adjectives (pre- and postposed).
- **Equating**: apposition, intensive predicator, lexical choice (sense relations).
- **Contrasting**: negation, lexical choices (sense relations).
- **Enumerating and exemplifying**: lists, intensive predicator.
- **Assuming**: presupposition
- **Implying**: implicature
- **Creating time and space**: tense, time adverbials, deixis, metaphor.
- **Presenting processes and states**: transitivity.
- **Presenting opinions**: modality, presentation of speech and thought.

This is not intended to be a comprehensive list of all that texts can do, but it attempts to draw together some familiar and some less familiar operations which might be considered in some sense independent of particular languages and in principle independent of text-type, though it is likely that some genres are more prone to some of these functions than others.

Feminism, theory and the body

Constructing the female body

The title of this book, as will be evident to some readers, takes a particular theoretical viewpoint. This has already been previewed in the earlier sections of this chapter which introduced the particular critical discourse analytic approach that is taken here. The material world is assumed to be at least partially experienced through the way it is described and thus 'constructed' for us. Thus, it is assumed that there is likely to be some effect on the reader's perceptions if it turns out that the data portrays the female body in particular, ideologically significant, ways. However, it is worth considering this assumption not only as part of a generalized CDA approach to texts, but in the context of feminist theory, and particularly feminist linguistic theory relating to the body. This section will attempt to contextualize the work in such a way.

The motivation for the research reported here, apart from a personal one, was that women have to deal with their material bodies on a daily basis,[7] and in the face of whatever construction the culture currently puts on their bodies. I wanted to see what some of the apparently helpful texts in women's magazines were actually doing to perceptions. At first sight, the texts studied all appear to be aimed at helping the contemporary female cope with the 'problematic' body. This construction of the body as a problem is one of the overwhelming impressions one gets, even just flicking through the pages of women's magazines. Though this is not a comparative study, the same impression is not given by the increasing number of men's magazines on the market. In the women's magazines, even the texts which aim to celebrate the body's normal functioning, such as pregnancy texts, operate within the mainstream ideology of the problematic body.[8]

Cameron (1998: 11) makes the point that it is not only the way that a language names the world that might be seen as sexist:

> In my own view, sexist language is not best thought of as the naming of reality from a single, male perspective. It is a multifaceted phenomenon, taking different forms in different representational practices, which have their own particular histories and characteristics.

This book contributes in a small way to the analysis of this complex picture of how representations of the female body may have contributed to the perceptions of the female form at a point in the early twenty-first century, in the context of mainstream periodical publications for women.

Price and Shildrick (1999: 2) note that early feminism concentrated its efforts on challenging the dominant view that women were in some way less than fully human, partly because they were tied in to bodily functions (menstruation, pregnancy) which were associated with 'gross, unthinking physicality'. They add that feminism was partly responsible for making the connection between the way that women were treated as driven by bodily function and similar views of black people, working-class people, animals, and slaves. They add:

> Whilst all such marginalized bodies are potentially unsettling, what is at issue for women specifically is that, supposedly, the female body is

intrinsically unpredictable, leaky and disruptive. Price and Shildrick (1999: 2)

The apparently unstable female material body, viewed negatively from a patriarchal viewpoint, has been one of the ideologies that feminism has sought to question and/or celebrate. It is also one of the great challenges to women in the twenty-first century, presented, as they are, with ever more technological ways of making their bodies 'perfect', so that there is less excuse for imperfection, and thus more potential 'blame' attached to the imperfect female. If some of the 'imperfections' are associated with those bodily functions that attach to the specific biology of being female, then controls on menstruation (e.g. through the pill) childbirth (e.g. through elective caesarean for convenience) and menopause (e.g. through HRT) are clearly two-edged swords. On the one hand these technologies clearly help women to live fuller and less biologically-determined lives, on the other they bring side-effects which are sometimes physical (high blood pressure, higher risk of breast cancer, and so on) and sometimes emotional or mental (expectations of control over our bodies that are convenient to a male-created society).

An increasing technologization of the body, also, has changed the way that plastic surgery and other similar interventions are viewed socially. Though the texts in this data are still a little ambivalent about these things, there is a definite sign that the development of an acceptance of changing our bodies to suit the prevailing view of perfection is under way, and that texts such as these are part of the process of that change. Of course, this acceptance is partly a product not only of patriarchy, but also of first-wave feminism, as Price and Shildrick (1999: 4) describe it:

The way forward was not to reclaim and revalorise the body, but to argue that the ideal standard of disembodied subjecthood was as appropriate to, and attainable by, women as it was to men.

What may seem strange at first is that the first wave of feminism has had such success, whereas the second wave of radical feminism, which attempted to put bodily difference at the centre of its politics, has had less apparent effect on mainstream portrayals (constructions) of the female body. Thus, the 'revaluing' of the specifically female – and maternal – body as a site of empowerment, seems to have had less impact on the mainstream magazines investigated here, except perhaps

in the more perverse and general of ways; the legitimizing of focus on the specifically female. This danger of radical feminism is pointed out by Price and Shildrick (1999: 4–5):

> The stress given to the embodied nature of sexual difference has been, then, a powerful advance for feminism, but nonetheless in its unproblematised form it runs two related risks: one the one hand it may uncritically universalise the male and female body, while on the other it appears to reiterate the biological essentialism that historically has grounded women's subordination.

What first, second and more especially third-wave feminism have offered to the powerful patriarchal producers of mass-circulation magazines is a rationalization of whatever position it suits them to take. If selling diets or plastic surgery is the aim, then the control of the body by technology and mediated willpower can be framed within a first-wave, rationalist perspective, where women, just as much as men, can 'rise above' the dictates of their bodies. It is a challenge that many readers would be reluctant to avoid taking up, since succumbing is weak, and being weak is not acceptable. However, and without any sense that it is contradictory, these texts simultaneously use the second-wave argument that the female is different, and should be valued as such, to underpin the selling of sexual technique, the rationale for the search for perfection (to attract a mate) and the excuse for women being at times 'at the mercy of' their bodies.

The rise of 'third-wave feminism', first as a reaction against the dominance of white women's experience and later as younger generation's reaction against second-wave feminism (see Henry 2004), provides the media with the opportunity to serve both their commercial interests and also pay lip-service to feminist concerns. As Price and Shildrick (1999: 7) point out, there is now a postmodern feminism that asks a different kind of question, rather than 'Can we change our bodies to become more acceptable?':

> To say that the body is a discursive construction is not to deny a substantial corpus, but to insist that our apprehension of it, is necessarily mediated by the contexts in which we speak... It is then the forms of materialisation of the body, rather than the body itself, which is the concern of a feminism that must ask always what purpose and whose interests do particular constructions serve?

This 'different kind of question' is 'can we change the way that discourse shapes our bodies?' They argue that what is needed to avoid the traps of both first and second wave feminism is 'the constant reinterpretation of the body, textually constructed'. The advantage of this approach, from a practical point of view is that instead of trying to deny the material physicality of bodily experience, the emphasis is on denying its stability. We will see some examples in the textual analysis later, which demonstrate the problems with the stable materiality of the body, and the pressures it puts on women to preserve a particular (young, slim, pre-maternal) version of their body throughout life.

> Theorists such as Susan Bordo (1993) and Sandra Barky (1988) have been in the forefront in analysing how the processes of surveillance and self-surveillance are deeply implicated in constituting a set of normativities towards which bodies intend. The practices of diet, keep-fit, fertility control, fashion, health care procedures and so on are all examples of disciplinary controls which literally produce the bodies that are their concern. (Price and Shildrick 1999: 8)

This understanding, that what is theoretically constructive in affecting the ways that women perceive their bodies, may also have a material effect on the shape and functioning of their bodies, is one that many theorists mention. If we are to have control over the shape, size and function of our bodies, it is, as Gatens (1999) points out, vital to know what power relations are superimposed on top of this apparent control:

> If discourses cannot be deemed as 'outside', or apart from, power relations then their analysis becomes crucial to an analysis of power. This is why language, signifying practices and discourses have become central stakes in feminist struggles. (Gatens 1999: 231)

Gatens argues that it does not make sense to simply decide that women should have access to power, since the cultural formation of their bodies does not fit the shape of the power.

Butler (1999: 240) makes clear that it is not that discourse actually creates the body, but that the body cannot be accessed or referred to without discourse. This means that every reference to the body will construct the body *in some way*. The ideological effects of this are unavoidable:

> To claim that discourse is formative is not to claim that it originates, causes, or exhaustively composes that which it concedes; rather, it

is to claim that there is no reference to a pure body which is not at the same time a further formation of that body. In this sense, the linguistic capacity to refer to sexed bodies is not denied, but the very meaning of 'referentiality' is altered. In philosophical terms, the constative claim is always to some degree performative.

This claim might make the well-intentioned writer of women's magazines want to give up, since there is clearly no neutral way in which s/he can write supportive articles, problem-page answers or hints and tips pages. But this, in a sense, is the point; that since neutrality is impossible, then the ideology of the text should be acknowledged, and all pretence that there is anything essential about femininity or womanhood should be abandoned explicitly.

Some of the writers in Price and Shidrick's collection make points that are not immediately applicable to the current research, but on closer inspection have some contribution to make to the theoretical background behind it. Thus, Bakare-Yusuf (1999: 314) discusses torture and silence, bringing into relief the connection between body and mind which is highlighted by this bodily practice aimed at making people speak. The connection between suffering and silencing, which is the experience of many oppressed people, not just women, is one that is important in looking at the data collected in the current research. Not only the absence of women's own voices in some of the articles themselves, but the absence of different kinds of women's voices, including black women, lesbian women and others, is an absence, like all absences, which is hard to trace, and easy to ignore. I will return to the question of the marginalised female and female body in the final section of this chapter and in the conclusions.

Battersby (1999) relates the experience of encountering the Cognitive Semantics proposed by Lakoff and Johnson (1980) which proposes a universal bodily experience as the basis of the many entrenched metaphors that suffuse our everyday experience. Battersby argues that their conception of the bodily lived experience does not reflect the experience of many, including women, black people, people (mainly women) with anorexia and so on:

> For feminist theorists who have long complained of the neglect of the body by western philosophers, the development of cognitive semantics might seem a promising move. However, as I read Johnson's and Lakoff's accounts of embodiment, I register a shock

of strangeness: of wondering what it would be like to inhabit a body *like that*. Battersby (1999: 342)

Her argument rests on the notion that unlike the 'universal', that is male, body, the female experience is one of permeable boundaries, where another being may grow inside one's own body and then separate itself (through labour), where the constructed experience of (heterosexual) sex is one of penetration and intrusion into the female body, and as a result of both the lived experience and its lack of match to the discursive 'norms' of the body Battersby (1999: 346) explains her 'failure to register my body as a container with a self safe "within" and the dangerous other on the outside' as partly due to the fact that this permeability and penetrability is 'typical of women'. In other words, the normalizing of the female form as aberrantly unsafe and 'leaky', in opposition to the sealed and 'clean' masculine form, is one of the sources of the female anxiety in relation to the body, including its extreme forms such as anorexia and bulimia.

A woman's life – the data

The data for this research were collected in the month of February 2000. In order to reflect the publications that would be available to teenagers and women at that time, the data were collected from all the women's magazines available in the main newsagents (W.H. Smith) in the centre of Leeds (West Yorkshire, UK) in that month. Some of these were dated March, some Feb/March and some February, but they were all available on the same day.

The only specialist magazines included in the data were those which concerned the body in particular ways. These included slimming, pregnancy and plastic-surgery magazines. All other magazines were generic. I did not include magazines which concerned the house and garden or cooking alone. A quick glance at them confirmed the assumption that there would be no data of interest in them as there were very few references to the female body. This choice, however, does explain one of the features of the data in this study, which is that it tends to assume that the reader is relatively young. There are a small number of magazines (for example, *Woman*) which address more mature women as well as including articles about the bodily experience of that age group. A very large number of other magazines, however, seem to assume that the life of middle-aged and older women is almost entirely taken up with the concerns of creating a beautiful home, garden or dinner party.

Another factor in the choice of data that has influenced the direction of this book is that I have had to leave out the early stages of a girl's life, since it is in books, rather than magazines, that early perceptions may be founded and they are not comparable with the data analysed here both because of this fact and also because they do not constitute comparable entertainment for children as for women and teenage girls. Children will rarely freely choose such reading matter and the range of genres and topics tends to differ considerably.

One slight dissatisfaction with the data, which turned out to be beyond my control, was the fact that having decided to choose data that would be readily available to all women, I discovered that there were no specialist magazines for lesbian women, and only two for black women in the shop at that time, though it is probably the largest outlet of magazines in a large northern English city. These latter were published in the USA and in some ways, therefore, are not comparable to the other magazines, all of which are either UK-based or have UK editions. Specialist magazines for lesbian women do exist, as my students have pointed out, but as they are not readily available in the usual outlets, readers would have to make a concerted effort to acquire them. The result is that the market is dominated by magazines which assume a heterosexual, mainly white and probably middle-class readership.

Once I had acquired the magazines, I extracted all articles, advertisements and other texts which had references to the female body. In the end, some of the more culinary articles had too little in the way of bodily references to include, though those which dealt with dieting or pregnancy were included. The final total of texts was 86, though some of these were compilations of short texts on the same topic or from the same publication.

The next stage was to write a comprehensive commentary on each text, using the textual functions listed in the first section of Chapter 1 as the analytical categories, keeping in mind that these functions do not have one-to-one relationship between form and meaning, and the analysis is therefore not an automatic process. Each text, therefore, was analysed a number of times, using each function as a 'filter' through which to see what kinds of structure and strategy were being employed. The potential effects of foregrounded features were noted in the commentary, but repetitive features of relevance were also noted for their potential in naturalising ideology.

Originally, the plan for this research was to divide up the data according to the stage of life that the texts related to; puberty, sexually active, pregnancy, menopause and so on. However, I soon found that the analysis done that way would be excessively repetitive, since the same strategies and features kept appearing across the data. The result is that instead of organizing this book according to the stages in life of women, I have organized it according to linguistic and rhetorical features. This has resulted in less repetition, though, as we shall see; there is a certain amount of overlap in the effect of some of the features included here.

2
Genre, Text Type and Rhetorical Strategy

Although most of this book is concerned with quite detailed analysis of localized stretches of language in texts, it turned out at an early stage of the project that it was going to be important to think a little about global questions of what kinds of text I was dealing with, and also what kinds of strategy were being used to present information, or sometimes simply opinion, to the readers. The result of these more general investigations is reported in this chapter, and I have, for convenience sake, divided these observations under the headings of 'Genre and text types' and 'Rhetorical strategies' respectively.

The term 'genre', like other similar terms which attempt to classify text types, is fraught with difficulty, but nevertheless, researchers find it useful and relatively recognizable, despite the difficulty in defining the term precisely. The most obvious definition, largely in terms of linguistic characteristics, can be seen in the following from Trask (1998: 105):

> A historically stable variety of text with conspicuous distinguishing features... The key fact about a given genre is that it has some readily identifiable distinguishing features that set it off markedly from other genres, and that those features remain stable over a substantial period of time. In most cases, a particular genre also occupies a well-defined place in the culture of the people who make use of the genre.

Another definition, from Swales (1990) emphasizes the communicative function of genres, arguing that the linguistic features of their style are subordinate to function:

> A genre comprises a class of communicative events, the members of which share some set of communicative purposes. These purposes

are recognised by the expert members of the parent discourse community, and thereby constitute the rationale for the genre. This rationale shapes the schematic structure of the discourse and influences and constrains choice of content and style. Communicative purpose is both a privileged criterion and one that operates to keep the scope of a genre as here conceived narrowly focused on comparable rhetorical action. (Swales 1990: 58)

Between them, these definitions help to mark out a useful approach to the current data which could be said to have a recognizable set of purposes including informing and entertaining women on the subject of their bodies as well as (in some cases) selling products and services to enhance their bodies. In addition, Trask's reference to historical stability and cultural recognition also seem to be relevant here, as the women's magazine genre is one that has been current since at least the eighteenth century (see Zuckerman 1991 and 1998; Wolf Thomson 1947), and has had many of the same general functions and text types throughout its history, despite the changes in content and explicitness that followed from social changes in the position of women.

The question of text types is one that has been addressed by Stockwell (2002) who uses the term 'genre' rather differently in a way which makes it hard to see at first how the term could be applied to magazine data:

mode	poetry, prose, drama, conversation, song
genre	comedy, tragedy, gothic, surrealism
sub-genre	mock-epic, comic opera, airport fiction, war novel, political memoir
type	sonnet, ballad, email, one-act play, short story
register	reporting language, letter-writing, narrative, lyricism
	(Stockwell 2002: 34)

Stockwell is mostly concerned with literary categories, but his 'register' categories include some which might be seen as non-literary. What is less clear is how such a system of overlapping categories could be expanded to include non-literary texts such as women's magazines. An attempt to do so could be as follows (in bold):

mode	poetry, **prose**, drama, conversation, song
genre	comedy, tragedy, gothic, surrealism, **information**

sub-genre	mock-epic, comic opera, airport fiction, war novel, political memoir, **women's magazines**
type	sonnet, ballad, email, one-act play, short story, **problem page, reader's story** etc.
register	**reporting language, letter-writing, narrative, diary-style,** lyricism

(adapted from Stockwell 2002: 34)

We could, therefore, use the terms sub-genre and type to refer to the data in this study, though in order to discuss what Fairclough (1995: 171) calls 'genre mixing', we need to be aware of both Stockwell's terminology and the Swales and Trask definitions.

The most general observation that can be made about a text's style is that some characteristics, both of language and layout, can indicate that it belongs to a particular sub-genre or text type that the reader will recognize. The placing of a text in a particular context (such as a women's magazine) will narrow down the anticipated range of text types in the reader's expectation though, as the analysis in this volume will show, these expectations can be undermined and played upon by disguising one text type as another (most obviously advertisement as article) and blurring clear divisions between types (for example advice and entertainment genres (see Cook 1992). In some contexts, the reader will know exactly which genre or text type s/he is faced with at any one time, so that the mixing of styles is playful and entertaining. More insidiously, in the data considered here, the confusion of types may mean that the reader is not consistently aware of the genre, and is thus less well-prepared for critiquing or resisting any naturalized ideologies that may be implied. Fairclough (1995: 172) describes the potential effect on the audience in the following way:

> The generic mix I have sketched out above leads to a text with complex and contradictory meanings, in terms of the identities set up by/for participants and audience, the relationships between participants and between participants and audience and the 'knowledges' which are constituted in the text.

Although, as we will see, there are links between text type (or genre) and rhetorical strategy, they are also independent of each other, as Halmari (2004: 23) found in relation to a range of rhetorical studies of political data:

What emerges from the chapters is, on the one hand, an understanding of the sensitivity of the linguistic form to the genre in question; on the other hand, what also emerges is the – in many ways surprising – similarity in the linguistic realization that persuasion may take across a range of very different genres. As long as the goal of the language user is to influence, change, and manipulate, persuasion will find its discourse-pragmatic and lexico-grammatical realizations, no matter what genre is used as the outlet.

This statement implies that rhetorical – that is persuasive – uses of language operate at the micro-structure level as well as higher levels. To the extent that the texts in the current data are persuasive, it could be argued that this whole book is engaged in analysing the techniques that are used in persuading women and girls to accept certain ideological constructions of their bodies. However, the emphasis here is more upon the potential influence of this kind, rather than the conscious intention on the part of the producers in every instance to be persuasive in a particular way.

Nevertheless, there seem to be some textual practices, overlaid upon genres, which have a very strong potential rhetorical effect, and this tendency is worthy of closer study. The rhetorical strategies used in these texts can be the carriers of ideological meaning, and if this ideological meaning is naturalized, the likelihood is that it will be effective in persuading the reader that this is how the world is. For example, there are a very large number of stories with 'happy endings' in this data, where a seemingly overwhelming problem arises, and further problems abound, and then something happens to make it all come right in the end. Another strategy is the use of 'perfect' examples, to indicate what a reader ought to do. This links with the use of implicatures (see Chapter 5), but is a more general characteristic of some articles and texts which seem to choose this counsel of perfection as a general strategy, whereas implicatures are usually more localized.

The rhetorical strategies discussed later in this chapter are all based upon some textual practice, whether that is narratorial, like the use of happy endings, or content-based, as in the exemplary women stories.

Genre and text types

Although we may use the word 'genre' quite happily in everyday life, and feel that we know what it means, it is much harder to pin down its meaning for academic purposes. Thus, whilst on the one hand we might wish to refer to the genre of women's magazines, we may also find ourselves wishing to refer to readers' stories, or glossaries (see below) as a different kind of genre, which cuts across the more reader-oriented labels such as 'health magazine' or 'angling magazine'. It would be difficult to order these cross-cutting categorizations in anything like an economical hierarchy, since there will always be repetition, wherever the first division is made. Thus, one could divide the world of magazines (to restrict ourselves to these) into sewing magazines, angling magazines, health and beauty magazines and so on, and each of them would then be divided into the types of text, including, for example, letters and responses; 'how to' instructions/advice; advertising and so on. Conversely, one could identify these latter 'types' of text, and then divide them into those which occur in the different kinds of magazine. Neither of these priorities is intrinsically superior to the other, though one may serve a particular purpose better than another.

The solution, as all librarians know, is to postulate a set of characteristics which can be attached to any text, and these will jointly confer sub-genre and text-type status in a way that unordered categories do in many computer-databases that we are familiar with. This 'keyword' approach is one that underlies internet search engines, and thus is becoming a more readily-assimilated sorting mechanism for present-day readers.

This preamble sets the scene for my use, in the current context, of the category 'women's magazines' as the sub-genre, and its division into text types as they occurred in this data. No assumption is being made about the hierarchical relationship, but since I was interested to investigate the nature of the language in women's magazines, the ordering of categories was essentially one of the 'givens' of the project. What I hadn't expected at the outset was to find that the sub-categorization itself would prove to be an interesting journey, and that the text types to be found would be so uniform across the range of women's magazines that I was studying.

I had wrongly assumed that there were a certain set of basic text types that I could predict, including, for example, problem-pages, advertisements and feature articles, and these would be established before, rather than in response to, the data. In fact, the text types were so much more interesting than this crude categorization that the analytical method had to change to incorporate a record of the text type as the first observation on each data item. The results of these observations are reported below.

Question and answer

There were, of course, as predicted, problem pages in many magazines, and similar 'Question and Answer' formats used in many others. The standard problem page is one in which there is a single 'agony aunt' who responds to letters purportedly written and sent in by readers. These correspondents are often given a first name to indicate that they are real and that there is a single identity behind the question being asked.

Examples of this kind of problem page were found in many magazines. Here is one typical example, from *Bliss*, and one which will be quoted a number of times in this book:

LUMP ALERT

At the top of my vagina I can feel a slimy ball the size of a 2p piece with a space in the middle. My tampons must hit it and it's bound to get in the way when I have sex. Am I deformed? Very worried, 16, Cambridge
You've located the neck of your cervix – the neck of your womb. Your womb is the size and shape of an upside-down pear, positioned at the top of your vagina. The bottom 0.5 cm, the cervix, projects into the vagina and feels like a nose with a dip in the centre. This dip is the opening to the womb, and it's the diameter of a thin straw, so tampons can't go through it (although sperm slips in easily and it's capable of expanding to fit a baby through). Don't worry, it won't get in the way during sex. It's good to find out how your body works, but don't push fingers or other objects too hard into yourself in the process.

Whether or not this is a genuine letter is academic, since the tacit agreement between the magazine and the reader is that this is how it is to be treated. What is more relevant to the question of defining a genre in this context, is the use of headings above each letter, which is not universal, but fairly common, and the entirely predictable first and then second-person narrative to be found in the letter and its answer respectively. With regard to the heading, it is noticeable that in this case, far from being a useful shorthand 'headline' to help readers locate topics that they might be interested in, it is rather misleading, and also quite sensational, given that the letter itself does not hint at cancer, the most likely interpretation of the word 'lump' in this context. Not all problem pages entitle their letters in this way, and some are quite straightforward, with titles such as 'Are we bulimic?' and 'I weigh so much' being typical of this more direct approach.

Of the 24 examples of problem pages or question and answer pages in the data, most follow the format shown above. There are, however, some variations, such as a reminder of the identity of the respondent at the beginning of the answer, as in the examples from *Sugar* where the response begins with 'Sarah says'. This text as we shall see is also interesting in that it consists of a single letter and answer, on the topic of breast cancer, and is followed by a 'how to' advice section (see below) on the importance of self-examination and instructions for doing so. This otherwise straightforward approach is somewhat undermined by the heading used over the 'how to' article on breast examination, which is *It's good to fondle*. Such a sexually suggestive heading belies the content, and serves no obvious purpose, except possibly to entertain or simply to attract attention. We shall see, later, that there is considerable blurring of sub-genres or text types (Fairclough's genre-mixing) in these data, and this suggestive title on a health-related piece is just one symptom of the larger issue.

Another of the variants of the problem page is one where there are a number of questions posed by the writer of the article on behalf of the readers. This happens in a question and answer piece themed around the topic of periods from *Fresh*, a teenage magazine. The questions are in the first person, such as 'When will I start?' and 'What kind of protection should I use?', and the answers read very much like the answers in a conventional problem page, as they are written in the second person and could be interpreted as written either for a single correspondent or for the general reader:

> Anything you normally do, you can do during your period. You can even go swimming if you are wearing a tampon.

Although problem pages are found much more commonly in teenage than other women's magazines, the question and answer format is used throughout the data in various guises. One example of its non-conventional use is embedded within another type of text, the diary-style article. *Our Baby*, for example, has a pregnancy diary telling pregnant women what to expect at each stage of the pregnancy. This is mostly a bullet-pointed list of what to do and what to plan for, but there are also text boxes scattered throughout the text and containing a question written 'as if' from a pregnant woman (for example, 'Should I avoid hot baths now I'm pregnant?') and answered by one or other of the 'experts' such as 'Dr Ilona Benfedy' or 'Midwife Brenda Docherty'. There is no pretence that these questions are from 'real' readers, but the convention is clearly that the question might be the kind of thing that is worrying a newly pregnant woman.

This blending of different kinds of text is common throughout the data in this study, and we will look at particular cases which may cause concern in a later section. It is worth noting here, however, that the pregnancy texts tend not to have single-function problem pages, but interspersed question and answer text boxes of the kind described in the last paragraph. This happens, for example, also in texts from *Pregnancy and Birth* concerning such topics as ante-natal visits and the size of a pregnant stomach.

The sexual and general health texts, however, do conform to the more normal problem-page format, with mostly straightforward (that is, not jokey) titles, such as 'Does circumcision affect sex?' (*Body Beautiful*) and 'I only want sex once a week' (*Woman*), letters in the first person such as 'Why do my legs tingle?' (*Woman*) and answers in the second person as well as wide-ranging statements, such as the following from *Woman*, that can apply to readers more generally:

> There's no such thing as normal when it comes to having sex. Libido, or sex drive, is a highly individual thing – some women feel the need for sex every day, others only once or twice a week, or less. But a sudden falling off in your normal level of sexual desire might be a sign of a problem.

Another variant on the normal problem page can be seen in *Slimmer Magazine*, where, instead of *Ask Emma (More!)*, this item has a panel of four experts who can give advice on relationships, diet and health according to their expertise. This variation on the unqualified (but possibly quite experienced) agony aunt is quite common, particularly in themed magazines such as those addressing the pregnant or the overweight woman. The tendency is typified by a problem page from *Body Beautiful* magazine, and is part of a sequence of items on plastic surgery. The problem page consists of a series of questions in first-person letter form and the answers are advertised at the top as being given by 'Dr John F Celin, Knightsbridge Plastic Surgeon and author of several books on the subject of cosmetic surgery'. This need to give credibility to the writer of answers to problems is particularly strong in this field where the suspicion of the motives and qualifications of those involved in making money out of people's vanity can be quite strong. There is no evidence for the assumed significance of the mini-CV of Dr Celin. He is styled 'Dr', which readers may take to mean that he has done six years of medical training, but no references are given for his books, and the significance of his place of work, Knightsbridge, is mainly that it conjures up images of wealth and leads the reader towards the view that he treats the rich and famous and must, therefore, be good. A similar effect can be found in an article on clothing from the same magazine (*Body Beautiful*) where the answers to the questions raised by readers' letters are provided by Mia Coleman, who is 'a personal shopper with a degree in fashion design. She shops for people with no time, and her clients include MPs and celebrities'. Again, there is no detail to substantiate these claims, but the impression is of someone who has good credentials for this role.

What is slightly odd about the letters in both of these problem pages in *Body Beautiful* is the fact that the names are unusually given in full, with their place of residence (for example *Tricia Welles, Suffolk* or *Susan James, Halifax*). This is unusual in the context of potentially embarrassing letters, and may, conversely, indicate invented readers, rather than very frank ones.

A fitness-related problem page in *Woman* mixes letters and answers with 'fact-file' sections and tips. The text-type boundaries break down here as some sections are full letters and others are simply headed by questions 'as if' from the reader's point of view (*Does my bum look big in this?*). This kind of mixing of text types is common in the adult magazines, though the boundaries persist more clearly in the magazines aimed at teenagers.

I would not suggest that all such confusion of genres is necessarily ideologically-driven, except insofar as the tendency toward short stretches of text colludes with the popular notion that young people cannot concentrate on anything longer, and require short, snappy texts to entertain as much as inform. However, we shall see that there are occasions when the genre-mixing or blurring is significant in its potential to confuse the roles of producer and reader.

Readers' and celebrities' stories

One of the most pervasive text types in women's magazines is the 'reader's story', or sometimes the 'celebrity's story'. These occur in the data in teenage and adult magazines, and on topics ranging from breast size to surgery and exercise. They are most common in the pregnancy and slimming magazines where the range of experiences can be quite wide, and the reader may read a number of stories finding parts of each story that match her experience to prepare her for a range of different scenarios or simply for prurience. The common stylistic feature of these stories, of course, is that they are normally written in the first person, and at least ostensibly in the words of the narrators themselves, though there may well be some editing and/or ghost-writing involved. Celebrity stories and some readers' stories often blend this kind of first-person narrative with an adapted interview. The questions may then be used as the headings to paragraphs, or the narrative may be in the third person with extensive first-person quotation and often lots of free indirect speech, as we shall see in Chapter 7.

Teenage magazines, insofar as they use readers' stories, tend to make sure that they represent at least two (and sometimes more) contrasting experiences. Thus one text from *Bliss* has two named (and photographed) readers explaining how they have changed from being unhappy with their big/small breasts respectively to being contented with them.

The readers' stories in pregnancy magazines are ubiquitous and range in style. Some overlap with other text types, such as the diary format. One article in *Our Baby*, for example, follows Jayne through the nine months of pregnancy in a pseudo-diary which begins before conception:

weeks 0–4

For the last six months I've been getting ready to conceive, following my GP's advice on diet and exercise, and we've been trying for about three months now. I can't wait to be pregnant.

Though this is presumably in some sense a 'real' account of the pregnancy, it is unlikely that the diary was written in real time, and the reader certainly experiences it after the event, so the use of the fictional present tense is a device to engage the typical or anticipated reader who is assumed to be somewhere on the road between conception and delivery herself. A different kind of item based on readers' experiences is also common in pregnancy magazines. This is where three or more readers give their account of a particular topic, such as labour and delivery, as in one text where the accounts, in first-person narrative style, are prompted by questions such as 'When did you go into labour?' and 'what did you feel when you first saw Ellie?'

These 'normal-range' stories serve a pedagogical function, of course, in telling novice mothers about the range of possibilities they face. There are others, equally pedagogical in effect, which chart the experiences of readers who have had life-threatening or other traumatic experiences, such as the loss of a child. One such text from *Our Baby* tells the story in first-person narrative mode of a woman who had a premature baby who died followed by an ectopic pregnancy from which she nearly died herself. She didn't expect to conceive after this, but now has two healthy children. We will return to the question of happy endings in a later section, but note here that the option to leave the reader with an unsatisfactory ending does not seem to be part of the normal range of features in this text type. Although the ostensible function of these stories may be pedagogical, there is also the potential for an 'entertainment' value which is served by the possibility that many readers will experience the lows and highs of these stories vicariously, so it is important from the commercial point of view that they are left with a positive outcome.

A slightly different, but also potentially pedagogical, purpose is served by another kind of reader's story, in this case written in the third person and blended with a second-person thread which acknowledges that the reader of the article will be going through similar processes. One example, from *Pregnancy and Birth*, narrates Mel Peter's first appointment with the midwife, and the reader is explicitly invited to 'sit in' on the experience in the sub-heading. Here is one extract from the article itself:

> swimming is one of the best forms of exercise for Mel (and pregnant women in general) because the water makes her weightless.

The consistency of narrative style in this text makes for some oddly uncomfortable reading in which the reader knows that points are aimed at her, but they are narrated apparently all for Mel's benefit. This kind of genre-merging is perhaps less successful than a straightforward juxtaposition of a range of genres, such as where an advice-giving feature article incorporates text boxes containing small reader's stories relating to the topic. This happens in a text from *Pregnancy and Birth* which discusses the issues surrounding the size of an embryo, and gives examples of people who had small or large embryos. A similar technique is used in an article from *Woman* which discusses infertility problems and pregnancy complications, and uses text boxes to tell readers' stories – all conspicuously about people who successfully conceived and bore a child in the end.

One of the stranger stories told in the pregnancy texts (*Pregnancy and Birth*) is the celebrity newsreader Katie Derham's story of her pregnancy.

This is written in the third person, but with a lot of direct speech and free direct speech too, so that the result is a 'voice' that mixes Katie Derham with the writer. The point of stories like this in pregnancy texts is similar to celebrity stories elsewhere – to give readers a role model who can provide answers to the questions that arise, in this case in relation to how to deal with pregnancy in the context of a busy professional life. The result is extracts like the following:

> She's selected her maternity wear with care – a few pieces from Nine over Twelve that she'll get maximum wear from until the baby's born.

Note the overlap here with advertising, as a particular outlet is mentioned 'in passing'. We will return to blended genres later, but it is noticeable that the information is given in a way that would allow readers to take their lead from Katie Derham, and the apparently straightforward description is therefore more a kind of indirect exhortation to the reader to model their behaviour according to this prime example.

The question of the stylistic authenticity of readers' stories when they are first-person narratives arises repeatedly in this data. One article from *Pregnancy and Birth*, for example, is made up of the stories of three pregnant women who have rather different experiences. They are in the first person and seem to be genuinely 'written' by them. There are a few clues, however, that indicate another 'voice' in the text. For example, two of the stories use exactly the same clause about a successful pregnancy: 'It's made this pregnancy even more special'. Whilst this may be a coincidence, it may also be a marker of the presence of another 'author' who tends to word similar feelings in the same way, whereas we might expect the readers concerned to use slightly different words. The additional 'voice' of the narrator or commentator may allow the reader to 'see' Katie Derham or other exemplars through a filter of advice, which effectively implies that readers could do worse than modelling their behaviour on theirs.

The only type of article that is similar to the 'reader's story' on the topic of sex is one where sex tips or techniques are tried out, usually by friends or colleagues of the writer, with short, first-person comments on each one. There are two such articles in the data, from *Shine* and *Minx* respectively, and they both seem aimed at making fun of ideas for sexual innovation, mostly for the purpose of entertainment. Because they are contextualized by the description of the technique itself, the comments are largely in direct speech:

The caterpillar walk was really lovely and sensual. But then he started sucking my toes and I just couldn't stop myself from thinking 'Oh my God, my size sevens are in Mike's mouth!' I'm afraid it took me quite a while to get back in the mood after that experience.

The preponderance of readers' stories in the slimming magazines meant that only six were chosen to be included in the data (Chapter 1, p. 23 *f*). These stories include one from *Diet and Fitness*, which is written in the third person:

When Diane Dowling walked down the aisle on her wedding day, she wore a long white gown, just as she'd always dreamed she would. Unfortunately, she didn't quite fit the fairytale princess figure of her childhood fantasies. She couldn't. Not in a size 24 wedding dress. Although only 25 years old, Diane was 18st and looked old and matronly. Her vast double chin protruded beneath her big, moon-shaped face, the tops of her arms spread massively beneath short sleeves.

Although people who lose large quantities of weight may indeed feel disgusted with their earlier selves, it is hard to imagine them describing their overweight version in quite such vivid terms as this. It is therefore a convenience to use the impersonal narrator to carry out this function, and to use direct speech to give the protagonist a voice. The prurience of these extreme stories of weight loss is partly achieved by the graphic description of the excess weight, and this is absent in the more solution-oriented articles, such as a text from *Best Diet Now* which has the stories of six successful slimmers in first-person narratives, and with no graphic description:

The turning point came when I saw a photograph of myself at a friend's wedding.

Other stories may also be quite solution-oriented as well as telling a particular person's story, and these tend to use the third-person narrative, but with lots of direct and free direct speech. Those which overlap with advertising, for example to promote the Rosemary Conley exercise classes, are not so inclined to indulge in gruesome descriptions, and lead much more quickly to the beginning of 'salvation':

Amy took herself to a local Meeting and, for the first time in years, got on the scales.

Readers' stories occur throughout the data, including examples relating to cosmetic surgery (*Body Beautiful* and *Woman's Own*) and exercise (*Diet and Fitness* and *Woman*). All these texts use the same format of third-person introduction followed by first-person narrative, though some are relating the story of only one person and others tell the stories of up to six people. The function of this choice of text type seems to be that the protagonists are role models for the reader, though the choice of the most extreme cases also suggests a prurient function which sells magazines.

Factual articles

The use of straightforward feature articles to discuss issues of the female body is reasonably well-represented in the data, though they tend to be short and are often restricted to the 'expert opinion' in a text box, or as a comment on a personal story. They deal with a range of topics including breast cancer, ectopic pregnancy, pregnancy itself, surgery, exercise, clothes and looking young. Not many of these more conventional articles occur in the teenage magazines.

Such articles, then, tend to be less significant in terms of giving advice than many of the other text types that we have already met, and others which follow, in particular those that use either instructions and step-by-step advice or divide the advice they are giving into sections according to the kind of woman they relate to, the time scale that they refer to, or even, and this is quite common, the body part they are focussing on. The reason for the lack of long, textually dense, factual articles can only be surmised, but is again probably related to the expectation that the attention span of readers for this kind of article is limited.

Diary-style articles

We have already noted that some of the readers' stories may overlap with a diary-style presentation, but this also seems to be a text type that occurs independently. There are some bodily topics that lend themselves to this kind of presentation, most obviously the menstrual cycle, and pregnancy, though there are also some texts which treat sex in this way. In this data, one text from *More* is a day-by-day guide to 'out-of-this-world orgasms', and is therefore broadly-speaking in a diary format, though it also divides each day into a number of steps, and thus crosses into another text type which is considered below. In this case, the text is in the second person, and since it is advice-based, its style is also marked by a number of imperatives:

Step two: exercise your bits. If you can't 'grip' his penis with your vaginal muscles during sex, then your internal vaginal muscles are too flabby!

More conventional diary-style texts include a text in *Our Baby*, which is headed 'Week-by-week action plan', and typically includes an initial statement in each section, followed by advice or instructions, using the second person to address the (presumably pregnant) reader:

4–8 weeks Congratulations – you're pregnant at last!

What to do now See your GP

We will consider other aspects of this text later, including the presupposition that the reader is and wishes to be pregnant, and that it took a long time to achieve this state. For now, let us just observe the norms of a fairly standard text type, and note that in this particular case it is supplemented by a set of question-and-answer boxes, answering imagined concerns, such as 'Should I avoid hot baths now I'm pregnant?'.

The variation in the style of these diaries depends on their focus. Texts in *Our Baby* and *Bliss* are explicitly directed at the reader, the latter having a circular-shaped 'diary' of the menstrual cycle, which sets out the different stages in each month with sentences such as 'The days when you bleed are called menstruation'. There are other diary-style texts, such as one from *Our Baby*, which chart the first-person diary of a particular woman, in this case Jayne:

Weeks 9–12

I'm a bit fed up about things but I don't want to blame my hormones – not all moods should be blamed on pregnancy! I'm finding it hard to concentrate on my studies to be a hypnotherapist, plus I'm nauseous.

Here, as in the readers' stories, the link to the reader is implicit, and is based upon the rhetorical strategy of the role model (see below p. *46 f*).

'How to' instructions/advice

A different way of breaking down advice into manageable chunks is to give a series of instructions or step-by-step advice, as in the breast-checking advice given in one text from *Sugar* and how to measure your bra size in a text from *Mizz* which begins as follows:

- Place a measuring tape around your rib cage, just underneath your bust.
- Check that the tape isn't too loose or tight.
- If the measurement is an odd number, add 5 in (12½ cm), if it's even, add 4 in (10 cm). Note down your number.

The main stylistic feature of such advice is, of course, the imperative verb aimed at the reader, as we see from the following extract from text from *Women's Health*, recommending an exercise regime for after pregnancy:

> Buttock Squeeze
> Breathe in, then out, lifting your hips off the floor slightly. Contract your abdominals and your pelvic floor muscles, then squeeze your buttocks. Hold for five seconds, release and relax. Build up to eight repetitions.

There is some advice that seems less likely to attract this kind of direct imperative approach. This is mainly in relation to sexual activity, where the second-person address mode is usually mixed with third-person reporting of trials of the advice given. This happens in texts from *Shine* and *Minx*, both concerning sex tips. Though the heading of one is an imperative, *Turn your body into a playground*, much of the article is either general (*The feet have a meridian line that runs through them*) or third-person (*When I started sucking Rachel's toe, she stopped relaxing*) and very few imperatives are included (*Get your partner to try a caterpillar walk with his fingers working down the sole of the foot, taking little bites as he progresses*).

Not all sexual advice articles are as reluctant to be directive as this, however. *Cosmopolitan*, for example, advises the reader to give *sex as a present*, and follows up the general advice with very specific instructions:

> When he can't hold on for much longer, allow him inside you then slowly squeeze your pelvic muscles.

This kind of instruction is modelled on the more common exercise routine imperative, such as is found in texts from *Woman's Own*, *Woman* and *Ebony*, the latter providing the following illustration:

> To work the obliques, or side muscles, curl up one elbow or side slightly above the other elbow and use your torso to do the turning.

Compared with the implicit advice to follow the example of role models, these articles are very straightforward in recognizing that the (typical) reader is looking for advice on particular subjects.

Categories of women

Slightly more unexpected, perhaps, than sections by time or by activity, are those which are divided according to categories of women – normally by bodily shape, but sometimes also by star-sign or even in one case by overeating style in a text (*Woman's Own*) which asks *What type of overeater are you?* and then names seven categories, including *comfort eater*, *habit eater* and *problem binge eater*, alongside a list of signs that will allow you to recognize your category and 'Self Help' tips for each case.

Another text from *Woman* concerns health and fitness, and uses individuals in different age groups to exemplify the issues and solutions that present to that particular decade. Each age is introduced in a general way:

30s

Juggling family life and a career is the biggest stress for women during this decade. Or you may hear your biological clock ticking louder and louder and wonder if Mr Right will ever come along. If you're in a rut, now's the time to make healthy, positive changes in your life.

The specific advice under each heading is filtered through the experiences of a woman who fits that age group.

The most frequent categorization by type of woman is to be found in the teenage magazines, where there are exercises advised according to star sign (*Bliss*), advice about bra styles according to breast shape and size (*Mizz*) and implicit advice on breast satisfaction from two different readers (*Bliss*), which begins:

Whether you're big, small, pointy, saggy or pert, chances are you wish your boobs were different.

Perhaps the most expected of these categorizations is according to overall body shape, such as *pear shape* or *hourglass figure*, which is found in texts from *Shout* and *Sugar*, the latter including a celebrity in each section to demonstrate that there are 'successful' people out there with the handicap of that particular shape:

You are Long and slim, with narrow hips, a small bust and long legs.

Star with your shape Gwyneth Paltrow.

Wear it Make the most of the gingham prints, which are *sooo* trendy this season.

Some informal reader research[1] amongst young women and girls indicated what I suspected, that they tend to read all sections of such articles, not just the one or two that they think apply to them. A different kind of project would be needed to investigate thoroughly the extent to which the reader identifies with the category of woman in each case, but I suspect that there is quite a high capacity for the reader to read 'as if' from the position of the relevant category, and even to imagine that she has the particular challenges of that category of body shape, breast size, and so on.

Advice in sections

In addition to dividing up advice according to reader-type, there are many articles, on all topics, which divide the advice that is being given according to body parts. Thus, as well as beauty advice by body part there are a number of texts giving advice about sex which are organized into body-part sections. These include a text from *Body Beautiful* which has an emphasis on sex as exercise, and advises on the *top five calorie-burning positions* as well as proposing the best sexual positions for enhancing the look of bodily features:

DOGGY STYLE

BEST FOR: Big bums

With the added bonus that all men love this position, it makes even the largest of bottoms look pretty attractive.

Less surprisingly, perhaps, the articles on cosmetic surgery tend to divide into sections by body parts or sometimes by the kind of procedure. Thus, in a text entitled *Body Parts* from *Body Beautiful*, the headings include *Nose jobs, Fat injection* and *Facelifts* whilst another article in the same magazine uses the perceived problems as its headings, with 'Acne scars', *Leg veins* and *Eye bags* being typical. Other, less invasive, beauty articles also organize on the basis of body part, as we see from the beginning of an extract on arms from *Looks*:

Feeling a bit baggy in the upper arm area? Yeah, yeah we all know exercise is the solution, but we want results and we want them now!

As we will see later, the language of these texts naturalizes a number of ideological views of the female body, including the notion that it is made up of parts, rather like a machine. This mechanical view of the body, whereby problems in particular areas can be sorted out, is part of the technological ideology that bodies, like cars, can be fixed.

Glossaries

Diary-style texts and many other health-related articles about the female body have an overt pedagogical aim, as I have noted earlier, though this may be mixed with the aim of entertaining. Perhaps the clearest example of this desire to teach is the glossary text type, which tends to occur most often where there is a plethora of technical terms (for example in relation to pregnancy), but also in teenage magazines where there is an assumption that some readers will not know the meaning of both technical and also more everyday words. One text from *Bliss*, for example, as well as having the diary of the menstrual cycle, also has a glossary covering toxic-shock syndrome and pre-menstrual syndrome as well as tampons. Texts from *Our Baby* and *Pregnancy and Birth* explain terms relating to labour and pregnancy respectively, in the first case in a column alongside the readers' stories, called *Explaining the jargon* and in the second case on the photo of a clipboard alongside the description of an ante-natal clinic visit, and headed 'Breaking the codes'.

What this apparent pedagogy confirms ideologically is that knowledge is power; that others (such as medical staff) have authority and thus power over us and that the magazine is on the side of the underclass, that is the reader. That this ideologically strong effect may be present does not necessarily negate any informational content that is actually given, and which may indeed help some readers to negotiate ante-natal clinics, doctors' surgeries or slimming regimes.

Advertising

The other main genre that is found throughout these magazines is the advertisement. We will see in the next section that there is no clear boundary between advertisements and other text types, but here we will simply establish the fact that magazines, being dependent on the income they produce, normally include a large number of them. The few to be mentioned here are those advertising tampons

(*Bliss* and *Shout*) surgery (*Body Beautiful*), products to beat cellulite (*Slimmer Magazine*) and a herbal remedy for the menopause (*Diet and Fitness*).

Personal opinion pieces

So far, the text types discussed have included almost all of the occurrences of body-references and discussions in this data. There are, however, two small groups of articles which make up the last two categories found here. These include personal opinion pieces, similar to the kind of text that makes up a newspaper editorial. In our data there are only two such texts, giving, as it happens, a male view of nutrition in pregnancy (*Slimmer Magazine*) and a male view of the way that young teenage girls dress and make up (*Jump*). I have no evidence that this situation (that is the male writer) is typical of opinion pieces more generally, though they certainly provide an interesting contrast with some of the other data in this study. The undoubted authority of a piece written by a nutritional 'expert' is perhaps invested still further with the authority of the gender of this piece. The other article is explicitly founded on the notion that a 19-year-old man has the authority to tell readers what men like in young girls:

> They're such attractive qualities in anyone, especially a young woman. Trust me, I'm a guy.

Note that we have no evidence that the writer is actually a man in this case, and there can be considerable doubt about the identity of authors in this kind of material. However, the implied author is indeed a man here, and this is the information on which the reader will base her reactions to the text.

Quizzes[2]

The final text type to mention here is the quiz, which is perhaps the stereotypical genre from the young-adult magazines for women, such as *Cosmopolitan*. However, there has either been a change in the market in relation to quizzes, or perhaps it is more the case that the topics I am interested in, relating to the body and bodily perceptions, do not lend themselves so readily to the quiz format, which is normally concerned with attitudes. The two quizzes that do occur in the data relate to sex (*Slimmer Magazine*) and fitness (*Woman's Own*) respectively. Here is a short extract from the former, to demonstrate:

Which would you prefer to wear to a party:

a A shocking pink dress that shows off your new shape, but is just a bit too tight for comfort?

b Your favourite black dress – you feel great and it hides a multitude of sins?

c Something inconspicuous, you don't want to be seen?

This illustrates the ideological issue with quizzes, which is that they are constructed around 'correct' answers, though of course they sometimes soften this with intermediate positions, where you can find yourself in the middle of a range between right and wrong. We will see a great deal more about correctness in the chapters that follow, but this structural feature of the quiz genre helps to naturalize such ideas.

Blurring of categories

The discussion of sub-genres and text types in the previous section has referred more than once to the fact that these category boundaries are not absolute, indeed that there are many texts in this data which either combine two or more text types or blend the features of text types, producing a hybrid text type. This is usually simply a question of ringing the changes, often also a way to make the potentially dry information-transfer a bit more interesting by breaking it down into manageable chunks or using different styles and approaches to get the same message across. Prototype theory from Katz and Postal (1964) was referred to in Chapter 1 as a way of avoiding the pitfalls of strict categories in describing the perceptions of female bodies as influenced by texts like the current data. Here, we may again invoke the prototype as a model of the related text types that appear to be distinct in their most central examples, but which overlap and merge at the boundary.

In this section we will consider a slightly more insidious and question-able practice, where the boundaries between informational text types are blurred with those of advertisements, and we find that the clarity of function that we might wish for begins to be clouded.

The cases of advertising being blended with the problem page format seem to occur mainly in the teenage magazines, and normally in conjunction with tampon advertising. One text from *Sugar* has a problem page relating to periods and also a diary-style description of the menstrual cycle. In the centre of the problem page is a photo of a Tampax box, and the further information section refers to the *Tampax Consumer Careline*. At first glance, this page would not look like an advertising feature, though the photograph is immediately recognizable so the advertising is not completely hidden. A similar text from *Shout* is more straightforward, with the column headed *TAMPAX*, and entitled *Tampax Period Column*. There is also a box with a free offer further down the page.

These texts raise some important questions about the role of advertising in information delivery. There are a number of possible reactions from the readers' perspective, ranging from being impressed at the social responsibility shown by a company that pays to give readers useful information to the opposite extreme of being annoyed by an advertisement that purports to be a neutral piece of advice. The cynical view is that this particular company is trying to get their name imprinted onto the minds of very young readers, with the consequence that they will use Tampax products for their whole menstruating lives, a time period of approximately forty years.

A similar kind of blending of text types occurs in a text from *Our Baby* which is entitled *FIVE STEPS TO A FLATTER tummy*, and subtitled *With a little help from Sweetex it's easy getting back to your pre-pregnancy shape*. The page looks like an article about those exercises which will help to get a new mother back into shape, with a photo of a 'cute' baby and mother in the centre of the five steps advice. The right-hand side of the page has a column offering a free Sweetex kit to *ten lucky winners*, and there is a photo of the product and other information in the bottom right-hand corner.

There are many articles in women's magazines which, whilst mentioning the detail of products, are not tied to a particular product, and at least appear to be a genuine attempt to review the range available for strengths and weaknesses. An example of this kind of blending comes from *Cosmopolitan*, which reviews the latest trends in dieting, and in doing so gives the full publication information on the diets mentioned:

There's also *The Body Code*, by Jay Cooper and Kathryn Lance (Piatkus Books, £9.99) – a new age eating plan which divides dieters into four groups: warriors, nurturers, communicators and visionaries.

If there is any product-placement here it is hard to tell, but other articles where only one or two cosmetic surgeries are mentioned, or which are placed in a whole magazine devoted to the Rosemary Conley slimming industry, are more obviously advertising by another name. Readers' stories, for example, usually have a crucial turning point (see rhetorical strategies below) in which the desperate yo-yo slimmer finally goes to a

WeightWatchers meeting, or a Rosemary Conley exercise class, and the slimmer starts to make progress:

> Then one day, in June 1997, Ros's sister-in-law, Christine, suggested that they try to lose weight together by going to a Rosemary Conley class...Ros managed to lumber through the exercise session that night, and by the time she arrived home, a mental transformation had taken place. 'I opened my member pack containing the Flat Stomach Plan diet and I was overcome with willpower' she says.

This kind of advertising is not surprising in the magazine produced and promoted by Rosemary Conley, but once the reader is halfway through reading it, it can be a surprise, and one might almost have to check the magazine's cover to be sure that this was an advert rather than an innocent mention of which particular class the protagonist happened to attend.

Rhetorical strategies

The ten rhetorical strategies identified here are all those recognized in the data and it was interesting to find how many of them were repeated in different contexts, and relating to different topics. The division of this chapter into the previous section on text types and this section on rhetorical strategies raises the question of how these differ, and to what extent the choice of text type is in itself a rhetorical choice. Thus, the blended genre categories in particular could be said to have a rhetorical aim in making the reader feel that they are being given neutral information, when in fact they are having a product-name reinforced. I will refer to such overlaps where relevant in the sections below, but there does seem to me to be a qualitative difference in principle at least between texts which are if not overtly, at least intentionally persuasive, and the choice of text type or other features which may have the effect of naturalizing an ideology, though this effect may of course be an unconscious result of the writer's own cultural assumptions.

Pseudo-science

This strategy involves the use of scientific terminology and authoritative-sounding experts to make the product or process appear up-to-date and technically well-grounded. It is not as common in the data as one might have expected given its ubiquitous presence in TV advertising, particularly in relation to household products and electrical goods. One text from *Slimmer Magazine* discusses 'Feminine Foods' and gestures towards a scientific rationale for its assertions about gendered eating habits:

> The way that men and women vary in their food choices has recently been closely examined by Katherin O'Doherty Jensen, Assistant Professor of Sociology at Copenhagen University.

The only other examples of scientific-sounding statements are in the data on cosmetic surgery, where the detail is likely to put off more readers than it attracts, such as this extract from an article in *Woman's Own*:

> During the operation, a narrow tube is inserted through a tiny cut and used to vacuum the fat layer deep under the skin…This technique is known as tumescent or wet liposuction

For whatever reason, though, there is generally very little of this kind of rhetorical appeal to the more rational side of the reader. We can speculate about the reasons, which may include the fact that the topics relating to women's bodies are too personal to the reader for a cold, technical, approach to be appealing. It is certainly interesting that the pregnancy texts, though they often explain all the 'jargon', do not emphasize the technical side of the processes involved, and usually minimize the detail, as in this text from *Our Baby*:

> Certain tests check for birth defects. Most take place at 16–20 weeks; a few hospitals offer a nuchal scan at 11–13 weeks, which checks for Down's syndrome.

Unlike in the cosmetic surgery texts, then, the pregnancy texts, on the whole, do not give a detailed, some would say graphic, description of what actually happens. The mystification of all such procedures under the term 'test' is quite a surprising finding within a context of apparent support for information and education of pregnant women. The ambivalence that these texts seem to feel towards women readers reflects the tension between first and second-wave feminisms, where the treatment of women as rational beings with the same mind–body split as men is in conflict with the revaluing of intrinsically female experiences, including the bodily experiences of menstruation and childbirth.

The result, in texts like these, is often a rather unhappy combination of appearing to be scientific and full of information, but not really going into the kind of detail that would help, for example, a reader who needs to take decisions about which tests to have. For these decisions, the health services normally have specific leaflets and pamphlets, so it leaves the magazine articles really only performing an orientation task, in which the information content is quite low.

Fictionalized heroines

Some readers' stories frame the person at the centre of the tale as a fictionalized heroine, using the style and narratorial techniques of fairytales or horror stories. One text from *Bliss*, for example, has sections dealing with different consequences of puberty, and each section has a sub-heading *The scenario*, which explicitly sets it up as the setting of a horror movie:

> You're minding your own business sitting on the loo, when you suddenly spot something in your knickers. It's alien stuff – whitish or yellowish gunk, almost like a gel.

These sensationalist beginnings are normally mitigated by the following sensible advice and reassurance, and it may be that the opening is aimed at making the most of the revulsion that girls can feel in relation to their own bodies in order to make the reassurance (we're all the same) the more effective. It does, however, also have the potential effect of reinforcing the horror. It is clear that this exaggeration of the alien nature of the leaky, unstable female body fits exactly with the feminist view of the problems constructed by patriarchy:

> That sense of the abject as both the alien other who threatens the corporeal and psychic boundaries of the embodied self, and as an intrinsic, but unstable, part of the self resonates with the widespread cultural unease with bodily, and especially female bodily, fluids. In the effort to secure the 'clean and proper' male body, the body that is sealed and self-sufficient, it is women who are marked by the capacity of that which leaks from the body – menstrual blood is the best exemplar – to defile and contaminate. (Price and Shildrick 1999: 7)

They point out the *cultural unease* with which women's bodily functions are viewed, and though the article quoted does try to give girls some strategies for dealing with the 'horrors' of the body, the opportunity to challenge this view of them is not taken up, indeed the horror is emphasized, and thus confirmed.

Happy endings

There is a widespread tendency for all stories in the data, whatever the topic, to have happy endings. This is not surprising, as magazines which make the readers feel upbeat about their lives are more likely to sell. An example of many from the slimming and fitness-related texts is an article from *Slimmer Magazine* which tells the story of Lynne Robinson, *the UK face of Pilates*:

> A history teacher with back problems, Lynne had difficulty finding a form of fitness that would help her and not aggravate her existing back pain... 'My backache disappeared as did the headaches.'

Other slimming texts also tell happy stories, and in some cases, they include a direct exhortation to the reader not to give up. One reader's slimming success story from *WeightWatchers* magazine does just this, in the words of the slimmer herself:

> To other WeightWatchers Members I can only say that if you really want it, if you work hard enough and dream long enough, it WILL happen.

Whilst it is not surprising to find that articles suggesting a course of action (like taking up Pilates) end on a positive note in order to encourage problem-solving, it is less clear that all pregnancies can possibly end happily, and certainly the solutions are not always completely within the woman's control. Nevertheless, all the pregnancy texts in the data end happily, even when the women featured have been through a great deal of pain and bereavement beforehand. Thus a text from *Our Baby* details the life of a woman who loses a first, premature baby, then has an ectopic pregnancy and finally has *two beautiful children*. The story ends on the following note:

> We haven't forgotten Christopher, but I'd really like people in a similar position to know that you don't have to give up. It may take time, but if you keep on trying there's no reason why you can't get there in the end.

This final statement is evidently untrue, and slightly disturbing in the context of a woman who also claims to be *incredibly lucky*, a sentiment that conflicts with the notion of *trying* and the implicit control that is conjured up in the above extract, so long as you don't give up. What kind of torment this would be to a woman faced with a similar situation is hard to imagine, so it is also hard to think who the article is supposed to be helping. Not those in the lucky position of never having had a pregnancy-related health problem, I suppose, though they may take vicarious satisfaction in reading what they have missed perhaps. A similar effect is seen in an article on getting pregnant from *Woman* which focuses on infertility problems and includes two readers' stories, both of which looked hopeless cases at one point, but each of which ends with a healthy baby.

This rhetorical strategy, reminiscent of the *Reader, I married him,* endings of nineteenth-century novels, is one that takes a singularly optimistic view of problems that do not always end happily in *Reader, I had a healthy baby.*

Real women

The use of 'real' women, as opposed to celebrities with impossibly perfect bodies for example, is one of the strategies used to persuade the reader that the magazine/article is down-to-earth and realistic in its view of the ideal woman. This technique has been used more frequently recently, even by advertisers, but in the women's magazine it is not new.

One of the techniques related to this strategy is to choose women with different extremes, such as large/small breasts (*Bliss*) or who have a range of different experiences in relation to labour (*Our Baby*) or who are willing to tell their own story in detail, as an example of one possible scenario for the reader to experience vicariously. This happens in an extreme form in *Our Baby* where a home birth is recorded photographically as well as in a commentary:

> Midwife Marlene (right) arrives soon after Claudia goes into labour. Claudia, who's 31, can't believe how much stuff Marlene's brought, especially as she's planning to give birth without medical pain relief. But a midwife has to be prepared for all eventualities.

There is an inevitable sense in a present-tense story like this that the reader is effectively being shown how to do it properly, and the reader may well feel under some pressure, at least whilst reading, to 'be like Claudia', whether that means to have a home birth or refrain from pain relief, these 'real' women are in some sense the female reader's role models, whether we like it or not.

Exemplary women

Related to, and sometimes the same as, real women, are the exemplary women who are held up as an example in a slightly more explicit way. The ancient Christian practice of setting up saints and other good women as 'exemplary women', which is shared by other world religions (see Clancy-Smith 2006) seems to happen quite regularly in the context of these magazines, emphasizing the importance of women behaving virtuously in relation to their bodies. Whilst this virtue may no longer emphasize chastity as the highest form of female virtue, there are nevertheless aspects of the current data which approximate to this kind of pressure. The new orthodoxy is the responsibility we each have to look after our bodies. Whilst not a religious message in itself, the rhetorical stance is not dissimilar to the Christian notion of stewardship, which is normally related in the Christian context to the idea of looking after a God-given Earth, but also encompasses the personal body. This includes, in the current data, dieting, sexual health, proper behaviour in pregnancy to ensure health and a return to the perfect body shape afterwards, the importance of making the most, visually, of the body you have, the use of technology (for example surgery) to enhance your natural features, and the responsibility on us to exercise for health and attractiveness.

One kind of exemplary woman, despite what we might know about their flaws, is the celebrity, and *Body Beautiful* discusses the relative merits of those stars, like Pamela Anderson, who have:

> finally cottoned on to what many of us have known for years: that the brash 'look at me, I've had plastic surgery' look from the 1980s is old hat, and in its place comes a more subtle approach to physical alterations.

However, the following extract from the same text indicates that the celebrities are criticized for being subtle too:

> She said that those stars who had obviously had it done and looked better for it, but wouldn't admit to going under the knife, were being dishonest. They were encouraging other women to have unrealistic expectations about how they themselves could look naturally, and to believe that they should look as good as the stars without having the surgical help.

These exemplary women, then, are not blamed for the amount of surgery they have, nor for wanting to look younger than their years, but for not being open about how they achieved this effect. The example that the commentator wishes them to make, apparently, is to praise the effects of cosmetic surgery.

Another kind of exemplary woman is based on the real woman of the last section. Most of these are women who are presented as a good example of how to react to different bodily issues. In the case of an article in *Woman* it is the importance of keeping your body fit and healthy at different stages of life:

> Janet's making the most of her retirement. In the last 12 months, she's lost 3st and started taking more exercise, She's tuned in to what she needs to do to stay fit, active and healthy in her 60s – and it's working.

Similar effects are to be seen in readers' stories generally, and celebrity interviews too. Here, there is a clear overlap with what I have been labelling text-types, and yet it seems logical to focus on the possible rhetorical effect of a text-type choice as a slightly separate issue. Thus an article which is based on an interview with pregnant newsreader Katie Derham (*Pregnancy and Birth*), gives an example of someone who becomes pregnant without being aware of it:

> Off on honeymoon touring California, Katie felt 'slightly odd' but put it down to jet lag. 'But tiredness is one sign I now realise is a dead giveaway! And although I love exotic food, on this holiday all I wanted to eat were plain, simple meals – shepherd's pie was a big hit.'

Perhaps the most widespread impression that the exemplary pregnant women give is not of particular activities or principles, but a generally engaged and informed attitude towards their pregnancy. Thus, Jayne in the diary-style article from *Our Baby* shows her balanced view of the options in labour:

> I'm still opting for a vaginal birth if possible, but I'm well aware that how the baby comes into the world is less important than his or her safety and health.

This display of reasoned thinking sets up an example to readers of how to react to the pressures on them to opt into or out of medical intervention in labour and sounds like a 'display' of the narrator's good sense. Similarly, in the slightly-fictionalized account of Mel Peter's first ante-natal appointment (*Pregnancy and Birth*), we find a third-person example being given of how to behave as a pregnant woman:

> From 32 weeks, Mel may recognise a pattern of movement. If this is different from normal, or if the baby moves less, Mel should tell the midwife.

We will be dealing in later chapters with the linguistic mechanisms by which these women become exemplary. Here it would appear to be a strong implicature that what Mel should do, all pregnant women should also do.

Puncturing myths

One rhetorical strategy in this data appears to be the setting-up of myths that are presupposed to be popularly believed, so that the article can knock them down. This is sometimes paired with a set of facts that are questioned, but turn out not to be myths after all. The first example in this data comes from the teenage magazines, where part of a text from *Bliss* gives the lie to myths about the menstrual cycle:

Myth 1

You can't get pregnant when you've got your period

Busted: A sperm can live inside you for days, which means it may still be alive in your womb when you start ovulating. And what does egg + sperm equal? Er, a baby.

The myth-puncturing style leads to an approach which, like the quiz structure discussed earlier, is simplifying almost to the point of being black-and-white. The desire to prevent unwanted teenage pregnancies leads to as firm a statement of the risk being taken as possible, with the more likely belief of most young people ('It's less likely you'll get pregnant if you have your period') being firmed up to the more extreme version given here, mostly in order to account for the small number of girls who may take such a risk.

Woman's Own takes a slightly different approach by alternating myths, that readers might think are true, with facts that they may find hard to believe. Here is a pair of this kind:

FACT Dieting can dull the mind

Studies have shown there is a link between dieting and mental performance. The reduction in working memory occurs because slimmers' brains become so preoccupied with dieting that other brain processes don't get a look in.

MYTH Obesity is genetic

Only 1% of obese people can blame their parents for passing on a 'fat gene'. The obesity epidemic is down to sedentary lifestyles with energy-rich and fat-laden diets.

Notice that the so-called 'fact' is not a scientific one in the usual sense that the mind is working less-well chemically, but relates to the obsession which dieters can build up. Notice that the rather vague reference to *studies* gives no clue as to what kind of research we are talking about. The message of this paragraph is ironic in the context of an article on dieting in a special issue of *Woman's Own* on dieting. It contrasts interestingly with the next myth, which is not letting the reader off the hook as regards obesity. The message, presumably an implicature, is that obese people should diet, though they can expect their brain function to be less effective as a result.

Sermon-style

Whilst we may recognize a more straightforward preaching style as being a kind of sermonizing rhetoric which tells the reader directly what she should or should not do, there are only two texts in this data that can be characterized as having something of the sermon about them. They are both claimed to be written by men. The first text (*Jump*) is a diatribe against the dressing up of young girls in a sexually enticing fashion. On the surface, it appeals to many of the ideas that sensible adults would concur with, such as the notion that it is important to give girls a chance to be children before putting them under pressure to look sexually attractive, and advises the reader to develop other attributes instead:

> Confidence and charisma will never go out of fashion. In fact, the older you get, the more important they become so you might as well try to develop them now. They're such attractive qualities in anyone, especially a young woman. Trust me, I'm a guy.

We will encounter this text again later, but here it is just worth noting that the preaching is not overt here, but is achieved by the technique of the implied author, who is a 19-year-old man, saying what he finds attractive and what he finds unappealing, with the flouting of the maxim of quantity resulting in an implicature that young female readers of the text will see that they should take note of his preferences.

The other sermon-style text is an article, also written by a man, on the subject of nutrition for pregnant women (*Slimmer Magazine*). Magnus Mumby discusses the ideal diet for pre-conception, and takes a very firm line with his readers:

> The diet isn't much fun it must be said, but it is only for two weeks and if you are not prepared to make small sacrifices for your child's well being then maybe you should consider if you are ready to become a parent.

This text is more obviously sermonizing, as it questions the commitment of someone who is not prepared to diet before conception. It has a great deal of deontic modality as well as being written in the second person, which gives it this authoritative quality. We will revisit this text in discussing particular stylistic features like these.

Steps (toward salvation)

The concept of structuring advice into easy steps towards a goal has already been commented on in relation to text types, but it also seems to describe a rhetorical strategy of trying to make the reader think that something very difficult can be achieved more easily in small steps. This may reflect some religious types of practice, such as steps to salvation, but these are perhaps more familiar to us in secular contexts as pseudo-religious forms of behaviour-changing, as practised by Alcoholics Anonymous, WeightWatchers and other similar organizations.

The examples in the current data include a text from *Ebony*, which is entitled *10 Steps to a FLATTER STOMACH*, and text from *Our Baby*, which has a similar title, but only half the number of steps: *FIVE STEPS TO A FLATTER tummy*. The latter text, as we saw earlier, is a cross-over text which advertises sweeteners as well as giving advice about exercise. A similar idea is found in *More*, which offers *out-of-this-world orgasms if you follow our seven-day sex plan*.

Damascene conversions

Continuing on the religious, particularly Christian, theme, there is a common rhetorical strategy which is familiar to many as the 'sinner

that repented', or from the story of St Paul who converted to Christianity on the road to Damascus. This kind of sudden conversion is thus sometimes known as a 'Damascene' conversion, though it would be surprising if such a story structure did not pre-date the biblical account of this incident. The rhetorical force, of course, of such a story, as the bible writers would have been aware, is to convince the reader that even the most heinous 'sinner' (in whatever sense) can be 'saved'.

This rhetorical strategy is related to strategies discussed earlier in that some real and some exemplary women are shown as having been through a Damascene conversion to convince them of the need to change/diet/have surgery and so on. Ferguson (1985) sees similar parallels between the religious cult and women's magazines:

> I have argued that women's magazines collectively comprise a social institution which serves to foster and maintain a cult of femininity. In promoting a cult of femininity these journals are not merely reflecting the female role in society; they are also supplying one source of definitions of, and socialisation into, that role. (Ferguson 1985: 184)

Both teenage girls in a typical text from *Bliss*, for example, are described as having been unhappy with their breasts at an earlier stage, and both now claim to be happy:

> Nowadays I'm perfectly happy being small. I'm glad I am what I am...I'm much more comfortable with my breasts now. I like them and I'm glad they're not big.

Whilst the reason for this change is not clear here, the change of heart is probably the point of the story as an example to other teenagers who are going through the earlier phase of being dissatisfied. The slimming texts tend to have a clearer conversion moment. Here are two examples, from *Slimmer Magazine*, and *Woman's Own* respectively:

> At my lowest point, I saw an article about how TV personality, Carol Vorderman lost weight using a programme called Slim from Within. I was inspired by what I read and as it seemed different to other diets I'd tried, I sent off [for] the programme.

> Amy took herself off to a local Meeting and, for the first time in years, got on the scales: 'I was dreading it. The lady who helps out said to me in a very quiet voice, "You're 20½ stone" and I thought,

Oh God, that's even worse than I thought! But then I thought, That's the worst bit over and you've taken the first step.'

These stories are advertising Slim from Within, and WeightWatchers respectively, though the latter is not a direct advertisement but a reader's story. The pattern is so strong in texts on this topic that the reader certainly has a sense of the absolute need for a moment of conversion, which though it is combined with willpower, control and self-determination, is also dependent on some outside agency, in this case not God but Rosemary Conley or WeightWatchers. The rhetorical strategy, then, is to persuade readers that they *can* slim – indeed anyone can slim – but not without that all-important trigger moment which requires signing up (and paying, though this isn't mentioned) to some outside agency.

Summary

Fairclough's notion of genre-mixing, a term he used to describe television interviews and debates, turns out to be useful here to describe the patchwork combinations of text types that these texts seem to favour. There may, however, be a justification for talking in terms of genre-blending where there is no clear dividing line between two or more genres, but rather a merging of their features. This, still more than the confusion of role predicted by Fairclough, may confuse or mislead the unwary reader, most particularly where advertising is slipped into the structure of another genre, or wears the clothes of a different genre.

As for rhetorical strategies, whilst these texts are not obviously using classical rhetorical figures, they nevertheless seem to exploit at times the *logos* or appeal to the intellect (for example in puncturing myths) and at others the appeal to the *pathos* or emotions (for example in the emotional appeal of readers' stories). Perhaps the most interesting, because the most clearly ideologically-loaded, are the appeals to *ethos*, or the sense of correctness or morality. Many of the texts of different genres appear to construct a sense of the 'right' thing to do, whether it is in relation to what to eat in pregnancy or how to deal with being overweight.

The mildly religious connotations of the exemplary women, the sermon-style and the idea of steps towards a goal are echoed in many of the slimming stories, particularly where they are a covert advertisement for a particular regime or exercise class. One text from *WeightWatchers* magazine, for example, uses the terms *Meeting, Programme* and *Leader* as proper nouns, and uses *Goal* without a determiner, which is another echo of the language of salvation. There is a very strong sense of the religious group in the piece as a whole, not least in the title, which is *Reborn* and thus reminiscent of the idea of being 'born again' in Christianity.

Women's magazines, then, though ostensibly there to inform and entertain, also appear to have a normative or even restraining purpose in addition. The conduct book of the eighteenth and nineteenth centuries (see Jones 1990) may have evolved and become more subtle, but women are still under pressure, even from their 'own' texts, to do what is correct.

As we will see in later chapters, some of the detailed stylistic features of the language used in the text types and rhetorical strategies examined here work to reinforce the ideological effects already noted. This chapter has demonstrated that the choice of text type, and within this the rhetorical strategies used, are the context within which the micro-level ideological naturalization operates.

3
Naming and Describing

This chapter takes as its theme two related textual processes which both have the potential to cast the topics they describe in specific ideological terms. Whilst the impetus for these analyses was the grammatical process of nominalization, we will see that very similar analyses can be made of nominals that are not derived from verbs. The term nominalization itself refers to the morphological derivation of a noun from a verb. These would include, for example, *introduction, sleeping* and *significance* from the verbs *introduce, sleep* and *signify* as in:

> The introduction of stricter controls on fraud was a government ploy.
> Sleeping in a hammock is bad for your back.
> The significance of that relationship escapes me.

Whilst there are very many such examples of strict nominalizations in English, most of them do no more than provide some economy in the language, so that we are not obliged to put each process into its own clause. If we attempted to do so for the above sentences we would find ourselves spelling out the basic ideas underlying them:

> The government have introduced stricter controls on fraud and this is a ploy.
>
> Someone(?) sleeps in a hammock and this process is bad for your back.
>
> That relationship signifies something but it escapes me.

Notice that as well as being explicit, this re-writing has also shown up the fact that we sometimes use nominalizations for general reference, as in the second sentence here. Once we try to undo the nominalization it turns out that we do not have a clear grammatical Subject for the verb *sleeping.* What early accounts of CDA realized was that this perfectly useful grammatical process, whereby the verb changes into a noun and various other participants may be left unmentioned for good reason (such as not knowing their identity) may also be used for less straightforward processes, including hiding the identity of participants, reifying the process and creating existential presuppositions. Fairclough (1989) for example, glosses nominalization as:

> a process is expressed as a noun, as if it were an entity. One effect of this grammatical form is that crucial aspects of the process are left unspecified ... causality is unspecified. (Fairclough 1989: 51)

He also notes (Fairclough 1989: 124) that references to time (that is, tense) get lost in nominalized versions of events and processes, and that modality and agency are lacking in addition.

One of the clearest statements of the potential of nominalization comes from Fowler (1991: 80):

> Nominalisation is a radical syntactic transformation of a clause, which has extensive structural consequences, and offers substantial ideological opportunities ... we claimed that nominalization was, inherently, potentially mystificatory: that it permitted habits of concealment, particularly in the areas of power-relations and writers' attitudes.
>
> If mystification is one potential with nominalization, another is reification.

Fowler points out that the loss of tense, modality and agency is only one part of the power of nominalization. The other, reification, refers to the creation of existential presuppositions. Thus, the use of a nominalization, *confirmation* in the sentence 'The *confirmation* that we are at war is a real blow to anti-war campaigners' focuses not on the process of the announcement, but on the outcome. This has the effect of making the *confirmation* more like an entity and less like a process, and it is also presupposed to exist, as we can see by the fact that it stays constant in the negated version: 'The confirmation that we are at war is not a real blow to anti-war campaigners'. This reification is not, in fact, limited to grammatical nominalizations, but is also true of all definite and some indefinite noun phrases, particularly where there is other modification in the form of adjectives or subordinate clauses:

The disastrous outcome of the trial will be felt for years to come.
This unique opportunity to see the world is available to all soldiers.

The subject noun phrases in these two invented sentences demonstrate
the effect of building into the noun phrase some of the assumptions
and ideologies that it might suit the writer to include in such a way that
they are difficult to contest. The propositions of the two sentences are
able to be challenged:

No – it will be forgotten about in a couple of months.
No – some of them never leave Britain.

The presuppositions – that the trial was indeed disastrous and that there
is a unique opportunity to see the world – are not in question here.

I would propose, therefore, that the analysis of nominals in general
is one of the more useful tools for critical discourse analysts, and this
chapter takes such a position as its starting point. Naming is one of the
major ways of incorporating ideologies into texts and because the modification of head nouns is part of that naming process, I have decided
to include 'describing' in this chapter as a related textual constructor of
meaning.

Naming and describing

Functionally, one of the potentially most influential choices any writer
makes is the names s/he uses to make reference. This is both an 'easy'
concept to understand, and a difficult type of analysis to carry out. For
many referents, there is little obvious choice in the way that they are
named in English. There are, of course, differences of effect achieved by
choosing nouns with different connotations, including those of register
and formality. But these differences tend to be quite transparent and
are certainly fairly easy to point out, even if their effect is not always so
clear.

However, if we take the noun phrase as the basic unit of naming, as
well as the choice of head noun, there are choices to be made about
the modification of the noun. Adjectival choices are considered under
a separate heading here (see 'Characterizing' below) but in addition to
these, the use of definite and indefinite articles, possessive and demonstrative determiners, and postmodification by prepositional phrases or
relative clauses results in a naming strategy which can encompass
complex presuppositions about ideology.

My use of the functional term 'naming' to characterize this aspect of style, reflects a widening of the CDA category of nominalization. The grammatical process of creating a nominal out of a process (for example 'nominalization' itself), though treated as a transformation by Fowler (1991: 80), is conceptually similar to the process of putting anything into a definite noun phrase and treating it as a 'given' – the effect is to reify its existence. But the effect is not only one of existential presupposition (see Chapter 5), it is also the more subtle question of deictic properties being assigned by the demonstratives and possessives and the effect they have on the naming of referents.

Though many of the functional categories I am using here can be identified at a structural as well as a semantic level, they also all have realizations beyond their most stereotypical form. However, it is useful to note that the most typical vehicle for characterizing in English is the adjective. This function, therefore, is largely sought through the use of adjectival modification of nouns, although it is recognized that there is an overlap here with naming, since the choice of a head noun to refer to something is one of the ways in which a text characterizes that referent. As we will see below, the most significant finding in relation to adjectival use in this data is the concentration of evaluative adjectives, in particular those relating to the normality or naturalness of the item or process being described.

The naming and describing of women and their bodies in magazines written for them and for their benefit is the original motivation for this research. Given that English has too few 'normal' labels for women's sexual body parts, particularly those which might be considered relatively neutral in relation to formality or informality; it was potentially of some interest to see how these were named in published texts. Whilst we have *vagina* to describe the internal passage from the womb and *vulva* and *labia* to describe the outermost parts of the female genitalia, these are seen as relatively technical and therefore formal words with very specific meanings, and are not normally used as a generalized label for the female genitals. At the other extreme, we have *cunt* as a taboo but relatively general label, and more euphemistic but titillating labels such as *pussy, beaver* and so on.

None of these terms serves women in their daily lives, who might wish to refer to the reproductive and sexual parts of their bodies for health and other reasons – to health professionals, friends and confidants. This leads to real dilemmas for parents and others in relation to the labelling of girls' body parts, as they need to find some way that female children can communicate about the health and cleanliness of these areas of their body just as they do about their knees, faces and hands.

One of the tasks of the analysis, then, was to establish the naming habits of women's magazines in relation to all parts of the female body, both sexual and non-sexual, given that the topics of many of the articles and advice columns is the body, and particularly its sexual attractiveness and other functions (such as reproduction). There was no particular expectation that the magazines would do other than reflect and reinforce the usage of 'polite' society, but the range and detail of the body-part naming, particularly in relation to descriptors, such as adjectives, was revealing.

The other main aspect of naming and describing that was investigated here was the construction of women, mainly as readers, but also as professionals and advisors, and the relationship that such women appear to be constructed as having to their bodies and bodily processes. The identification of people by body parts, and the use of evaluative adjectives in relation to women and their bodies are of particular interest in this regard. Whilst the analysis is not quantitative, there are some features of language in the data that one might wish to describe as overwhelmingly present, and in these cases one might argue that there is the potential at least for a very strong ideological influence over readers' perceptions of women's bodies.

As we saw in Chapter 1, there are no simple one-to-one relationships between textual features and the stylistic functions that we are concerned with in this analysis. However, there are certain features that most obviously line up with each of the functions, and in the case of naming and describing, the obvious textual features relate to nouns, noun phrases and related adjectival modifications of nouns. Whilst this narrows the field a little, for example by enabling us to ignore verbs for the time being, it nevertheless leaves open a large number of considerations relating to nominal and adjectival constructions. These potentially include everything from the lexical semantic structure of the texts, in terms of lexical fields or use of hyponyms, for example, to the choice of euphemistic lexemes or the premodification of head nouns by definite articles or possessive adjectives.

The texts which form the data of this study were scrutinized for the manner of naming body parts and processes, the manner of naming women and the kinds of descriptions attached to these names. The checklist of textual features which were considered included the following, though there was no clear expectation about what kinds of patterning might be found under these headings:

- Use and reference of pronouns;
- Lexical semantic patterning of texts (including lexical fields and occurrence of other sense relations);
- Connotative features of the body part labels chosen;
- Nominal labelling of processes;
- Structural properties of noun phrases, including determiners and the choice and use of adjectives, in premodifying, complement and head noun roles.

What emerged from this particular analysis of the data was a remarkable set of consistent habits of both labelling and describing women and their bodies, though some of the features investigated were not as fruitful as others. For example, though the study of lexical fields can be of great significance in relation to the style of a poem or poems, the nature of the texts in the current data is such that the occurrence of certain lexical fields (of body parts, processes, and others) is firstly not surprising, and secondly of little significance in stylistic terms. What turned out to be much more interesting in this data is the precise choice of terms from the relevant lexical fields, and the implications that these choices may have for the reader's perceptions of the female body.

Constructing the reader

In a sense, all of the analysis in this book is aimed at finding out how the reader is potentially constructed by the language of the texts. However, in a very specific way, the writer may make presuppositions and implicatures about the kind of reader that is being taken for granted. We will look at other presuppositions and implicatures in Chapter 6, but here we will consider those which seem to relate particularly to the process of naming and characterizing or describing the readership.

People
It is no surprise, perhaps, that many of the texts address the reader directly using the second-person pronoun, *you*, and they just as often indicate that the referent of the pronoun is female:

Find out what's happening to *you* and *your* baby... (*Our Baby*)

Turn *your* body into a playground (with the highly underrated art of foreplay) (*Shine*)

Identify the reasons why *you* can't say no to food and *you're* more likely to succeed with *your* diet... (*Woman's Own*)

As these examples demonstrate, the second-person pronoun is often used in conjunction with other phrases making it clear that the supposed reader is not only female, but is also in a particular category; pregnant woman, sexually active woman, dieting woman or unsuccessful dieter.

The norm for many of the articles, particularly those giving specific advice, is to use the imperative form of the verb, with a second-person addressee, as in the following examples:

Use your fingertips gently to ease the area around the kneecap. (*Body Beautiful*)

Buy yourself a pocket-sized notebook and each day *write* down... (*Woman's Own*)

There will, of course, be readers of these texts who do not fit into the construction of very particular kinds of women, and this will include women who are not pregnant/overweight/sexually active/heterosexual as well as male readers. However, I would hypothesize that there is a particular reader-position of empathy which female readers tend to adopt in relation to their magazines and which would be less likely in the case of male readers.

One text from *Bliss* in the teenage data, consists of a set of exercises – a 'workout' – according to the star sign of the reader:

Scorpio: You're spiritual, so an airy exercise, like a roll down, will relax you.

Capricorn: Press-ups are perfect for you 'cause you've got loads of energy.

The referent in each of these sections is different, by definition, and yet as we saw in Chapter 2 it is unlikely that many readers will only read their 'own' section. Similarly with the article on fashion (*Mizz*) which categorizes girls by their bodily 'failings':

So you have a chest...
So you're smaller on top, bigger on the bottom!

The clothes advice is all about how to ameliorate the look of a flawed body and the advice of only one or two of the sections may be relevant to a particular reader, though as we saw in Chapter 2, readers tend to read all sections and imagine themselves to have the relevant body type. The pronoun is therefore of shifting reference here too, and the reader of such magazines will become accustomed to decoding the pronoun reference in such cases as they are very frequent.

A slightly different case holds for the many texts that take the form of some kind of question and answer, such as problem pages. In these cases there may be an actual referent of the pronoun, that is the letter-writer or assumed questioner (they are not always given an identity). But the referent of the second-person pronoun in the answers slides between the individual addressee, and the wider group of addressees in the readership:

> This lump is more likely to be due to the breast bud developing. I know *you* might find it embarrassing, but *you* should still get it checked out...It's better to have things checked than to let a major worry get *you* down. (**Sugar**)

I would suggest that there is contextual evidence here that the first and second occurrences of *you* refer to the letter-writer, and that the third one refers to 'people' or 'one', which may be taken as being addressed to the wider readership. These contextual clues include the use of *This* at the beginning, which has definite reference (to a particular lump) and the main clause introducing the second sentence: *I know*. This indicates that the advisor is aware of the feelings of someone, and it is likely to be someone specific, rather than the readers in general. The final use of *you* is in a generic sentence introduced by *It's better* and the phrase *a major worry* is used, rather than a particular concern about a lump in the breast, leaving the possibility open that other worries might also require the same kind of advice.

A similar move takes place in another answer to a teenage letter writer:

> First things first hun, *you*'re completely normal. It's very common for bleeding to be irregular when *you* start your periods. It can take months for *your* body to settle down...If *you*'re still worried then pop along to your GP. And don't be embarrassed, after all, all us girls have 'em! (**Mizz**)

The first *you* in this answer is clearly referring to the letter-writer, as it follows the endearment *hun* which is presumably intended to make the letter-writer feel cared for. The second, and more particularly the third, uses of *you* are very much wider in their reference, since they are discussing a range of scenarios rather than the specific worry described in the letter. It is also interesting to note the inclusive use of *all us girls* in the same answer. This is a common way of the writer identifying with the readers on the grounds of her gender. In the current case, this can sound slightly awkward, as it is clear that the writer is an adult, whilst the supposed reader is a teenager. The use of the word *girls*, then, is an attempt on the part of the writer to emphasize the similarities between her and the reader (that is, gender) and play down the differences (that is, age).

A more extensive version of this kind of identification with the reader comes in an answer to the question of whether looking at other girls in the shower at school makes the letter-writer a lesbian:

> All bodies are beautiful, so they're nice to look at (especially girls ones, less messy and no dangly bits). In addition, we normally cover our bodies up with clothes, so it makes it kinda weird when we see them naked, that why it makes us feel a bit funny inside sometimes. (**Mizz**)

We will return to this text a number of times, as it is one of the very few in the data which deals with sexuality. Here, we need only note that the advisor uses the first-person plural pronouns, *we* and *us*, to generalize about people, and thus to include the letter-writer as well as herself and the readers in the generalizations. The function of this usage is to make the letter-writer feel 'normal'. We will return to questions of normality below.

Whilst the naming of individuals and groups of people is not, in itself, necessarily constructing the female body in particular ways, it is noticeable that the population of these texts, apart from the addressee (usually the readership in general) is made up of allies (*your mum, my closest friends, my parents*), experts (*expert, your GP, midwives, their plastic surgeons*), exemplary women (celebrities, readers and others who do the 'right' thing) and the 'other', that is men (*guys, boys, he, my husband*).

The ideology of women being to some extent helpless victims of their bodies is partly supported by these categories of people surrounding the subjects of the texts, despite the many exhortations to take action. The women at the centre of the texts, whether real or generalized, famous or 'ordinary', are constructed as needing help – from their friends and family, and from experts or authority figures. The male is largely absent from the scene, except when the expert happens to be male, and is only referred to in relation to problems (in teen magazines and the black magazines); in relation to pregnancy and as a partner in relation to (assumed heterosexual) sex.

The other consideration which arises from the naming and describing of the people in these texts is the categorization by body shape or by relationship to the body: my big-boobed friends (*Bliss*). This example illustrates that the teenager is busy splitting up the world into different kinds of girl on the basis of the size of their breasts, just as some of the texts do. An article on slimming crazes in *Cosmopolitan* also categorizes people into the users and promoters of various diets:

> **Users**: devotees, a low-carb devotee, long-term convert, carbohydrate addicts
>
> **Promoters**: celebrity diet-trainer, nutritionists, american dieticians, nutrition experts, diet gurus, personal trainer

And finally, there are a number of texts in the data which divide subjects into various 'other' categories, whilst simultaneously trying to assert their similarity to *us women*:

> The hot stars; A-list celebrities; the stars; the women who seem to naturally look good; a heavyweight star; actress, wife and mother Cher.

This list, from *Body Beautiful*, is in an article about celebrity surgery, emphasizes the 'otherness' of celebrity women, because despite being 'normal' working women (*actress, wife and mother Cher*), they also manage to *naturally look good*. There is a potential paradox about many of the exemplary women, whether famous or not, which is that they both embody what we could be and are marked out as different from the rest of us. We will return to the idea of exemplary women in a later section.

People as body parts

One common tendency in many of the texts in this data is for people to be identified by the body part under consideration. The main mechanism for this is that the second-person pronoun (*you*) is used but with a clear referent of the body part rather than the whole woman:

Teenagers: A curved piece of wire is threaded underneath each cup giving you lift and support (*Mizz*);

Whether you're big, small, pointy, saggy or pert, chances are you wish your boobs were different (*Bliss*);

Pregnancy: I'm not very big (*Our Baby*);

'I was fully dilated by 9.30 a.m. (*Our Baby*);

Sex: A few weeks ago my boyfriend and I tried to have sex but he couldn't get inside me (*Woman*);

I'm so dry (*Woman*);

Slimming: 'you're 20½ stone' (*WeightWatchers*);

Surgery: I went from a 32B to a 32D (*Body Beautiful*).

In these cases, then, the reader is variously referred to as her breasts, her womb, her vagina, her body weight and her chest size.[1] We have seen in Chapter 2 the indication that dividing the body into parts can provide the basic structure of whole articles. This is another sign that women can find themselves identified by a significant body part, either by others, or as part of their own self-perceptions.

The ideological implication of these repeated tendencies is not easy to pin down, but it is clear that this metonymic habit relates only to the sexual and reproductive body parts, or the weight, which is usually considered to be a factor in (sexual) attractiveness. Note that there is no equivalent tendency to equate women with their hair (*you are greasy*) or feet (*you are sevens*). Female readers of such magazines throughout their lives will have the primary functions of sex and reproduction repeatedly conjured as the equivalent of their 'self', which may over time influence the woman's self-perception to concur with the centrality of such social functions.

Choice of adjective versus noun

The final way in which people are characterised in these data, which may be of some ideological significance, is in relation to the choice of an adjectival or a nominal form to represent their particular features:

My friend caught me looking at her and called me a lesbian, is she right? (*Mizz*)

Does this mean I'm a lesbian? (*Bliss*)

These two letters, and the answers given, use the nominal form of *lesbian* (indicated by the definite article, *a*), though the second one has a heading which uses the adjective *gay: Am I gay?* It is clearly the case that the use of a nominal form indicates a characteristic which is represented as more permanent and intrinsic to the person than the adjective. Thus, to call someone 'Jewish' is potentially less aggressive than to call them a 'Jew'. Whilst the permanence and intrinsic nature of Jewishness is not in question, the effect of using a label (that is, a noun) is more stark and likely to sound like a categorization than the use of an adjective, which simply notes a particular characteristic. Similarly, to use the noun, *a lesbian*, rather than the adjective, is to make clear that there are two kinds of people; those who are, and those who aren't lesbians, rather than, as some might prefer to argue, a heterosexual-to-lesbian continuum (Rich 1993), or if not a continuum then at least more categories of female sexuality than two. The answers to these letters, though willing to concede that some people might indeed be in the 'other' category, lesbian, nevertheless try their best to reassure the letter-writers that they are probably not 'in' that category (*it doesn't mean you're a lesbian*).

The reinforcement of strict categories of sexuality here is one of the byproducts of what is intended to be a reassuring answer. By contrast, the one text in the data which deals with bulimia, uses the adjectival form, rather than a noun:

> We don't binge on food and if anything we under-eat, but anything we do eat we throw up. Are we bulimic? (***Sugar***)

It is probably not common for people to be known as *a bulimic*, possibly because of its relatively recent development in the public consciousness. The condition of anorexia, which has been discussed in public for longer, does seem to have made that shift, so that people might well say *She's an anorexic*, just as they would say *He's an alcoholic*. The data under scrutiny here do not have such examples.

Parts, substances and processes

The naming of body parts, secretions and processes in the data is often straightforward, and need not concern us further here as far as non-sexual or taboo body parts are concerned. Thus, the regular use of normal vocabulary such as *leg*, *arm*, *face*, is evident throughout the data, as seen in these extracts:

Step onto right leg and kick left foot across in front. (*Diet and Fitness*)

Shiny tights can turn large calves into two pork sausages! (*Body Beautiful*)

Even here, it is noticeable that the overriding concern with looking 'normal' is paramount, and the text manages to imply that those with *large calves* should be trying to hide them in some way.

One of the significant distinctions that the texts tend to make is between the outer and the inner body parts of women. The emphasis on the inner sex organs of girls is made explicit in sex-education literature, as can be seen in the following extracts from Meredith (1985):

> Girls are often unaware of the changes in their sex organs because most of them are inside their body...
>
> It is easy for a boy to tell when his sex organs are developing because they increase visibly in size.

This distinction between the accessibility of the male sex organs and the relative inaccessibility – and thus mystery – surrounding the female organs remains implicit in much of the data under consideration here. As we shall see in the sections that follow, the distinction is reflected in the vocabulary and structure used in naming the female body parts in this data, with the reproductive organs (inside) being treated differently to the outer body parts, including those which provide sexual attractiveness.

Once we start considering the sexual or reproductive body parts of women, the vocabulary of English begins to be deficient, as discussed above, and these texts find themselves using a range of connotative forms which are, at one extreme, scientific or medical, and at the other very informal, verging on the taboo. There are also occasions when the writers resort to euphemism as a way out of the problem of what to call things.

The use of scientific or technical jargon is found particularly in relation to the inner body parts, mostly because there is no alternative available, these parts having been largely ignored (or not known about) over the centuries, and there being no neutral equivalent. Note that this is not a problem with all internal organs, as testified by the words *kidney, heart, lungs, liver* and so on. The internal sexual organs of the female, however, seem not to have developed a detailed everyday vocabulary, with the exception of the word *womb*. The texts dealing with these internal organs, therefore, find themselves using a range of vocabulary that sounds semi-formal and technical:

> Your fertilised egg (the zygote) is wafted down the Fallopian tube. It reaches the uterus around five days later ... (*Our Baby*)

In the texts relating to pregnancy, the use of technical vocabulary is extensive, particularly in relation to the complications and problems that can arise during pregnancy:

> 'They told me I had a blocked Fallopian tube and needed a laparoscopy and a hysteroscopy to check for fibroids' (*Woman*)

This kind of vocabulary use is probably unavoidable, and yet is in effect medicalizing the process of bearing children for *all* readers of the magazine, whatever their own personal experience. Although the articles in this case do not normally divide into sections ('what kind of pregnant woman are you?'), nevertheless, there are clearly many readers who do not fall into the categories of pregnant women that are described in this data. However, the reader-position of many women, whether pregnant or not, may be 'this could happen to me', and it is a qualitatively different experience from that of a male reader to whom it could not happen. The emphasizing of problems, then, with their attendant medical terminology, is one of the overwhelming effects of the pregnancy material.

There is, however, a clear sense that many of the texts in this data feel a pedagogical responsibility to explain not only terminology but the processes and mechanisms of the body. One of the techniques used to make the strange seem more accessible is to compare parts of the body, or the foetus/embryo with everyday objects:

> At the top of my vagina I can feel a slimy ball *the size of a 2p piece* with a space in the middle ... You've located your cervix – the neck of your womb. (*Bliss*)
>
> Womb – *the size and shape of an upside-down pear.* (*Bliss*)
>
> The opening to the womb, *the diameter of a thin straw.* (*Bliss*)
>
> Girls have an orgasm by having their clitoris (*tiny, pea-shaped knob of flesh* at the top of the inner vaginal lips), stimulated. (*Bliss*)
>
> Your cervix ... is about *the same size as a pin.* (*Bliss*)

I noticed a lump under the centre of my nipple. It's about *the size of a 2p coin* ... (**Sugar**)

The embryo now measures *about half the length of a grain of rice.* (**Our Baby**)

And your baby ... now measures around 13 cm (5in) – *about the length of a pen.* (**Our Baby**)

And your baby ... weighs 500 g (17 oz, *about half the weight of a tin of beans*). (**Our Baby**)

She's *the size of an envelope* (21 cm or 8.2 in long). (**Our Baby**)

The comparison with everyday objects gives a visual sense of what is being described. A more coy, but equally prevalent, way of referring to the more taboo parts of the body or bodily processes is by euphemism:

Tampons are inserted into your vagina to absorb *menstrual flow.* (**Bliss**)

There are two types of *protection* you can use to absorb *your flow.* (**Fresh**)

now I'm scared I've damaged *my insides* and won't be able to have children. (**Bliss**)

These examples tended to occur more in the teenage than in the adult magazines, though there are also euphemisms to be found in articles about sex for adults, often in the context of much more explicit language:

Now he can orgasm up to three times a night, he's never been happier – and I get a lot more *action*! (**Cosmopolitan**)

Step two: exercise *'your bits'*. If you can't grip his penis with your vaginal muscles during sex (**More**)

The probable use of such euphemisms in sex articles with otherwise explicit language is as a tantalizing technique, on the assumption that too much explicitness might sound too clinical. A different reason might be surmised for the euphemisms used in problem pages:

'My privates' are smelly ... I've noticed a strong smell coming from *'down below'*. (**Woman**)

Here, it is more the absence of appropriate vocabulary, and a reluctance to talk too explicitly about taboo areas of the body that limit the letter-writer to the euphemistic phrases. A similar avoidance of difficult subjects occurs in the pregnancy texts where the phrase *precious pregnancies* occurs frequently as a reference to pregnancies following miscarriage, stillbirth or other birth traumas. At the other extreme, there is some use of dysphemism when the topic is assumed to be one on which the readership would agree:

> Once upon a time, stretch marks were a taboo issue. If you had them it was assumed you were *a bit of a porker* (**Looks**)

This example aims to puncture the myth that people with cellulite are necessarily fat, and so it is 'safe' to use the uncomplimentary term 'porker', in the knowledge that it will not be taken to be applied to the readers, even if they have cellulite. One of the potential effects on some readers is to make them feel that they are in the category of non-fat women, and to allow them a small glow of satisfaction at not being *a porker*.

Perhaps the most noticeable vocabulary choice tendency in this data is the use of informal vocabulary, often in the same context as the formal and technical, and apparently used to undermine any sense of being over-serious or too pompous. The result is that the references to the stomach very often use the terms *tum* or *tummy*, and texts generally use *bum* in preference to the only slightly more formal *buttocks*:

> Marlene gently manipulates Claudia's tummy. (**Pregnancy and Birth**)
>
> I reckon I lost around four to five inches from around my lower tum. (**Woman's Own**)
>
> Feeling glum about your bum or your tum? (**Woman's Own**)

It is unusual to find anything more taboo than this, though there is one reference in the data to a *huge arse* (**Body Beautiful**).

The references to more obviously sexual body parts than the stomach or bottom, however, tend to vary a little more, as we have seen above, with euphemism often being the only alternative to the formal or technical. The possible exception is the range of words used to refer to breasts, which are often called simply 'breasts', but may at times be referred to as the 'chest' or the 'bust'. Quite often these terms are replaced with the more informal, and slightly jokey 'boobs', as we can see in the following examples:

You are long and slim, with narrow hips, *a small bust* and long legs. (*Sugar*)

If you have *a bigger chest*, try wearing... (*Shout*)

Girlies who have got *small breasts; bigger-chested* gals. (*Mizz*)

I'm much more comfortable with *my breasts* now. I like them and I'm glad they're not big. (*Sugar*)

My problem is I have *huge boobs*. (*Shout*)

In summer it is much harder to look good in a T-shirt and other tops when *your boobs are uncomfortably big*. (*Bliss*)

You are curvy figured, with broad shoulders, wide hips, a slim waist and probably big boobs! (*Sugar*)

Such patterns as exist here seem to clearly associate the word *boobs* with large breasts, and there are, indeed, more extracts mentioning large than small breasts anyway, the latter tending to use the neutral terms *breasts* or *bust* in preference to *boobs* or *chest*, both of which have a humorous connotation. So, whilst it is likely that in fact both extremes of 'abnormality' give women cause to worry, the greater obsession in this data is with large breasts, which are both celebrated and seen as a burden or cause for amusement simultaneously. It is hard to know whether magazine producers are consciously aware that this usage, read by the right readers (males who enjoy soft porn?) could encourage a kind of prurience. It certainly seems unlikely that it's purely there to be informal and colloquial, since the word *boobs* never collocates with *small*.

Notice, incidentally, that the examples above include one with a clear sense relation of hyponymy:

Breast enhancements include *breast* enlargements... *breast* uplifts, *breast* reductions. (*Body Beautiful*)

Here, the reader is, as it were, taught that the term *breast enhancements* is the superordinate to three kinds of procedure, and we are thus introduced to some of the terminology of cosmetic surgery. This field of activity in relation to the female form is particularly fond of nominalizations, which sound both reassuringly scientific and also, because of their nominal nature, quite simple:

Fat can be removed from the lower lids with a procedure known as *transconjunctival blepharoplasty*. The surgeon makes incisions inside the lower eyelid that leave no visible scar. (*Body Beautiful*)

Sometimes *liposuction* is the answer, sometimes *a mini-abdominoplasty* (small incision) is indicated, and for most advanced cases an *abdominoplasty* is advised. (***Body Beautiful***)

In some examples, like the first one here, the nominalisation is accompanied by a description of what is involved. In other cases, such as the second, the terms are assumed to be understood from the wider context of the article, where the need for loss of abdomen fat has been discussed at length. Other nominalizations in the data are not always so formal or technical, so we have more informal, everyday usages, such as *nose job, tummy tuck, overeating, childbirth, dieting* and so on.

The analysis of naming conventions in the data has demonstrated some tendencies towards constructing the reader in particular ways, sometimes by categorizing her as a particular kind of woman, and at other times referring to her as though she were identified with her body parts – particularly the sexually significant ones. The choice of nouns to refer to body parts reflects the problem in English more generally, where there is a lack of everyday words for some of the more sensitive or taboo parts, and the result is a tendency towards euphemism or technical jargon. Nominalization itself seems to be the preserve of the over-formal scientific topics such as surgical operations.

Whilst the naming itself is interesting ideologically, the ways in which the nominals are modified is also very important. The next section, therefore, examines noun phrase modification and other kinds of textual describing.

Describing

Determiners

The use of determiners before body parts and processes is not the most obvious place to look for features of interest in describing bodily features, but in this data it turns out to be one of the more significant characteristics of the texts.

In listing the nominal phrases that were used to describe body parts and processes, individual texts which were written in the second person with the reader in mind, seemed to be showing a pattern that was not universal, but nevertheless had a tendency to use the definite article in relation to internal and taboo body parts, and a possessive adjective in relation to external and less taboo parts. Let us take some longer extracts from a complete text to illustrate this point:

You and *Your Body*
Love 'em or hate 'em, periods are all part of being a girl. There is
nothing to be afraid of, ashamed of or embarrassed about – because
we all have them! Read our easy guide for everything you need
to know.

Q What are they?
Periods are a physical sign that *your body* is ready to reproduce. Every
month, one of *the ovaries* releases *an egg* which travels down *the
Fallopian tube* to *the uterus (womb)*. *The uterus* prepares itself for *a
fertilised egg* by thickening its lining with blood. If *the egg* is not
fertilised then it is expelled from *the body* along with *the lining from
the womb*. This is *your period*, and it will last from three to seven days.

Q When will I start?
The average age to start having *your periods* is about twelve, although it
can be from any time between the ages of nine and sixteen. You can't
tell when you are going to start, although *your breasts* will usually
have started to develop.

What kind of protection should I use?
There are two types of protection you can use to absorb *your flow*.
Sanitary towels are worn inside your knickers, and come in a great
range of shapes and sizes to suit everyone's needs. Remember to
change your towel on a regular basis. Tampons are worn inside *the
vagina*, and should also be changed at least every eight hours. You
can start using tampons as soon as you start your periods, and using
a tampon does not mean losing your virginity. You cannot lose a
tampon *inside yourself*. (***Fresh***)

What we see here is a typical movement between the possessive presentation of things that are not too unmentionable (periods, breasts etc.) and
the distancing mechanism of the definite article being used for those
body parts that are more taboo. Thus we have initial sequence introducing the context as second-person, with repeated uses of *your body*,
which give way very quickly to *an egg*, followed by *the uterus, the body*
and *the lining from the womb*. I would surmise that *the body*, here uses
the definite article because it is caught up in the middle of a definite
sequence, and couldn't so easily slip back to the possessive. However,
once the difficult business of discussing internal matters is over, it is
'safe' for the text to return to the possessive, in *your period*. The next
answer to a question continues in this vein, with *your period* and *your*

breasts, and the following answer also manages to maintain the second-person theme, by using the euphemism *your flow*. However, the need to mention where tampons are *worn* means that *the* vagina uses a definite article in the middle of a possessive sequence, which finishes with another euphemism, *inside yourself*, rather than resorting to a possessive adjective, followed by *vagina*.

There is no universal law operating here, and some texts do use possessive adjectives with *vagina, womb* and so on, particularly in magazines written for adults. Nevertheless, there are some texts throughout the data that seem to have a similar pattern of determiner use. One text from *Our Baby* which we have already considered and which has a second-person 'diary' of pregnancy, contains the following body parts/processes:

your +	the +
period	fallopian tube
fertilised egg (zygote)	*uterus*
pregnancy	*uterus wall*
Baby	amniotic fluid
digestive system	umbilical cord
pelvis/pelvic bone	embryo
body	*placenta*
hair and skin	linea negra
nipples	
uterus	
waist	
breasts	
palm	
temperature	
blood	
navel	
abdomen	
cervix	
placenta	

One of the differences here, is that the internal parts, particularly in this case *uterus* and *placenta*, appear at first with the definite article, and then, almost like guests that have now been properly introduced, they start to appear later in the article with the possessive, *your*. There is relatively little mention of the internal sex organs beyond the teenage and pregnancy texts, not surprisingly. The slimming, sex, plastic surgery and fitness texts are mostly concerned with outer body parts, and inner parts are normally only muscles, such as *your deep postural muscles* (**Marie Claire**).

However, there is some indication that the distinction I have made above between the use of the definite article and the possessive adjective also distinguishes between body parts in some of the other data, not on the basis of whether it is internal and taboo (versus external and/or not taboo), but on the basis of whether it is evaluated as good or bad. **Woman's Own**, for example, on the merits of lipsuction, begins by addressing the reader:

> You've given up junk food, taken up exercise and STILL you can't manage to shift *that lingering roll of fat*. So, is surgery the answer?

What is noticeable about the problems being addressed here is that although the reader may be the addressee, the perceived bad features that are the subject under discussion are not preceded by a possessive adjective, but by a demonstrative. We see this in the opening sentence above, with *that lingering roll of fat*, and the same transition from personal to demonstrative occurs in the next paragraph too:

> Go one step further, and you could also say goodbye to *those baggy folds of skin* and get *those unwanted slack muscles* tightened up.

This psychological distancing by the use of distal deictic terms (*those*) has the interesting effect of producing simultaneous but possibly conflicting implicatures that the reader *has* these features (produced by the definiteness of the demonstrative adjective) but also that these features are not an integral part of the reader (produced by using distal deictic terms, rather than possessive adjectives). Note the effect if these passages were to be rewritten reversing this determiner usage:

> You've given up junk food, taken up exercise and STILL you can't manage to shift *your lingering roll of fat*. So, is surgery the answer?
>
> Go one step further, and you could also say goodbye to *your baggy folds of skin* and get *your unwanted slack muscles* tightened up.

It seems unlikely that the reader would respond well to being told so plainly that she has these problems (even if it is true) and so the distancing deixis is perhaps less likely to alienate the reader.

The article continues to describe in some detail the process of liposuction, and often uses generic sentences as well as definite articles to avoid drawing the reader in too closely, and possibly insulting her:

> However, liposuction offers a way to completely remove unwanted deposits on *the* tummy, neck, arms, hips, thighs, knees or even ankles... During the operation, a narrow tube is inserted through a tiny cut and used to vacuum *the* fat layer deep under the skin. The process removes fat, leaving *the* blood vessels and nerves intact.

There is a very fine balance being struck by these writers, and the interplay of the different determiner usage seems to be an important part of this process. The article does 'frame' the potentially disturbing detail of the process with more personal references to your body shape, but the level of detail in these sentences is very much less:

> As there are now fewer cells to take up fat, any changes to *your body shape* should be long-lasting... Current surgery techniques can help to improve *your body shape* but only under certain circumstances.

These two sentences occur near the beginning and end of the article respectively, and between them there is much more detail about the procedures, none of it related to the reader through the second-person pronoun. The writer thus manages to relate the article to the reader in general ways, whilst not causing her to be put off by imagining these processes actually happening to her. One of the sentences that appears to be actively avoiding such an outcome is as follows:

> In circumstances where *someone* has lost massive amounts of weight, a tummy tuck *can be carried out* to remove excess or baggy skin. This *is done* by cutting away the skin (stretch marks *may be cut out* too during this process) and loose muscles *can be tightened up.*

Here, the use of *someone*, specifically avoids referring to the reader, and the procedures are then dealt with hypothetically by use of the passive voice. This is another method of separating the action from the reader, so that those with a squeamish reaction to the detail may not relate the procedures too closely to themselves, whilst still considering themselves amongst the addressees of the article.

A similar effect is achieved in a very different article in **Body Beautiful** which also aims to 'improve' the body shape of the reader, but by careful choice of clothes. First, there is a very long introductory section, detailing what the reader should and shouldn't do in the way of choosing a wardrobe, and using the second-person pronoun:

> You may have beautiful skin, but wearing pale colours will make you look tired.
>
> Your wardrobe should consist of about 60 percent colour (blues, green, pinks etc.) and 40 per cent basics (navy, black, white, stone, brown and grey).

We will revisit this text later in relation to modality, but the interesting aspect of the language for us here is that after the generalizations, and once the text begins to tackle perceived problems of body shape, the second-person progressively drops out and the definite (or indefinite) article takes over:

> Therefore, a white, silky blouse will make *the bust* appear larger; satin trousers will enlarge *the bottom* they encase; a shiny dress or suit will add inches to *the entire body*; and shiny tights can turn *large calves* into two pork sausages!

Although, in the early stages of this article, there were some references to the reader's own body shape (*If you are short or overweight...*), the example above, towards the end of the article, represents the climax of a more and more negative picture of the possible problems with the female form, culminating in the *pork sausages* reference. It is therefore, perhaps, not surprising, that though the article may intend the reader to identify with some of the problems, it is left to her to make the connection, and the second-person possessive is omitted in favour of articles or plurals with no determiner (*large calves*). The article, like the cosmetic surgery article discussed above, finishes as it starts by referring more directly to the reader again, but not with any uncomfortable detail about unattractive body parts:

> You must be realistic about your assets and faults. If short jackets are fashionable and they suit you, wear them and vice versa.

Here, the reader is reminded that they have faults, but only in general terms, and the alternatives of wearing something fashionable that suits you and not wearing it if it doesn't suit you are opposed, but the latter, where there is the potential for negative feelings, is subsumed into the phrase *vice versa*. Thus, the reader is left with more of an impression of the good side of that equation – what it's like to be able to wear fashionable clothes, knowing that they suit you.

This pattern of article, starting and finishing with second-person addressee, and tending toward the more distancing effect of definite articles and demonstratives in the central part of the article, where potentially the most disturbing information is found, is repeated again and again throughout the data. Here are three sentences from the beginning, middle and end of an article on nutrition and weight gain in the menopause years from *Diet and Fitness*, which demonstrate the same phenomenon:

> Keeping *your weight* in check can help keep the ageing process at bay.
>
> around the time of the menopause and thereafter, the decrease in the amount of oestrogen produced by *the body* increases the likelihood that fat will be deposited around *the abdomen*.
>
> Exercise will help to maintain muscle tone, keeping *your body* in good shape and preserving *your physical strength*.

Note the use of the second person in the first sentence in relation to the relatively safe topic of *keeping your weight in check* whereas the second sentence discusses the technical aspects of the relatively taboo menopause, while the last sentence returns to the here and now and discusses external features like the body shape and muscle tone and returns to using the second person again.

Adjectives

The patterning of determiner usage discussed in the previous section was less anticipated than some significance in the patterns of adjectival modification of nouns, either within the noun phrase, as a premodifier, or as the complement of an intensive verb, as for example, in clauses like *her weight was excessive*.

Perhaps the most overwhelming pattern amongst the adjectival usage was to find that the large majority of adjectives could easily be interpreted in the context as hyponyms of either *good* or *bad*:

> I used to have quite large breasts but after breastfeeding they became *empty* and *floppy*. So I decided to have them filled up again, which is exactly what the surgeon did for me. They're *brilliant*.

This extract from a reader's story in a cosmetic surgery article in **Body Beautiful**, demonstrates a phenomenon that happens repeatedly throughout the data. Adjectives describing the bodily 'before' and 'after' situations are either positively or negatively evaluated. Thus, it is possible to equate all of these adjectives with *good* and *bad* as appropriate:

> I used to have quite *large* (= *good*) breasts but after breastfeeding they became *empty* (= *bad*) and *floppy* (= *bad*). So I decided to have them filled up again, which is exactly what the surgeon did for me. They're *brilliant* (= *good*).

It may not be surprising to find such good–bad distinctions in this data, which by definition is aimed at helping women with their bodily problems, so that we would expect the problems themselves to be cast in a negative light, and the solutions in a positive. One of the difficulties of analysing data in our own culture, with which we are very familiar, is that it is hard to step outside our own conditioning and see other possibilities. How else could women's bodily problems be addressed other than in black-and-white terms or with problem-and-solution strategies? In this case, of course, the problem is an entirely constructed one, in that the unsatisfactory breasts are only seen as such in relation to the ideal of a pre-maternal, young and 'full' shape. If the ideology of our culture celebrated the different shapes of breast, not only between people, but throughout a woman's life, this problem would simply not exist.

One of the more common themes in the data, particularly in the teenage data, is the distinction between that which is normal, natural or healthy in relation to the body and that which is abnormal, unusual or unhealthy:

> 'I thought I must be *abnormal*', says 18-year-old Sally from Glasgow.
>
> 'I thought my vagina felt so weird I even peeked in one of my brother's horrible porn mags. Eventually I asked my doctor and he said I was *normal*. (**Bliss**)
>
> Am I *normal*? How long are they supposed to last? . . . First things first hun, you're completely *normal*. . . . And don't be embarrassed, after all, all us girls have 'em! (**Mizz**)
>
> Listen up girlies, looking at other girls' bods in the showers is completely *natural*. (**Mizz**)

Teachers play an important role when we're at school, so it's *not unusual* to feel this kind of attraction.... It's perfectly *healthy* to have questions about your sexuality, and sharing your worries can make things more clear. (**Bliss**)

but he says all girls enjoy this and there must be *something wrong* with me. Is he right?... Your breasts are *normal*. (**Bliss**)

Masturbation is a *natural* part of getting to know your body. (**Bliss**)

For many girls, whatever their age, heavy periods are *normal, healthy* and *natural*. (**Shout**)

vanity is a *normal* and vital part of us. The world without vanity would be a far duller place. (**Body Beautiful**)

Some texts are built entirely upon the distinction between what is normal and what is not. For example, a problem page in **Woman** has the heading 'Am I normal?' as a summary of all the problems dealt with on the page. These questions and answers deal with a range of sexual problems, from pain and vaginal dryness to lack of desire. The subheading sums up the rhetorical thrust of the piece:

It's hard to know where to turn if you have a problem relating to your sex life and all too easy to jump to the conclusion that you must be *abnormal*. But many 'problems' are surprisingly *common*...

This extract illustrates a logical anomaly in the whole normal–abnormal line of reasoning. For a bodily feature to be normal, it needs to be statistically at least in the majority, rather than a minority. Most of the problems which cause concern to readers of these magazines, by their nature affect a minority of people. It is therefore illogical to claim that something relatively unusual is also normal. However, it is a habit of this kind of advice-giving to make just such claims, as a way of reassuring the readers, as if there is then no action that needs to be taken, because normality has been established. In fact, the details of the answers in this case do not fulfil this logic, and contradict the rhetoric of the introduction:

If you get itching and an *abnormal* discharge, a vaginal infection is likely to be to blame.

There's *no such thing as normal* when it comes to having sex. Libido, or sex drive, is a highly individual thing.

Other texts, such as the following one from **Cosmopolitan**, compound this (lack of) logic explicitly:

> But remember: not all women come every time they have intercourse, some women do not come at all. So relax, you are perfectly normal!

A similar anomaly occurs in relation to plastic surgery. Although it is clearly very far from being 'natural', one of the tests of its success is if it looks or feels so:

> The implant was inserted behind the breast tissue so when you touch the breasts they actually feel very soft and *normal*...I had silicone put in so they're firmer than *normal* tissue but they still feel like part of my body. It doesn't feel like there's anything there at all. I think it feels *very natural*. (**Body Beautiful**)

Related to this normal/abnormal distinction, but with a slightly more ominous tone, is the only slightly less common distinction between what is *correct* and what is *incorrect*:

> As for your *correct* weight, this depends on your height and frame, not your age. (**Sugar**)
>
> Are you wearing the *right* bra? (**Mizz**)
>
> What is the first thing you do with a part of your body that you don't like? Cover it up? If you do it *correctly* that is great. But if you do it *incorrectly*, you may hide your assets at the same time. (**Body Beautiful**)

Whilst there is some concession made to difference in the first of these answers, there is nevertheless a notion of correctness even here. And in the second and third extracts, the idea of a fairly rigid set of rules for dressing according to body shape is implicit.

Lining up with the good/bad implications of these two distinctions (*normal/abnormal* and *correct/incorrect*) are other general distinctions between things that are pleasurable, pleasant or attractive about the female body, and aspects that are painful, disgusting or in some way unattractive, in other words, distinctions which have *good/bad* connotations:

> Stop reminding everyone who will listen that you've got *a huge arse*. One advantage of this superficial world is that everyone is too

obsessed with themselves to really notice *your lumpy thighs!* (***Body Beautiful***)

Discharge might seem *yucky* but at least it proves your body's in working order. (***Bliss***)

The second text here seems to be emphasizing the abnormality (from a male perspective of the complete, clean body) of regular body parts/processes in the female. The list of negative-sounding adjectives in this text (remembering it's for teenagers) includes:

hairy; thick, dark hair; unlikeliest bits; freaky; alien; whitish or yellowish gunk; itchy; dry; putrid-smelling; green; yucky

This list of features is probably intended to be light-hearted, as well as comforting, in the sense that it recognizes the squeamishness of teenagers, faced with the reality of bodies. However, the ideology of the whole piece reinforces the notion that whilst these processes may be natural, we should nevertheless hide, minimize or correct such features of our bodies in order to approximate to the unattainable ideal body.

Although some texts, such as the one above, focus on the negative, the data show a greater tendency to emphasize the positive extreme, often in the form of superlatives:

This type of bra is *perfect* for girls who love slipping into a boob tube (***Mizz***)

Long, slinky catsuits look *amazing* on slim frames; a whole outfit in one dark colour makes the most of those *gorgeous* curves. (***Sugar***)

many doctors recommend that, prior to pregnancy, women should try to get as close to their *ideal* weight as possible (***Ebony***)

To achieve a *perfect* body all you need to do is understand which lengths and styles work for you (***Body Beautiful***)

The use of words like *perfect* and *ideal* are both a reflection of the type of overstatement that women and girls might use in a conversational context and also a reinforcement of the targets that they may be setting themselves. Since such words are used frequently in the data, they reinforce the ideology of the ideal body each time they occur.

In many texts, there are multiple examples of negative adjectives and corresponding lists of positive adjectives relating to the health and/or fitness of the body. One text in ***Women's Health*** deals with getting back a flat stomach after pregnancy, and talks about *good posture, ideal posture* and *keeping the spine strong and supple* as contrasted with:

> When the abdominals are *weakened* and *stretched* (as after pregnancy) the pelvis *sags* backwards, the spine *curves excessively* and the back becomes *vulnerable* to *damage* and low-back *pain*.

There is an emphasis in this text on bodies and body parts that are healthy, strong and natural. The implicature, rather oddly, is that what happens to the body after childbirth is unnatural, unhealthy and weak, and in other texts that what we are granted by nature in the way of body shape or size is also somehow the opposite of natural. This may indeed seem true to evenly-proportioned and healthy women who have grown up expecting their bodies to continue to function in the same manner throughout their lives, but it is an ideology, rather than being in any sense absolutely true. Thus another ideology, of the unchanging body, is reinforced repeatedly through these texts. The body is portrayed as serving the individual, as able to let us down, and to some extent able to be 'fixed'.

Beauty advice in pregnancy also manages to stress the negatives as we see in these extracts from **Pregnancy and Birth**:

> During pregnancy hormones can cause your hair to become *greasy* and *lifeless*... The weight you carry around in pregnancy can take its toll on your feet, leaving them with *hard, calloused* skin... Although creams can work to firm the skin and keep it looking *supple*, the best way to prevent *saggy* boobs is to wear a well-fitting, supportive bra.

Where more positive adjectives are used, they are often connected with products that are being advertised, albeit obliquely:

> This *wonderful* new skin saver from... will leave your skin *glowing* and your mind feeling *invigorated*... is available exclusively from...

In relation to pregnancy more generally, the overwhelming occurrence of adjectives in relation to the pregnant woman concern her emotional, rather than her physical state, and in all cases, these emphasise the two extremes, so that in one text we get *doomed, terrified, very emotional, a bit frightened, very upset, devastating* contrasting with *absolutely fine, so lucky, grateful* (*Our Baby*). This emphasizes the ups and downs of the hormonally-affected emotions, as well as reflecting this reader's own experience. The reinforcing effect of repeatedly reading such stories might well be expected to influence the expectations and highlight the fears of pregnant women.

Interestingly, one of the pregnancy texts, which has three readers' stories which focus on all sorts of horrible problems, ends with the following advice:

> Women who have 'precious pregnancies', where they've had previous miscarriages or fertility treatments are, naturally, anxious during pregnancy. But it's best to focus on the *positive* aspects of pregnancy. Try not to get sucked into *negative* thoughts. (***Pregnancy and Birth***)

Whilst keeping pregnant women ignorant about the potential risks of pregnancy, and signs to look out for which may need intervention is not ideologically acceptable, there are, nevertheless, an inordinate number of articles which dwell on the problematic, and it is quite difficult to see how even a very healthy pregnant woman reading these magazines might not become very anxious about all sorts of imagined symptoms, and find it difficult to *focus on the positive aspects of pregnancy.*

By contrast with these general articles dealing with problems and 'real' women, articles on celebrities in pregnancy tend to treat them as exemplary women who may encounter a few problems, but on the whole are rather good at dealing with them, and have a generally positive experience, as we can see from Pregnancy and Birth where one article charts the pregnancy of Katie Derham, a broadcaster and newsreader:

> this current change in her own life has left her 'excited, but slightly bemused'...she and her management consultant husband, John, are thrilled and delighted...she hopes for a natural birth.

The worst that seems to befall Katie in this account is that the surprise of her pregnancy leaves her *slightly bemused*. This is very much less negative an emotion than those found in the more general articles, or those dealing with readers' stories, for whom the problems they have is their only claim to being included at all. This is even true of those stories where there are no significant problems being discussed.

As we might expect, most of the articles and texts dealing with sex are full of positive adjectives relating to sexual activity. One text in ***Shine***, which reports on different aspects of foreplay, is full of such descriptions as applied to different techniques:

If it [the knee] is touched in a *sexy* way...

If...he slides his hand round onto your bottom, it can be highly *erotic*...

Get him to knead, nibble or stroke your cheeks –...it's all very *suggestive*.

...any attention to her mitts makes her come over all *lustful*.

Because this is all about sensual pleasure, there is no mention of negatives here of course. It is also noticeable that some of these adjectives (for example *lustful*) have positive connotations, but may be negatively evaluative in other contexts (for example in evangelical religious tracts). It isn't always the case that in magazine data the evaluation of sexual activity is all positive. In one of the texts which dealt with the weirder end of the sex-tips range, there were just as many negative as positive descriptions, mainly from the people who tried them out:

It seems a bit *unfair* that I put in all the work and got nothing out of it.

Crap, says Amanda.

How extremely *humiliating*.

Mate, it's *brilliant*.

'My God, I had no idea we sounded so *unsexy*.'

The norm, however, seems to be that the introductory and theoretical parts of articles on sex (and indeed on fitness, slimming, clothes, and beauty) tend toward the positive adjectives:

Not only does sex help keep your body *toned* and *shaped*, but women who have *regular* sex (meaning at least twice a week) have been shown to live *longer*, to have *lower* blood pressure and to look *younger* than those who don't. (**Body Beautiful**)

Note that although many of the adjectives labelled positive or negative have these connotative polarities irrespective of context, there are others which acquire their polarity only through their collocation with other lexemes. Thus, *longer* and *regular* are both positive in relation to living and sex respectively, though *longer illness* or *regular abuse* would clearly reverse this polarity and *longer dresses* and *regular rainfall* may be neutral with regard to evaluation. By contrast with the more general treatments,

these texts also include a large number of negative adjectives in the sections where they describe either actual readers, or hypothetical ones, in the process of trying to achieve perfection:

> Doggy Style... With the added bonus that all men love this position, it makes even *the largest of* bottoms look pretty attractive.

> Missionary... and elongating your limbs makes *saggy* bits look less *saggy* and *chunky* bits less *chunky*. (**Body Beautiful**)

It is as though the reality of all of these solutions to bodily imperfections shines through when the detail is discussed, and the achievable aims diminish from perfection to *pretty attractive* or *less chunky*.

Texts which deal with specific problems, such as the difficulty for some women of getting pregnant, of course might also be expected to have descriptive vocabulary which is either positive or negative. This is the case with one text in *Woman* which looks at a range of infertility problems and some readers' stories. The overriding ideology is one of fixing problems, and this results in phrases such as the following:

> ... or where infertility is *unexplained*.

> Miscarriage – the most common cause is that the baby *hasn't developed normally*.

> 'Hanna is a great joy' says Avril, after *a healthy pregnancy*.

Of course, many problems with infertility and complications of pregnancy can be ameliorated and/or solved by medical intervention, and I wouldn't suggest that these advances in medicine are a bad thing or that magazines should ignore them. However, the underlying ideology that all those who wish to have children ought to be able to do so, and that it is in some sense unnatural not to be able to conceive and bear children successfully, adds to the burden of those for whom none of the solutions work. The happy ending stories in such articles are both encouraging to people in such situations, and potentially devastating for them too. The requirement of success, the sense of responsibility (and therefore guilt at 'failure') and the exhortation to readers to make adjustments in lifestyle as well as monitoring their own symptoms, all add to this pressure on the individual:

> Get to know your cycle.

> Make love every other day, especially around the middle of your cycle.

Give up smoking...

Cut down on alcohol...

Eat a healthy balanced diet and take exercise.

Try to relax and get enough rest.

As we saw in Chapter 2, the lengths to which 'fixing' things is taken is evident in this text from *Slimming Magazine*, which concerns diet before and during pregnancy, and includes the father as well as the mother, who are advised that if they are reluctant to modify their diets for two weeks before conception, *you should consider if you are ready to become a parent*. The writer goes on to point out that a third of all conceptions spontaneously abort in the first three months. This is followed by:

If both partners are *well nourished and healthy* then these odds are significantly reduced.

The writer doesn't, of course, cite any evidence for this view, and he doesn't deal with the many reasons why these early spontaneous abortions might be a 'natural' way of avoiding birth defects. In each article of this kind, there is an over-simplistic reliance on the notion that whatever advice is being given, it is the panacea for the problem that is being addressed.

Perhaps the most clearly positive–negative structure of descriptive vocabulary comes in the slimming texts where there is a clear paradigm of positive and negative adjectives building up through the data including the following from a problem page on slimming in *Slimmer Magazine*:

Positive: fit and healthy; balanced; content and happy; healthy active interest; healthy lifestyle

Negative: overweight; ugly; poor body image

There is an emphasis in the slimming texts on weight and proportion, the latter often being tied in with the toning associated with gym membership and fitness classes.

A specific area of description which is prominent throughout the data is that of size, whereby on the whole *big* is negatively evaluated and *small* is positive. This is noticeably reversed in relation to breasts, where the evaluation of large breasts as good is evident even where the texts deal, as they often do, with people complaining about both ends of the spectrum. The following extracts are taken from readers' stories in *Bliss*:

> At that point my breasts *weren't very big*...
> There are two things I don't like about having *a larger bust* though.
> I don't know anyone with *bigger boobs* than me.
> I'm perfectly happy *not being small*.
> ... even if I had *bigger breasts*...

Although this text is superficially even-handed about the perceived difficulties of being either too big or too small, the nature of the descriptions of both cases seems to dwell more on the description of large than small breasts. There is also sometimes a direct contrast between phrases containing the 'big' adjectives, which may premodify the personal noun and those containing 'small' adjectives, which are more likely to function as the object of a possessive verb such as *have*. This pattern is confirmed by the following extracts from **Mizz**:

> are great for girlies who have got *small breasts*
> an ideal everyday bra for *bigger-chested* gals

This difference of presentation is more than a superficial stylistic variation. The pre-modifiying *bigger-chested* adjective phrase indicates a more intrinsic feature of the body than the mere 'possession' of small breasts. The latter, of course, in sexual terms, are deemed more undesirable, though this is not stated directly. The fact that they might be able to be fixed is not the subject of this text, but in the context of other texts about surgery its grammatical placing as a part of the body that is 'possessed' is significant, as it indicates at least some potential for separation or exchange for a 'better model'.

Note that there is also some phonological and morphological symbolism going on here, with the use of *girlies* referring to young women with small breasts and *gals* referring to those with larger breasts. The relatively close vowels of *girlies* and its morphology, with a diminutive ending, seems to indicate that it had been particularly chosen for its size implications. By contrast, the open vowel of *gals*, which is more open than the central vowel of the standard word, *girls*, can be taken to reflect a larger size, in the same way that many sound-symbolic words in English do (for example *teeny* versus *large*). One could also argue that there is a connotative difference between these two words, which may both denote young females, but seem to connote immaturity in the case of *girlies* and street-wise brashness in the case of *gals*.

Whilst these phrases, even accepting the analysis above, might be dismissed as the product of a single writer, and therefore of little wider ideological significance, nevertheless, the inter-textual context indicates that these views are embedded more generally. Thus, the texts dealing with surgery on the whole are more interested in breast enhancement than reduction, though the latter may have physical and medical reasons, and the former cannot be anything other than cosmetic. Similarly, the linking of sexual maturity (but not old age) to size of breasts is confirmed by readers who claim to feel more womanly as a result of a breast implant:

> I feel so much more *womanly* now...I believe that if anyone wants a breast enlargement, they should have it done. It really does make you *happy*. (**Body Beautiful**)

One letter in **Bliss** which deals with having small breasts, receives an answer which seems much more interested in big breasts:

> At 13 you are just starting to develop, and your breasts may grow *larger* over the next few years. You will find that those girls with *very big breasts* aren't that happy either. In summer it is much harder to look good in a T-shirt and other tops *when your boobs are uncomfortably big*. If you are doing sport of any sort it is harder if you have *very heavy breasts*. In General Practice we often see women that come in complaining of back and shoulder pains because *their breasts are too large* and want to have them made smaller. You often hear boys saying they like *big boobs*. They often 'talk' about it. The truth is that when you start having a boyfriend who really likes you, then you will see that the size of your breasts is not a problem. It is the person he will want to be with and he won't mind the size of your breasts.

Whilst it would be difficult to attribute intentions to the writer of this answer on the basis of the text alone, it is striking how 'obsessed' with larger breasts the answer seems to be. The implicature in the final sentence that it is indeed a problem having small breasts, though one which can be got over, emphasizes that this answer only confirms the fears of the letter-writer; that she is at a sexual disadvantage compared with her peers.

There is a tendency for this data to avoid being too categorical about features of the body which might be seen as negative, particularly where the text is applying the term to the readership in some way. One solution, which avoids insulting, whilst still enabling the reader to relate to the points being made, is to use comparative forms of adjectives, but without a basis of comparison, thus leading to their possible interpretation as categorical adjectives:

> If you have a *bigger* chest, try wearing...So you're *smaller* on top, *bigger* on the bottom! (**Shout**)

This usage allows the reader to interpret the text in a number of ways, including:

> Bigger/smaller than it should be for perfect proportions;
> Bigger/smaller than normal;
> Bigger/smaller than I would like to be.

More importantly, it allows for readers to consider their body parts to be bigger/smaller by any amount, from a little to a lot. This may make the girl with very large/small body parts feel better (it's only comparative, not an absolute, like *huge* or *fat*) and yet it may also encourage the relatively well-proportioned girl to think that there's a problem because her body part(s) are even slightly bigger or smaller than some fictional 'ideal' would require.

Other uses of the comparative form are more genuinely comparative, but the implied comparator is with the current self:

> Five steps to a *flatter* tummy... By following the simple five-step plan devised by Sweetex, below, a *trimmer, slimmer* you is just around the corner. (**Our Baby**)

Again, we see in these examples the ideology of the unchanging ideal body, in the context of the reality of ever-changing bodies. This striving against the lived experience of a changing shape is repeated in so many texts that it is naturalised almost to the point of being hard to pick out as other than the 'truth'.

There is another tendency in some texts to overstate the positive in such a way that it almost has the effect of very positive modality; one that sounds the more insecure for having to be so effusive:

> I used to be *extremely fit*; the rest of my body was in *perfect* shape; it's made a *huge* difference; I always used to be *so aware* that I had a

bump there; Now it's *wonderful* to be able to wear what I like; Now I'm *so much more confident*: at least I've got a *wonderfully flat* tummy.

In this article in **Woman's Own**, the intensifiers and use of superlatives push to the boundaries of the positive, and this has the potential to ring hollow in the reader's mind. One of the potential problems of these texts, even within their own terms, is that the use of extremes can have a less persuasive effect when repeated too often. Another of the plastic-surgery stories emphasizes the negative of excess fat in various phrases such as *baggy folds; baggy skin; loose muscles; slack muscles* and *loose skin*, but uses absolutes for the positive effects of surgery: *miracle cure; the perfect body; marvellous*. By contrast, the fairly gruesome-sounding techniques of liposuction (*vacuum the fat layer deep under the skin*) are softened by the use of adjectives emphasizing their small size:

a *narrow* tube is inserted through a *tiny* cut

Again, this pattern seems to show the extremes of bad and good in talking about the problem and its solution theoretically, whilst mitigating these extremes when discussing the practical aspects of a solution.

Much of the discussion of body parts, and the clothes they can be covered by is concerned with what is wrong with them. There is thus a great deal of intensification of adjectives with negative evaluation, as we see from the following:

but avoid anything that's *too* tight; You might want to avoid anything *too* big and baggy; avoid anything *too* long and loose; You might want to avoid anything *too* fussy! (**Shout**)

don't mix and match *too* many patterns; frills and bows around a neckline might make you appear *too* busty. (**Sugar**)

There are also particular intensifiers which seem to crop up in magazine registers. These include *super-* as a superlative intensifier and *less-* as a negative modifer of adjectives. These occur more than once in a text in *Cosmopolitan*, which concerns the diet fads of celebrities:

there's a long list of *super-slender* success stories: Friends star Jennifer Aniston is a low-carb devotee as is her co-star Courtney Cox and *super-skinny* Calista (Ally McBeal) Lockhart.

there are other *less extreme* versions such as The Balance

. . .

Less enticing is his decree that dieters should take plenty of cod liver oil, which apparently helps to keep the insulin levels down.

The use of adjectives to describe successful slimmers is, on the whole, one of extremes, though often focusing on the large or negative:

> Her *vast* double chin protruded beneath her *big, moon-shaped* face, the tops of her arms spread *massively* beneath short sleeves ... 30-year-old Diane, now a *fantastic-looking* blonde in size 10 *fashionable* clothes, (**Diet and Fitness**)

Note that these two sentences, which follow each other in the text and seem to represent the two extremes of Diane's weight, are contrasted by the use of *vast, massively* and *big* on the one hand, and *blonde* and *fashionable* on the other. We will return to this issue in Chapter 4, but it should be mentioned here that the clear implications of this contrast are that it is impossible to be *fashionable* or *blonde* (assuming sexy or attractive, rather than a literal meaning) if you are overweight. Note also that some of these descriptors turn up in non-adjectival uses, though the descriptive force remains. Thus, the use of the adverb *massively*, rather than an adjective, *massive*, allows the upper arms to be perceived as actively spreading, and leads to a sense of being out of control. By contrast, the use of *blonde* as a head noun, rather than an adjective, implies a closer and more permanent link between Diane and her blondeness. If this feature (her blondeness) is also symbolic of her new image (of attractive slimness), then its occurrence as a permanent feature emphasizes the other extreme from her earlier, out-of-control, self.

Another repeated pattern in slimming texts is the tendency to line up emotional and physical features as equivalent:

> *Fed up* and *desperate*, she broke the yo-yo chain by *learning to slim from within* ... I have always been *unhappy with my figure* ... I'd end up feeling so *unhappy*.

These extracts from **Slimmer Magazine** in an advert for a slimming programme based on psychological changes, set up the situation in which a successful slimmer begins her story as a binge-starve dieter. In the pattern of these narratives, she has a 'Damascene' moment:

> At my lowest point, I saw an article about how TV personality, Carol Vorderman lost weight using a programme called Slim from Within.

The rest of the story reiterates a number of times, the before and after effects of watching the tapes associated with this programme:

> *Now*, I'm very happy with my husband and I have a rewarding job as a childminder.

There is no mention in this story about the slimmer having been unhappy with either her husband or her job when she was overweight, but the presuppositions in this extract are just that. In other texts the claims for the additional effects of slimming (beyond being slim itself) are varied, and include the discovery of a birth mother by an adopted woman and the achievement of life goals such as the finding of new and better jobs.

This equating of slimming with happiness and success in general is underlined by the repeated occurrence of transferred epithets, whereby the adjective which might be used of the achievement of slimming is oddly attached to the amount of weight loss itself:

> Today she's a *fantastic* 8st 5lb lighter (**Slimmer Magazine**)
> When Ros Thatcher lost an *amazing* 9st. (**Diet and Fitness**)

These transferred epithets also occur in other texts, such as those for teenagers and fitness instructions:

> Tampons and towels are so *discreet* that there is no need for anyone else to know you have your period unless you choose to tell them. (**Fresh**)
>
> Being such a perfectionist, everything you do has to be just right. A *neat* arm workout is the best exercise for you. (**Bliss**)

In the first case, the tampon itself is described by an adjective that would normally collocate with a personal noun. The effect is the equating of tampons with discreetness, rather than with an ability to behave in a discreet manner. In the second example, the exercise is described as *neat*, though this adjective could be more appropriately applied to the desired shape of the arms. This transferring of attributes from the personal onto other artefacts or processes is indicative of the positioning of the woman in these texts. It is not what slimmers do that is amazing, but the conceptual mound of bodily fat that carries this description. It is not the proper and effective use of sanitary products that can be discreet, but the very existence of tampons themselves. And note, in passing, that in itself the desire to hide all signs of menstruation, whilst universally accepted, is nevertheless an ideology in itself, and reinforces our greatest remaining bodily taboo.

The desire for beauty and sexual attractiveness underlies many of the texts in this data, and there are two contrasting methods of convincing readers that they can achieve these goals. On the one hand, there are a number of compound adjectives which are used to imply that the advice being given will make the reader irresistible:

> For a sexy, *come-to-bed* style, first give your hair a lift... Cosmo's *get-beddable* beauty guide. (***Cosmopolitan***)

These examples demonstrate the direct link between beauty and its ideological aim, which is to have sex. Whilst young (and not so young) women may claim to be doing things 'for themselves', this text, and indeed many of the others in more-or-less direct ways, acknowledges that this is simply not true.

By complete contrast with this rhetorical method (it will get you 'laid'), there are also texts which emphasize the scientificness of the advice they are giving, without apparently expecting much in the way of technical understanding:

> An increased *trans-epidermal* water loss... These ingredients form an *occlusive* barrier (***Women's Health***)
>
> specially designed *thermographic* scanners... a newly developed *hypo-dermal* technology (***Slimmer Magazine***)

In the first three of these cases, the adjectives add very little, if anything, to the head nouns. Thus, water loss from the body is likely to be through the skin (trans-epidermal), barriers are by their nature occlusive, and scanners tend to use heat. The final example is a little different, but equally vacuous. The head noun, *technology*, means very little (a pencil could be called technology). The adjective, in this case, is there to tell us where this technology takes place (through the skin). It adds very little, whilst appearing to 'firm up' the content of a rather general word (*technology*). But content or information is not the point of these terms, whose job is to make the reader feel reassured about the reliability of the techniques being described, and their foundation in science.

As explained in Chapter 2, there is little in this data which relates specifically to the older woman, despite some of the magazines being aimed at this age group. The poignancy of the one advert for a product which would minimize the effects of the menopause may be a good place to end this discussion of the description of women in this data:

find the *real* you (***Diet and Fitness***)

As we have seen, the texts aimed at younger women spend pages of print on issues which divide up the body into sections at the same time as seeming to indicate that the construction of the reader is in the hands of not only a series of experts, but is flexible, alterable and ever-changing. This advertising slogan, hints towards an earlier, non-postmodern world in which the self had not only integrity, but also an unchanging core identity which would not be affected by the superficial bodily changes of life. The irony, of course, is that this advertisement undermines such a message in trying to sell the reader a (albeit natural, herbal) remedy to mask the 'natural' effects of the ageing process. The real self, then, though existent in this text, is still a younger self, a fitter self, and one which has no pain or emotional distress.

Summary

With a couple of exceptions and contrary to the original impetus of this research, the actual naming of body parts was less interesting than how they were set into their surroundings. Thus, the naming of breasts in particular seemed to emphasize the importance of size in attracting male attention, in itself to be desired, and this was reflected in the use of *boobs* for only large breasts, whereas the more neutral term *breasts* tended to be used for small breasts. The other more sexual body parts were either mentioned using the medical terminology (*vagina*, and so on.) or not mentioned at all. If anything, there was an absence of sexual body-part vocabulary, reflecting perhaps the inadequacy of everyday language as much as a reluctance to mention these parts.

The findings of this investigation in relation to naming and describing focused more on the modifiers of the head noun with determiners being of particular interest. It seems that there remains a tendency to regard the female reproductive organs as slightly alien in the sense that they are hidden and somewhat mysterious. This results in the use of the more distancing definite determiners often being used with the more technical words referring to the internal organs such as *uterus* and *fallopian tube*, even in texts where the norm is the second person possessive (*your*).

The descriptive vocabulary, in the form of adjectives, highlights what is confirmed by the construction of opposites; that the overwhelming pressure on readers of these texts is to create the *perfect, natural* and *normal* body by any means possible.

4
Equating, Contrasting, Enumerating and Exemplifying

This chapter introduces some forms of analysis that are not the usual tools of analysis in CDA, but are analogous to the regular apparatus in that they appear to construct meaning textually, and have a particular, repeated semantic process that operates on the basis of a range of textual triggers. The semantic relations that are being constructed textually are those which relate to similarity and difference of meaning (equating and contrasting), and those which produce examples of a general case either by enumerating all the different variants or by using one or more examples.

Textual construction of sense relations

One of the most important things a text can do, locally, is to create sense relations such as synonymy and antonymy between lexical items. This will have meaning for the purposes of that text in the first instance, but may have repercussions beyond the scope of the text if similar sense relations are repeated, or if the text has a particularly strong effect, as some advertisements, for example, do. This hegemonic tendency is particularly likely in the case of the data being analysed here, which is read regularly by many women and girls and treats the subject of their bodies about which they are often quite insecure. The creation of opposites and equivalents relies largely on the syntactic frames that set up these semantic possibilities, though the semantics of the words may themselves also contribute to the effect. This textual creation of what are normally seen as context-free lexical semantic meanings is just one of the ways in which we can see the symbiotic relationship between code and usage or between langue and parole. The recognition and understanding of opposites, for example, relies on our prior understanding of such a relationship including the core examples that speakers have learnt, often as children, and which seem as a result to be in some sense 'given'. However, readers of texts are not beyond understanding completely new opposites, which have no prior existence in our conceptual apparatus, but they do so on analogy with those that are already known. We will see the mechanisms for creating opposites in more detail later, but the kinds of syntactic frame that create textual opposites include parallel structures and negative / positive pairs of structures. Jones (2002) provides the most comprehensive account to date of the occurrence of conventional opposites in context, and Mettinger (1994) also provides insights into the contextual behaviour of conventional opposition. Mettinger explicitly distinguishes between what he calls systemic and non-systemic opposites, but spends no time on the latter:

> It might be noted that non-systemic semantic opposition has not attracted the attention of many structural semanticists. It would, however, be a profitable field of research for any kind of conceptual approach towards the study of meaning-relations. (Mettinger 1994: 74)

There is no study of the creation of unconventional opposites currently published.[1] Note that Cruse (1986) provides the definitive work on lexical semantics and then (2004) moves towards including contextual meaning by including pragmatics, but perhaps surprisingly does not extend his lexical semantics to include the contextual creation of sense relations.

A similar contextual creation of a sense relation can be found with synonymy, though it is often less dramatic in its effect. The main apparatus for achieving some kind of equivalence is apposition – at all levels (word, phrase and clause). These equivalences can have the apparent aim of educating (for example explaining or expanding upon a term) or more significantly making an assumption about an equivalence which would not be automatically obvious to all readers – and might indeed be controversial – but the nature of this function is such that the equivalence is not immediately open to question, and is taken to be part of the common sense ideology of the text. Jeffries (1994) explores the potential ambiguity that can be created by apposition, since the distinction between a list and co-referential apposition is not structurally clear and may be semantically unclear too.

In the context of the current data, the focus is on the part of this process which either reinforces or possibly also invents or reinvents such similarities and contrasts in meaning. There are many syntactic and semantic frames or structures that can cause such semantic relations to occur in a text. Here, we will look at a few of the most obvious ones.

As already mentioned, the clearest example of a frame which creates equivalence is apposition. This is the juxtaposition of two or more noun phrases in the same syntactic role, such as clausal subject, which either clearly have the same referent, such as *Mr Bun, the baker,*[2] or which are deemed by their very juxtaposition to have such a referent in common. The latter is probably the more interesting of the cases for this project, suggesting as it does that equivalence can arise out of the placing of noun phrases into such a relationship. We will see some examples of this in context later in this chapter.

Other possibilities for equivalence-creation are the positioning of noun phrases either side of an intensive verb, such as *be*, as in *She is my cousin's daughter*. This frame puts the relationship of equivalence under the spotlight in a way that apposition does not, and it is thus more open to debate by the reader or hearer. The proposition of such a structure is precisely that the equivalence relation exists, and this means that the reader or hearer can question and debate the assertion that there is equivalence between the two referents of the noun phrases. This, in terms of ideological assumptions, is therefore less hidden than the production of equivalence by appositional means, which is harder to query.

These are, of course, not the only structures which can create an equivalence of meaning, but the task of this book is not to investigate the range of form-to-meaning relationships in each section, but to explore the data along a number of dimensions. Other frames for equivalence, then, will be introduced in relation to the data as necessary.

As for the structural ways of producing opposition, these are many and varied, and are investigated in Jeffries (forthcoming) and Davies (forthcoming). Here, I will simply demonstrate some of the more common frames, and we will see in the analysis of the data below how these may trigger oppositional meanings.

One of the more likely places to find opposites is on either side of a coordinating conjunction such as *but* or *yet*. These, and to a lesser extent also *and* and *or*, often highlight the dimensions along which words or phrases are contrasted. Thus we may find conventional opposites, as in

The children were happy but everyone else was sad. But we may also find slightly less usual contrasts framed in the same way:

She felt uncomfortable but he seemed relaxed.

The process that is happening here, I would suggest, is for two words which would not be listed together in a dictionary of antonyms to be juxtaposed in such a way that they almost appear to be conventional opposites. Though, if asked, a native speaker would probably not say that *relaxed* is the opposite of *uncomfortable*, the context makes such a relationship seem natural. Still less clearly related words and phrases may also be put into such a frame, and in some contexts this will also result in the temporary oppositional relationship being highlighted. We will see some examples below.

Other likely frames for such creation of opposition include the use of parallel structures to focus onto the differences between two items. This can be seen in pairs of sentences such as:

Janet produced a delicious home-made lemon cake.
Sarah produced a packet of biscuits.

This rather cutting juxtaposition of the efforts of two women to feed their guests constructs an unusual opposition between lemon cake and commercially prepared biscuits. This, of course, is not something that is embedded in the core semantics of these words, and readers may find themselves searching for the 'real' underlying opposition. This will be found, perhaps, in the more conventional contrast between home-made (= good) and shop-bought (= bad) which is stereotypically part of the ideological outlook of certain female communities, particularly those with the time and money to spend on such things as home baking.

In addition to the textual construction of equivalence and contrast, there is also the potential for texts to construct other sense relations, such as hyponymy and meronymy, as well as more straightforward uses of lists to enumerate and other structures to exemplify the case being made, as we shall see below. One particular kind of enumeration, the three-part list, is recognized as having the status of a rhetorical strategy by many analysts, as we see from this extract from Tuffin (2002: 77):

Such lists were originally discussed in terms of their rhetorical effectiveness for political speeches (Atkinson 1984) and have since become an almost standard analytic tool. Edwards and Potter (1992) highlight, for example, how such three-partedness serves the useful rhetorical function of conveying an implication of completeness and representativeness.

Whilst this is not a rhetorical strategy on the large scale that was considered in Chapter 2, the effect, as some have claimed, may be persuasive:

> Gail Jefferson (1990) notes that in everyday conversation, lists are commonly delivered with three parts or items, since this is sufficient to indicate that we have instances that stand for something more general; hence, as Potter (1996) notes, they have a normative status. (Hepburn 2002: 278)

We will see later in the chapter (pp. 123*f*) the different ways in which the three-part list plays a part in normalising certain views of what is good and bad in the female body and its functions.

Equating

The occurrence and range of structures demonstrating the creation of similarity in meaning in our data is less widespread and perhaps less ideologically significant than the data on opposition. We will therefore look at it first. One of the more obvious purposes of equivalence or equating is as a pedagogical method to teach the reader what a technical term means, or to show that the writer considers two referents to be essentially the same.

The following, from an article on breast cancer in *Sugar*, makes two attempts to describe what the reader might be searching for:

> With three fingers on your left hand, feel for *lumps* or *thick tissue*.

It is noticeable here that the two references to the same thing are conjoined by *or*, and thus could theoretically refer to two rather different phenomena. However, this conjunction is often used in pedagogical contexts to offer alternative ways of describing essentially the 'same' referent, and this use shows an awareness of the inaccuracy of language to describe each individual's experiences.

Slightly less clearly pedagogical are those examples of rephrasing which may have an explanatory effect, or could have an emphatic effect.

In the following example from **Bliss** there is a rewording of *artificial* as *pretend*, and one might conclude that this is to explain the term *artificial* to those teenage readers who haven't come across this word before.

> The hormones in the Pill give your body *artificial* periods each month ... these *pretend* periods could be masking a problem

The equivalence here is achieved by the use of the demonstrative, *These*, which, with the noun *periods*, forms a cohesive tie to the earlier phrase containing the same head noun. The different adjectives, then, are put into a relationship of equivalence, and the reader is able to deduce that at the very least they both apply to the same phenomenon.

In the extract from **Woman** below, by contrast, the relatively conventional synonyms *stop*, *give up* and *quit* are used interchangeably to give a very strong and unusually direct message:

> *Stop* smoking. If you haven't *given up* smoking, do it right now and get your partner to *quit* too.

These pedagogical and directive uses of equivalence are ideological in an explicit way and do not present us with a sense of an ideology being naturalized by implicit means. Rather, we have a clear sense that the magazine is, in the last case, disapproving of smoking in pregnancy and anyone who might disagree or think the approach was too extreme would be able to take the opposing view with relatively little difficulty.

Returning to a more clearly pedagogical use of equivalence, we can see that the function of most of the comparisons of body part (or embryo) with everyday objects that we saw earlier is intended to explain to readers in terms that they can visualize. Here are two examples from **Bliss**, though there are many more in the data that have already been noted in Chapter 3:

> The opening to the womb, *the diameter of a thin straw* ...
> Girls have an orgasm by having their clitoris (*tiny, pea-shaped knob of flesh* at the top of the inner vaginal lips), stimulated.

Note that the equivalence in each case here is constructed by apposition. The parentheses in the second example make it clearer that this is a supplementary piece of information, but the syntactic relationship of apposition remains.

Another informative type of equivalence occurs where a general case is made more specific to inform the reader of a particular way of achieving some goal. In *Sugar*, for example, the intensive verb (*be*) is used to construct equivalence between getting in shape and activity/diet:

So *the best way to get in shape* at your age is *to get active and eat healthily.*

Here we have a general case, which is *getting in shape*, and it is made particular by the superlative, *the best way to.* This is then made more specific by the complement *to get active and eat healthily.* This example is odd in two ways. One is that it seems to link the need to be active and eat healthily to a particular age group, when this advice is surely relevant to all ages, demonstrating that the division of readers into age groups is often arbitrary and leads to such odd statements being made. The other striking point about this extract is that it states the obvious almost to the extent of being tautological.

A similar structure, using the intensive verb as a kind of equals sign, can be seen to have an effect of equivalence verging on the tautological as in the apparently empty statement that *Staying positive is a good coping strategy* from **Our Baby**. More clearly tautological statements can be found throughout the data, and one can only speculate as to their function and/or effect. The following are from **Bliss** and **Pregnancy and Birth** respectively:

You're quite vain, and always like to look your best ... Being such a perfectionist, everything you do has to be just right.

They are not compulsory and Mel can refuse any test she wishes.

Here, there are two examples conjoined by *and* which demonstrate that its reputation as a simple additional conjunction is inaccurate. The second part of the first example uses a subordinate clause (*Being such a perfectionist*) to duplicate the notion of *being right.* Possibly, in both of these cases, the writer is covering the eventuality that readers do not know what the words *perfectionist* or *compulsory* mean. The conjoined examples sound more tautological to the reader who knows these words, because there is an implication that something will be added, and then nothing, in fact, is. The first example, using the subordinate clause, seems to lead in the direction of a more specific case of being a perfectionist, as we saw in the example above. But in this case, the specificity is not there, and the concept of perfectionism is simply reiterated.

The following example demonstrates the lack of clear boundaries between the textually constructed semantic relations in this chapter, as it is on the borderline between apposition and list – and implies some kind of equivalence between doing wrong and being a lesbian, since the negative of these two structures is juxtaposed in a series of clauses that syntactically could be either list or apposition:

> *You've done nothing wrong, it doesn't mean you're a lesbian* and if anyone says you are just ignore them and they'll soon forget about it, I promise. (*Mizz*)

The two clauses here can be seen as additional to each other, but they also both refer to the same incident and to that extent seem to be appositional too. The conclusion we can draw is that the two things that the letter-writer fears are also linked. Thus, being a lesbian would be implicitly connected to doing something wrong.

We will return to clearer listing and exemplifying examples below, but first there is the question of the impact of created opposites on the ideological messages about the body in this data.

Contrasting

The ideological significance of created opposites in these data seems to be much greater than that of the equivalence relations. The latter were mostly intended to inform or teach, and though this strengthens the authoritative status of the magazines, there is little in the way of direct equivalences being set up to create a particular view of the female body.

Constructed oppositions, however, seem to fall into themed groups across the data, and the most comprehensive of these can be categorized under the superordinate heading of *good* versus *bad*. They clearly overlap in this case with the descriptive features discussed in Chapter 3.

Much of the advice in these magazines in relation to the body is very clear about what is or is not desirable, to the extent of indicating that some actions or approaches are right, where others are wrong:

> Make the most of your height by standing straight and walking tall – slouching around will make your clothes look terrible! (*Shout*)

This extract uses the imperative (*make*) to indicate what should be done and a negative value judgement (*terrible*) to indicate the opposite (*slouching*). Interestingly, this contrast appears to be quite embedded in the language, as the word *slouching* itself has negative value connotatively, and it is hard to think of a neutral word with similar denotation. If this example can be glossed as 'right' versus 'wrong', and these are, in turn, specific examples of *good* versus *bad*, then the tendency to categorize notions as myth or fact exemplifies a different kind of right versus wrong. In this case, we are referring not to value judgements, but the truth or otherwise of ideas.

We saw in Chapter 2 that there are some texts in the data which structure themselves around the myth-versus-fact idea. This can be seen also in **Pregnancy and Birth** in an article which has sections of advice and product promotion in relation to pregnancy and body care. There is one section which is labelled *Pregnancy Myths This month: breast changes*, and is clearly one of a set which is spread over a number of issues of the magazine. There are three individual 'myths', each of which is followed by a paragraph of explanation, headed *Fact*. Here is one of them:

Myth: The darker colour of your nipples and the surrounding area is only temporary, and they will return to their normal colour after the birth.

Fact: This colour change occurs because ... This is in fact a permanent change.

The opposition here is based on a familiar, if not conventional opposition between things that are true and those that are untrue. Lexically, the words *myth* and *fact* may not resonate as antonyms, but it is clear that they work quite normally as complementaries, their negatives being equal to the other term. Thus, if something is *true* or a *fact* in normal usage, it is necessarily not *false, untrue* or a *myth*. This raises the issue of the textual reduction of many topics to a relationship of complementarity, where experience may actually indicate a more gradable or converse relationship, for example. The complementary, or mutually exclusive opposite appeals to news and magazine copy-writers because of its clarity, and to readers for the same reason. However, there are many issues relating to the female body that are nothing like as clear as this either–or kind of relationship, and the overreliance on relationships of complementarity by rhetorical strategies of this kind reinforces distinctions which may reflect prevailing ideologies, of the perfect female body, the intrinsic maternal function of women and so on.

By far the most common hyponyms of *good* and *bad* in the data are those which could also be seen as being in a hyponymous relation to *normal/abnormal* or *natural/unnatural*. Whilst these words are both conventionally opposed in English, and slightly different in meaning to each other, the way that they are used in the data makes them almost synonymous at the positive end in indicating a kind of prototypical body which is both *natural* and *normal*, with all variations from this ideal being somewhere on the cline from here to *unnatural* and/or *abnormal*.

To begin with the *natural* versus *unnatural* end of the spectrum, there are many examples in the pregnancy texts of readers contrasting natural childbirth with pain relief. Here are some examples:

> *Painkillers like ibuprofen* can help ease period pain... *Natural remedies* can also help (**Bliss**)
>
> I had a *normal birth* with *no pain relief* except gas and air. (**Our Baby**)
>
> she's planning to give birth without *medical pain relief*. But a midwife has to be prepared for *all eventualities*. (**Pregnancy and Birth**)
>
> ...says she hopes for a natural birth, 'though I'll probably start off with *whale music* and end up with *an epidural!'* (**Pregnancy and Birth**)

The triggers which cause these opposites (italicized) to be created are parallel structures in the first example and negation in the second. In the third example, the conjunction *but* introduces a contrasting situation, though the new term being opposed to *medical pain relief* is a euphemism, *all eventualities*, which hints at problems and their likely technical solutions, that is unnatural processes. The final example is a classic case of a created opposite which operates at a very specific level to exemplify a higher-level opposite, in this case *natural* versus *unnatural*. The trigger is the temporal contrast of *start with* versus *end up with*, and the opposition is set up between *whale music* and *an epidural*. The superordinate in this case begins to look a little odd, since there is nothing natural about women listening to whales when they give birth! We can therefore begin to see that what is popularly seen as natural in childbirth terms is actually closer to a conceptual opposite of *interventionist* versus *non-interventionist*.

This question of what is *natural* and indeed what is *normal* becomes still more cloudy when we consider the data relating to cosmetic surgery. We saw the following extract from **Body Beautiful** earlier and it gives a reader's reaction to the process of breast enlargement:

> I had *silicone* put in so they're firmer than *normal tissue* but they still feel like part of my body. It doesn't feel like there's *anything* there at all. I think it feels very *natural*.

The first contrast here is set up between *silicone* and *normal tissue*. Thus, *silicone* would not be opposed to *human tissue* in other contexts, for example in relation to its use in computer components. Here, the alternatives in fact are between ordinary breast tissue and silicone, and the contrast is highlighted by the comparative form, *firmer than*. This opposition is undermined a little in the next sentence which uses negation and parallelism (*doesn't feel* versus *feels*) to set up an opposition between what is *natural* and what would be (hypothetically) *unnatural*. The oddity of this example, of course, is the reader's assertion that it is the breast implants which feel natural by not seeming to be there at all.

The slightly jokey treatment of problems of puberty that is found in **Bliss** and was discussed in Chapter 2, relies on notions of normality and abnormality, but uses a scaremongering technique to contrast something ridiculously abnormal with the supposedly normal situation that is at the root of the problem. Thus, in the following extract the surreal suggestion that one might find a hairy caterpillar under one's nose is contrasted, by negation, with the reality, designated as *worse*, by a comparative form:

> Close inspection reveals that it's not a hairy caterpillar that's decided to take refuge under your nose. It's worse than that – it's a moustache!

This text, then, plays on the *good* versus *bad* superordinate by lining up the reality, which is *bad*, with normality, which is usually *good*. This is partly a rhetorical device which enables the text to first of all emphasize the feelings of revulsion that the young girl may be feeling, and then to continue in a more soothing tone to undo the very semantic relations that are being set up here. This reinforcement of the supposedly 'natural' reaction to the facts of the female form, that it is 'unstable and leaky', ends by trying to emphasize the fact that everyone has some body hair, making the abnormal in some sense normal, but not in the sense that it would be seen as normal for a male:

> **Smile 'cause:** Every one of your mates has a hair scare somewhere, and if you hate it, you can deal with it.

The concept of normality in many texts in the data is confused with ideal or perfect. This is particularly noticeable in the pregnancy texts where the tendency is to consider the pre-pregnant body as normal, and the post-pregnancy shape as being aberrant, as we can see in the following example:

If your life's been turned upside down by the arrival of a new baby, shouldn't your stomach have the good grace to return to normal? (***Women's Health***)

This extract is typical of the apparently universal assumption that there is a stable ideal body which can be achieved, even after the major disruptions of pregnancy. Though this may be easier for some to achieve than others, whether with additional help from exercise, diet or surgery, the fact is that pregnancy changes bodies, and these magazines are part of a large lucrative industry telling women a different kind of story.

If these potential influences on teenage readers' perceptions of their bodies is part of the reinforcement of more generalized ideologies about the perfect female form, the construction of opposites in relation to normal pregnancies versus problematic ones may have a more immediate effect on some readers. It is clearly to be desired that women have unproblematic pregnancies which result in live and healthy children, but the construction of complications in pregnancy as abnormal is potentially problematic because this lines up conditions like pre-eclampsia under the superordinate *bad*, and this may have overtones of responsibility associated with it, leading to feelings of inadequacy in the women affected. Here's a case in point from ***Woman***:

> After losing her son, Jac, just six days after he was born prematurely due to severe pre-eclampsia . . . She'd had two normal pregnancies and healthy children . . .

The word *normal*, then, has to do duty for a range of meanings, including unproblematic in this case. It marginalizes those with other experiences, and places only the most straightforward pregnancies in the centre of the prototype of normality.

One final example of the *normal* versus *abnormal* range comes from the text in *Jump* written by a young, male-implied author on the subject of unduly sexualized young girls. He describes himself early on as *a seemingly normal, red-blooded, 19 year old guy*, and then later, in case there's any doubt, tries to establish his credentials by distancing himself from abnormality in the following way:

> Nor am I the kind of guy who only goes for earthy types (you know, girls who prefer eco-terrorism to experiencing life and refuse to, like, shave and stuff).

This distancing from abnormality is achieved by the negation of a case which is exaggerated by a hyperbolic and negative description of *earthy types*. The constructed opposite between the normal male (who doesn't like such women) and the abnormal male (who does) is compounded by the constructed opposition between *experiencing life* and *eco-terrorism*, the latter in some sense being equated to not living a full life in the terms of this writer. Thus, we have the beginnings of a paradigm of people and their activity types emerging from this text as follows:

Good	Bad
normal, red-blooded male	abnormal male
doesn't like earthy types of women	likes earthy types of women
likes women who experience life (equals clubbing?)	likes women who don't experience life
likes women who shave	likes women who engage in eco-terrorism and refuse to shave

It is not difficult to see here that the normalizing of certain types of behaviour, in particular the construction of political interests in extreme ways (as terrorism) is being carried out here. The use of opposites is just one of the ways in which cultural and socio-political norms are created as over-simplistic binaries in texts, with the potential influence on readers being to embed such oppositions in their reflex/default perceptions.

Another pervasive contrast in this data, and one which also comes under the general heading of *good* versus *bad*, is the one between *healthy* and *unhealthy*. This can turn up in expected pairings, but quite frequently the aim is to construct particular, quite specific, contrasts such as between dieting and healthy eating, rather than the more expected pairing between dieting and putting on weight. This construction is very clear in responses to letters from teenagers who are complaining of being overweight, as this extract from *Sugar* demonstrates:

> Dieting is not the answer, a growing girl needs a healthy balanced diet.

Like this one, the other opposites constructed in the data in relation to food are often constructed by negation, with one clause being positive and one negative. In some cases, though, the two terms of the opposition may be all on the unhealthy side of the debate, as in the letter from two teenagers with bulimic tendencies:

We don't *binge* on food, and if anything, we *under eat*, but anything we do eat we throw up.

This is a clear construction of a problematic opposite (*binge – under eat*) by the young girls, who seem to have only aberrant relationships with food from which to construct their understanding of it. The answer to this letter, interestingly, sets up a different opposition, with undereating being opposed to healthy eating:

You need to try and eat a *healthy diet*, so that your body gets all the vitamins and minerals it needs to grow and develop properly. Please try not to *undereat*.

The opposition here is created by the triggers of parallelism and negation combined (*try and* versus *try not to*). What these conflicting oppositions show us is the fluidity of oppositions, depending on our lifestyle, experiences, outlook and also according to the prevailing conditions in any single context. The result is, in this case, a glimpse of the negotiation of semantic relations which is being carried out between the letter-writers and the advisor who is effectively trying to 'correct' the mis-constructed opposition that the girls have developed.

Other examples of the *healthy* versus *unhealthy* opposite are found in pregnancy texts, also often in relation to food:

The main thing is just to eat things that are made from *fresh produce*, avoiding *processed foods* or *frozen junk food*. (**Slimmer Magazine**)

In this extract the opposition in focus is a relatively familiar one, between fresh foods and processed or frozen foods. Though this is a common textually constructed opposition, it does not seem to have the force of a lexical relationship in the strong sense. Thus, native speakers would not necessarily show any consensus about which of the possible terms for non-fresh foods would be the opposite of *fresh*, and are just as likely to say *stale* as any of them if prompted, but given no context. However, this opposition is one that has grown up as a recognizable socio-cultural contrast in the recent past, since the forms of storage of foodstuffs has been increasing rapidly in range and type. It is therefore reasonably unsurprising to see it referred to in texts of this kind.

A slightly different interpretation of the word *healthy* is appropriate in the following extract from **Pregnancy and Birth**:

> The alpha-foetoprotein test (AFP) blood test is done between 15–18 weeks and measures the amount of AFP in the mother's blood. A high level shows an increased risk of spina bifida. A low level shows an increased risk of Down's syndrome. However, *healthy* babies can produce lower or higher levels of AFP.

Here, we have the two superordinate oppositions, between *normal* and *abnormal* and *healthy* and *unhealthy*, being brought together, since the phrase *healthy baby* does not refer to one that does press-ups and eats a balanced diet, but a baby that does not have any obvious health problems. The creation of the opposite, in this example, is more spread out, with *healthy babies* contrasting with the three preceding sentences where various difficulties are described, with the oppositional construction being somewhat retrospective as a result. The potential for feeling a sense of responsibility or guilt if your baby is not healthy may be reinforced by these sense relations.

In addition to those textually constructed opposites which seem to line up under the headings of *good* and *bad*, there are others which offer more detailed consideration of oppositions that we (think we) are familiar with. Thus, the following, from **Pregnancy and Birth**, demonstrates that insemination is not the same as impregnating:

> We had two attempts at intrauterine insemination (IUI), but I never fell pregnant.

Though these are not complementaries, since they are not necessarily mutually exclusive, their causal relationship seems to be called into question in this construction using the conjunction *but*, which normally favours opposites through the process which Grice (1975) would term conventional implicature. This reflects rather well the feelings of a woman who has been through technological processes to help her conceive and has not done so; the link between insemination and pregnancy may well, in that case, seem to have been severed.

Another group of created opposites in the data relate to time, and in particular to the permanence of certain bodily-related issues:

> But it's a good idea to get into the habit of checking your boobs *now* – as it's a habit you should keep *for life*. (**Sugar**)

It's important to ask yourself whether your feelings for this woman are about her being a special person in your life *right now*, or about your sexual feelings *in general*? (***Bliss***)

Myth: The darker colour of your nipples and the surrounding area is only *temporary*, and they will return to their normal colour after the birth... This is in fact a *permanent* change. (***Pregnancy and Birth***)

Although the final example uses conventional opposites (*temporary* versus *permanent*), the other two examples use the word *now* to indicate temporariness, and contrast this with permanence in the form of the phrases *for life* and *in general*. Note that the meaning of *now* has the potential anyway to contrast not only with *always* (as in permanent), but also with *then*. In other words, we might hypothesize two polysemous meanings of *now*, one of which means 'not-always' and the other of which means 'not-then':

Women *used to* be weighed routinely in pregnancy as a guide to their progress and their baby's development but the view *now* is that weight gain gives little indication of your baby's growth. (***Pregnancy and Birth***)

This extract exemplifies the latter contrast, between *then* and *now*, and the strong implicature is that *now* is better. In other words, this is another opposition with a paradigmatic relationship to the *good–bad* superordinates.

In addition to these, there are two sets of opposites that relate to the female body and which seem to construct it in a binary form. The first simply divides the body up horizontally between top and bottom. This is normally for fashion or beauty reasons, and is best exemplified by a text from *Sugar*, the whole of which is about setting up the top versus the bottom half of the body as separately variable sites. The categories are introduced as follows:

Triangle. You are Broad shouldered, with slim hips and a small bum. You may have a large bust – and always look great in a bikini!

Hour glass. You are V = Curvy figured, with broad shoulders, wide hips, a slim waist and probably big boobs.

This text, and others like it, may be aiming at encouraging the reader to see that we are not all the same, that there is no one ideal shape, and so on. However, the tendency is still to normalize, and to emphasize the clothes that will minimize any imbalances in the natural figure, rather than, say, flaunting such features. The reader of this last sentence might wish to pause and consider her (his?) reaction to it. If the reaction was to think that it was obvious that people would wish to balance out their bodily shape, and this is not ideological, but 'natural', then I would suggest that such reactions only serve to underline the strength of the cultural imperatives at work here.

The other major division that is evident is that between the physical and the emotional. Many texts make explicit this distinction, whilst also indicating that well-being in one goes hand-in-hand with well-being in the other:

> You are definitely *feeling better*, if not perfect. Yippee! . . . *your skin may become spotty*. Boo! (***Sugar***)
>
> Time to recover, both *physically and emotionally*. (***Our Baby***)
>
> This wonderful new skin saver . . . with tea tree, mint and herbs is a great way to *detoxify your skin and relax your senses*. (***Pregnancy and Birth***)
>
> . . . an instant facial sauna which will leave *your skin glowing and your mind feeling invigorated*. (***Pregnancy and Birth***)

These texts, then, reflect some of the third-wave feminist views of the holistic person, and are claiming to treat both aspects of the 'old' universal opposite of body and mind. Notice that apart from the second example, where the conventional opposite of *physical* versus *emotional* is used, the other examples all identify skin as the representative of the body more generally and oppose this to *feeling better, your senses* and *your mind* respectively. This variation, perhaps, reflects the socio-cultural ambivalence about this division of the person into a material being (the body) and some other less tangible kind of existence, which would once (in Western culture at least) have been an accepted binary of body versus the soul. The fragmentation of this certainty in the late twentieth and early twenty-first centuries is echoed, then, by the range of possible opposites for *body* and its synonyms.

Other issues relating to the use and creation of opposites include the common tendency to treat some contrasts as coexisting, rather than mutually exclusive. This might sound as though what is being created is a kind of converse, whereby the two terms are simply two ways of looking at the same phenomenon. In fact this is not the case, and the suggested co-occurrences usually imply not contented co-existence but the tensions that arise from that very relationship of mutual dependence, as in the following case from **Sugar**:

Remember, it's just as important to be *happy* as it is *healthy*...

The use of a non-conventional opposite (*happy*) to *healthy* raises the question of what this means. It certainly appears that there is an implicature caused here by the flouting of the maxims of relation and manner whereby we don't expect them to be contrasted normally and the contrast is achieved only by their foregrounding in the parallel structures. The implicature, then, causes these terms to be contrasted, so that the whole clause may have the force of 'Don't make yourself miserable dieting'. There is no sign here that the text producer recognizes that these two are not opposite, and the possible conclusion to be drawn by the reader might therefore be that dieting makes you unhappy and therefore is a block to the other necessary ingredient in life.

Whichever way the implicature is read in the last example, there is no doubt that the text is advocating trying to achieve both happiness and health, even if this is difficult to achieve. Note that these terms are both on the positive side of evaluation, and are aligned in some ways with the body and 'soul' distinction mentioned earlier. Other overlaps between co-occurrence and contrast occur when terms are used to invoke a range of possibilities. These may all tend to congregate at one end of a supposed spectrum, as in the following, also from **Sugar**:

Bumps and lumps are usually nothing to worry about – particularly in your teens.

This combination of the negative (that is, things that can appear to be wrong with your breasts) is intended to cover the possible options, in other words to represent all sorts of mishaps. Similarly, the following examples, from **Fresh** and **Woman** respectively, refer to two different points on a gradable range, both of which are nearer the negative than the positive end of the spectrum:

This can range from *mild* tummy aches or back aches to *painful* cramps.
It can be *dangerous*, even *fatal* to mother and baby.

Note that the use of gradable opposites, particularly textually-created ones, is much rarer in this data than the construction of complementaries, which are the mutually-exclusive type of opposite. This may reflect the ideology of this data, which reflects a desire for certainty in the culture with all contrasts being more like complementaries than gradable antonyms. It may also reflect the convenience of being able to describe bodily issues in terms which the reader will find very clear, and therefore know how to act upon them.

The few cases where the whole range of a gradable opposite is invoked have an apparent information value which is undermined by their lack of clarity, as we can see in the extract from *Pregnancy and Birth* that was quoted earlier:

> The alpha-foetoprotein test (AFP) blood test is done between 15–18 weeks and measures the amount of AFP in the mother's blood. A high level shows an increased risk of spina bifida. A low level shows an increased risk of Down's syndrome. However, healthy babies can produce lower or higher levels of AFP.

This extract has the appearance of being full of information, but beyond telling the reader when the AFP test will be done and two problems it can show up, it fails to make clear whether having a high or a low level of AFP is a good or a bad thing. Whilst there is an indication that both extremes have their risks, and no measurements are given to indicate what how or high would be in real terms, even this small amount of information is undermined by the final sentence which tells us that the high or low readings may anyway occur within normal distributions.

Enumerating and exemplifying

Fairly similar in some ways to equivalence, the textual construction of exemplification is based on generic categories and their examples, and in some cases enumerates a long list of the members of a category, often, but not exclusively, for pedagogical purposes. When it is not educational, these functions can also create categories and category members in much the same way that opposites and equivalences are described as being textually created above. By assuming such relationships, the text sets up a further ideological apparatus. As we shall see, there are overlaps here with the creation of equivalence or contrast, but there are also cases which perform a distinct function that has the effect of elaborating on the more general descriptions, bringing detail and examples into the text.

Examples and generalizations

We will begin by considering the case of the generalized label which is then made more particular, often by the use of a list of examples. At its simplest, this can take the form of a general case and a single example, as in these extracts:

Healthier choices, like fruit. (***Best Diet Now***)
STDs – especially Chlamydia. (***Woman***)

There appears to be an assumption in such examples that the reader will know the rest of the list, or that the most important one is mentioned anyway. There are other cases where the two most obvious cases of a general category are given as examples:

an eating disorder, such as anorexia or bulimia (***Pregnancy and Birth***)

Unsightly birthmarks, such as port-wine stains and broken blood vessels... (***Body Beautiful***)

cosmetic surgery – whether it was a nose job... or a nip and tuck... (***Body Beautiful***)

The two-part list in these cases seems to gesture towards a longer 'real' list, but indicates that the main cases are covered. In the final case there is clearly an indication of a range of procedures between these two typical cases, though the range is not ordered in any significant way, for example from mild to serious or from one part of the body to another.

The more pedagogically-oriented the text, the more likely it is that instead of a single example or a couple of important examples, there will be a true list of cases that expand upon the generalization. The following examples illustrate this direct informing process:

The symptoms usually occur between weeks four and 10 and can include long, painful periods; dark, watery bleeding; severe, low, one-sided abdominal pain; pain on emptying bowels; and shoulder pain. (***Our Baby***)

Foods to avoid include liver, liver sausage and liver pate; raw or lightly cooked eggs; peanuts; rare or undercooked meat or poultry; mould-ripened soft cheese; unwashed salad or veg. (***Our Baby***)

There is a sense, here, that the writer is trying hard to cover all the eventualities, to help the pregnant woman make sense of her symptoms in the first case and decide on dietary adjustments in the second.

All of the cases of exemplification we have seen so far have appeared to be truly informative, though more detailed in some cases than others. There are many other cases where the effect, if not the intention, of the exemplification may appear to be more than, or different to the 'pure' delivery of information:

> irregularities can start showing through. I've seen some *very poor results* – you could actually see *the tracks where the tubes had passed through the fat again.* (***Body Beautiful***)

This extract illustrates the general case of *very poor results* (of liposuction) with a specific example of the kind of result that is meant. The relatively emotive effect of the description of tracks under the skin is presumably intended to make potential customers think twice before they go to a cheap or under-qualified surgeon. Cosmetic surgery is the one topic that goes against the upbeat tone of most of this data, and is given to this kind of scaremongering, possibly for good, responsible reasons. However, it is also noticeable that there is barely a single article on surgery that doesn't have the name of a clinic or clinics in the text. Whilst they are not strictly advertisements, these articles, nevertheless promote particular clinics as being within the realm of the responsible, so the scaremongering tactics could be seen as promoting commercial advantage for them.

The converse of this motivation, the desire to protect plastic surgeons from blame for failures or relative lack of success, is also delivered in the form of exemplification:

> Surgery is not an exact art – there are too many variables, such as skin quality, social behaviour, different healing times and potential complications ...

This extract from ***Body Beautiful*** adds detail to the assertion that surgery is not an exact art by making it clear that the variables are too diverse to be able to predict the precise outcome. The slightly chilling, and throwaway, item in this list is the final one, *potential complications*. Though it does, indeed, present as one of the variables in all surgery, it is in itself a general case which covers all sorts of frightening possibilities. At this point, the text retreats from full explanation and lets the general term stand with no further exemplification which could discourage potential customers.

It is not unusual, of course, to find lists that have specific items at first, and then end with a catch-all category to cover anything that might not have been mentioned individually. The following is such a case:

> It is thus possible to improve long-term facial contours, for example by augmenting the cheekbones, the chin, the jaw-line or any other area that lacks definition. (***Body Beautiful***)

The reader who is considering facial surgery may read this list and check off the different areas of the face in relation to her own. The final item on the list makes it more likely that each reader will relate to the text personally, as they work out which parts of their own face might come under this description.

The structural techniques which set up exemplification are many and varied, but often include explicit reference to the fact that they are examples, using verbs such as *include* or adverb introductions like *such as*. For some cases, where the items in the list are clausal, and there is structural repetition, there may be a strong rhetorical effect reminiscent of Biblical or poetic parallelism:

> Good posture eases tense muscles; it makes balance easier; it leads to more efficient breathing and circulation, and the internal organs are better able to work well. It helps keep the spine strong and supple. It creates balance throughout the muscles of the body using minimal energy. It makes you look and feel good. Lastly, it will minimize the risk of back injury or pain. (***Women's Health***)

This list of what good posture does for the body is long, and has the effect of putting good posture into a conceptually superior role as the centre of all well-being and health.

Three-part lists

The difference between these genuine, if sometimes patchy, examples of lists, and the symbolic three-part list is striking. Though it cannot easily be 'proven' to be a different kind of textual practice, it does seem noticeable that when you read a three-part list, its significance is often more rhetorical than informational:

> There is nothing to be *afraid of, ashamed of or embarrassed about.* (***Fresh***)

This example uses three overlapping, though not identical, negative emotions, and could probably have added a few more, such as *horrified by, confused by* and so on. It is often claimed as discussed earlier in the chapter that the impact of a three-part list is to give the impression of completeness, rather than providing a comprehensive list of items that happens to have three parts. The examples in the data support this claim, as they nearly all seem to either reiterate essentially similar ideas, in order to achieve three parts and/or choose three items from a potentially much longer list.

We can see in some cases that the three-part list is a little forced, as in the following from *Pregnancy and Birth*:

> Midwives can tell all sorts of things by *looking, feeling and asking clever questions*.

There is something odd about the third part of this list, possibly because it is not a physical activity, but probably because it seems to be added on to make up the numbers. Other examples use the superordinate terms that we investigated in relation to opposition, which has an additional effect of completeness, as well as the three-part list effect:

> For many girls, whatever their age, heavy periods are *normal, healthy and natural*.

The use of *normal, healthy* and *natural* here is an emphatic statement of the message that the text is trying to convey, and could possibly have been achieved by different means, such as the intensification of any one of the words (for example *quite normal, perfectly healthy* or *completely natural*). In other words, the intention is to say that heavy periods are basically good, and this is emphasized by the use of three of the hyponyms of *good* that are repeatedly used in this material. Similar effects, using quite general and partly overlapping terms can also be seen in the following extracts:

> May simply want to look more *alert, relaxed and happy*...(***Body Beautiful***)
>
> She is a very busy woman – *actress, wife and mother*... (***Body Beautiful***)
>
> Every session is *pleasant, relaxing and invigorating*...(***Slimmer Magazine***)
>
> Before years of *laughter, smiles and tears have left their mark*...(***Body Beautiful***)

The rhetorical status of the three-part list is often underlined by some kind of phonological recognition of its status as a relatively undifferentiated unit, rather than a list of separate items. The following examples use rhyme and alliteration respectively with this effect:

> We guys go through it too...Think *unwanted zits, smelly pits and shaving kits.* (*Jump*)
>
> *Reshape, realign and rebalance* the Pilates way. (*Slimmer Magazine*)

Phonological clues like these seem to indicate a symbolic three-part list, and other candidates for this symbolic status include those where there is a sense that the list is really much longer, or the terms overlap more than strictly necessary. However, it is not possible to draw up a strict list of criteria to identify lists which have three items and are also one of these more stylised structures. There are, for example, lists which seem to genuinely have three things that make them up:

> Mel is weighed and measured and her blood pressure is taken.

This extract from **Pregnancy and Birth** does not appear to be from a longer potential list, and it has no phonological sign that it is symbolic. This is, indeed, what happens at the beginning of a first ante-natal appointment, so it has all the qualities of a genuine list. Another example, from the same text, appears at first sight to be a genuine list, but on closer inspection, we see that the second and third elements of the list are very much more general than the first:

> CVS This test is done to check for Down's syndrome, chromosome abnormalities and genetic disorders.

This seems like a 'real' list which just happens to have three parts, though the second and third in the list are rather general, and may encompass a number of conditions which are as specific as Down's syndrome. One could conclude that the list appears reassuringly complete, and it could also be argued that it informs less than it appears to. Pregnancy complications are two-edged for pregnancy magazines, which may want to be positive about all aspects of pregnancy, whilst informing their readers about the dangers. One of their techniques is the happy ending, as we saw in Chapter 2. This may be another one, whereby the three-part list glosses over the detailed facts and gives an impression of informing, whilst really smoothing over the potential anxieties of the pregnant reader by suggesting that everything is capably dealt with by the test concerned. The absence of any follow-up information about what would happen if the test showed up an abnormality may be significant here, as it confirms that there is an avoidance of difficult issues.

In the same vein, there appears to be a taboo surrounding large breasts, except in the context of sexual attractiveness. A straightforward advice article on measuring for bras, for example, uses a three-part list, plus *and so on* to indicate the formula for working out cup size:

> If it's the same as the measurement underneath your bust, you're an A cup; 1in ($2\frac{1}{2}$ cm) more, you're a B cup; 2in (5 cm) more, C cup and so on. (**Mizz**)

It could be argued that the pattern is established by the third case, in a way that it is not when only two sizes are mentioned. Thus, the larger girl can easily deduce what to conclude if her breasts are three or more inches larger than her ribcage. However, the effect, intended or not, is to make those larger girls invisible, and this could result in some of them feeling abnormal.

Whilst many of the pregnancy advice articles have a large number of three-part lists, and some of these may be more genuine than symbolic, there are cases in all text types where the number three seems to dominate for no reason other than a rhetorical one. In one article from **Woman**, which is about complications in pregnancy, we have a three-part list which becomes increasingly extreme as it goes on:

> Causing severe pain, bleeding and even death.

There may in fact be other symptoms of ectopic pregnancy, but the end of this list appears to be rather final. Other indications that the number three is significant occur in the quiz format, such as in **Slimmer Magazine**, where each question has three possible answers:

> You've just been invited out on a hot date. Do you: a. Rush out and buy a really tight dress? b. Treat yourself to a facial and a new lipstick? c. Panic! Start the starvation diet NOW – there's no time to lose?

Similarly, each of the seven days of activities in the build-up to a greater orgasm in **More** has three steps, and in the same text the explanation for the effectiveness of frequent *quickies* is also, apparently, tri-partite:

A quickie twice in one day will work for three reasons: 1) a frenzied bonk will boost your libido; 2) quickies break the routine and may spur your boyfriend on to greater things; 3) the adrenaline surge will give you a day-long, warm, fuzzy feeling.

There is no doubt at all that this writer could have come up with any number of additional reasons if pressed, but three is the convention in such lists and more might make clear the lack of substance in the article as a whole.

It is hard to be sure that there is not a good physiological reason for manufacturers of tampons making them in three different sizes, but in the context of the ubiquitous three-part list, it is hard to avoid the conclusion that such technical decisions might be partly influenced by the advertising attraction of being able to use three-part lists, as in this extract from *Sugar*:

Try the Tampax Multipack, which contains three different absorbencies: Lites, Regular and Super.

In fact, their products often come in four different sizes, which makes it all the more interesting that only three of them are mentioned here.

Note that the three-part list can operate at higher levels of structure, and sometimes occurs where parallel structures are being used. The following example uses three question forms to hypothesize about the reason for Pamela Anderson reducing her breast implants to a smaller size:

Was she worried by the recent health scares about silicone implants? Was it because moody musician hubby Tommy Lee had grown bored of her plastic chest? Or was it simply that she herself had tired of the old 'glitz and tits' image that she had fought so hard and become so well known for? (*Body Beautiful*)

There can be, of course, no comprehensive list of all the possible reasons for any course of action, so the writer falls back upon the three-part list as the standard number of options to give.

Summary

A general conclusion that we might draw from this analysis is that many of the texts in this data have an ostensibly pedagogical function, which may be served by the equivalence-construction of appositional and other structures, but is also undermined by the lack of genuine information, in some cases leading to the conclusion that the desire to inform is subservient to the desire to entertain. Nevertheless, that there is some 'teaching' going on is not in doubt, and the equating function of texts seems to perform this role more often and more sincerely than the other similar functions explored here.

The textual construction of contrast, or opposition, seems less clearly pedagogical or informative in nature, tied as it often is to the superordinate oppositions of *good–bad, normal–abnormal* and *natural–unnatural*. The overwhelming presence of evaluative oppositions, both conventional (see Chapter 3) and unconventional (see above pp. 109 *f*) indicates a hugely normative drive in this data towards an ideal, youthful and unchanging body shape, irrespective of age or life's experiences.

As for enumeration and exemplification, which are not clearly distinct from each other in function, they have a split effect, sometimes having a clearly informative or pedagogical role and at other times performing a symbolic but not genuinely informative function. The most interesting and ideologically-loaded type of enumeration or exemplifying is the three-part list, which is less truly informative than a 'real' list, and appears to reinforce the culturally dominant ideal body shape, maternal role and other stereotypes.

Note that in the context of so many three-part lists, many of which appear to symbolize completeness, the consequence for longer lists is that they may seem over-long by comparison. The following example from *Pregnancy and Birth* has a five-part list which may well represent a fuller picture, but also seems to symbolize the length of time that the ante-natal visit is taking:

Mel's booking-in visit seems to last forever! The midwife wants details about her husband and family and information on asthma, diabetes, epilepsy, heart problems, high blood pressure...

5
Assuming and Implying

If some ideology can be delivered through processes of equating, contrasting and exemplifying, the way in which the world is structured ideologically can also be naturalized very effectively through the assumptions and implications that a text makes. This chapter explores these processes in the data under consideration and demonstrates both the construction of an assumed/implied reader and the construction of the assumed/implied perfect female form.

Presupposition and implicature

The two categories of assuming and implying are the labels that I am using for what is technically known as presupposition and implicature by linguists. This chapter, then, considers those meanings which are often seen as less direct than lexical and sentence semantics, and as a result of this indirectness can be seen as helping to naturalize certain ideologies relating to the female body. What is particularly important about the functions of assuming and implying in texts is that these meanings may communicate themselves to the reader at a relatively subconscious level, and if reading texts of a similar nature repeatedly delivers the same ideological assumptions, the reader is vulnerable to the conceptual influences that such repetition could have on world view or perceptions.

Many of the assumptions and implications we address here will be part of a more general process of constructing an ideal or supposed reader. This process includes making assumptions about the general categories that the reader is likely to belong to (such as female, white and so on.) but it also includes, as we shall see, much more specific assumptions, for example about the kinds of problems the reader has, or the shape of her body.

The textual delivery of assumptions is normally by the mechanism of presupposition. There are many ways of building presuppositions into text; indeed it is impossible to avoid, at the most basic level. We will draw upon two categories of presupposition to investigate this data: existential presupposition and logical presupposition (see Simpson 1993: 125–6). The structural properties of these types of presupposition are different, and it is sometimes assumed that the logical presuppositions are potentially more ideologically loaded than the existential ones. This is because the latter are unavoidable, and many of them can thus be seen as innocuous in persuasive terms, being no more than an assumption that something exists. Thus, the following (invented) sentence includes three existential presuppositions, relating to the noun phrases, *the local baker, a part-time job*[1] and *his shop*:

The local baker was advertising a part-time job in his shop.

Such presuppositions are a necessary part of the normal exchanges that speakers make in everyday conversation and we have already encountered some nominally-based presuppositions of this kind in Chapter 3. They are useful to speakers and hearers because they trigger conceptual schemata without the need for further contextual inform-ation. More elaborate noun phrases may build-in a more complex set of presuppositions to the noun phrase, by the use of pre- and post-modification, as in the following (invented) sentence:

Your ugly sister wore that dreadful outfit again!

I have exaggerated the offence that could be given in this sentence, to demonstrate the difference that a couple of adjectives can make to the existential presuppositions. Instead of presupposing the sister's and the outfit's existence, as this sentence would have done without adjectives, it presupposes the existence of an *ugly sister* and a *dreadful outfit*, which is where the potential for offence comes in. Note that this production of existential presupposition, commonly by definite noun phrases overlaps in some ways with the naming function that we investigated earlier, though naming itself will not always produce such presuppositions.

The logical presupposition is triggered by one of a number of structural devices which embed some kind of assumption into the utterance (see Levinson 1983: 181–3). The following are the major triggers for logical presuppositions mentioned by Levinson, though he concedes that these can differ according to the definition of presupposition:

- Factive, implicative, judging and change-of-state verbs
- Comparative constructions
- Iteratives
- Non-restrictive relative clauses and counterfactual conditionals
- Cleft and implicit cleft constructions
- Temporal clauses

As we will see below, some of these triggers occur more frequently than others in the data. Those which do occur provide a basis for the naturalization of certain ideologies pertaining to the female body.

In addition to the presuppositions that contribute to the textual construction of the female body in this way, these texts also depend on conversational implicature to provide further ideological underpinning. Conversational implicature, a consequence of Grice's co-operative principle and its maxims, is described by Simpson (1993: 129) as:

> those meanings which unfold when it is clear that the semantic content of an utterance is alone not a reliable guarantor of the meaning of that utterance in context. In this way, implicatures can be regarded as inferences that develop from a mutual understanding between speakers engaged in interaction.

The context of the texts analysed here is different, of course, from the original conversational context envisaged by Grice (1975), since the texts are published and read at a distance from the production process, and there is relatively little genuine exchange between producer and reader analogous to the interaction that takes place in face-to-face conversation. Nevertheless, it is clear that implicature is now viewed as a potential carrier of indirect meaning in both written and spoken language, and the shared understanding that may underlie this mechanism is clearly both personal and cultural.

Thus, in discussing someone with a friend who also knows that person, there will be shared knowledge that may inform the conversational implicatures that arise. In reading articles relating to the female form in magazines, the reader will make assumptions about the norms and expectations of the cultural context in which the magazine is produced and read which will influence her understanding of implicatures in the texts she reads.

Note that this explanation of how the implicature may work in the case of published material also gives an insight into the reinforcement and reproduction of ideological norms, which are assumed to

be understood already for the typical – or 'successful' reader of these texts.

One example of this may be the use of implicature to set up the exemplary women, seen in Chapter 2 as a generalized rhetorical feature of these texts. The precise linguistic mechanism that makes the rhetoric work is, in many cases, the presentation of a woman who has had an experience relevant to the topic, and who apparently tells her story quite simply and straightforwardly. The following extract, for example, comes from a diary-style article about pregnancy:

> I'm extremely tired. I've got to look after myself, put my feet up and eat healthily. (*Our Baby*)

There are many such examples in the data, on all topics, and we will look at some of them in detail below. Here, the point is to notice that there is probably more information than the reader needs in the second sentence, unless it is not just a 'note to self' in the protagonist's 'diary', but is also a semi-coded message to all readers of the magazine that they too should do these things in the early stages of pregnancy. This self-consciousness of the multiple addressees of the text can be described with reference to discourse roles (see Thomas 1986). Thus, this text requires both the fictionalized self-addressing of the diary-style article and also the knowledge that there are other addressees, the pregnant readers, who will be expected to assimilate the information that these are good things for pregnant women to do. The message of this extract, delivered by implicature resulting from the flouting of the maxim of quantity, is that this is what the reader, also, should do. The mechanism is essentially circular; many such implicatures in fact do not seem to deliver any 'new' information, leaving the implicature, which amounts to 'you already know all this, but should act upon it' as the main message of the text.

Constructing the reader

The overwhelming majority of the texts in our data make the understandable assumption that the reader is female. This is demonstrated in a number of ways, but mostly by the use of the second person pronoun (*you*) or the possessive determiner (*your*) in conjunction with purely female conditions such as having breasts, periods or a vagina.

Thus in texts from *Bliss* and *Sugar*, for example, the reader is addressed by talking about *your vagina* and *your period* which form existential presuppositions, as the possessive pronouns are definite in meaning. Similarly in texts from **Mizz** and **Woman** (and many others), there are clear indications that the addressee is female because of the attributes described:

> Are you wearing the right bra? (**Mizz**)
> Be aware of changes in your cervical mucus (**Woman**)

Some texts make an explicit appeal to the solidarity of being female, by including the writer, as well as the reader in the first-person plural pronoun, *we*:

> Firstly, don't be embarrassed about your breasts – we've all got them! (**Shout**)

> periods are all part of being a girl. There is nothing to be afraid of, ashamed of or embarrassed about – because we all have them! (**Fresh**)

Apart from the occasional expert opinion or article, the data are mostly neutral with respect to the writer's gender, but these occasions when the writer makes an appearance in the text are striking in their attempt to cause the reader to identify with her.

Whilst it is to be expected that articles which purport to be of help to women might address all readers as female, there are also a very large number of presuppositions and implicatures which detail the *kind* of women that they are addressing. Whilst there is no explicit statement of expectation that the reader will have these characteristics, there is, nevertheless, the potential for a normalising effect where the same characteristics are assumed time and again.

Take, for example, the assumptions that everyone lives in a nuclear family, and in particular that everyone has a mum. **Bliss**, for example, presupposes just these things, by the mechanism of the same *your*+noun structure that we have already seen:

> you're also worrying about what *your mum* will say when she does your washing.

It is, of course, also noticeable that the stereotype of the mum that does her (teenage) children's washing is presupposed here as a result of the iterative meaning of *when* in this context. These norms of family life and gender roles may indeed still reflect many young people back to themselves, though the potentially alienating effect on those without the comforts of such a background, or with completely different, though equally supportive backgrounds can be imagined.

More widespread across all the data is the assumption that the reader is not only female, but heterosexual, and usually in a stable, loving relationship. The text world of these magazines is made up of couples, particularly where sex or pregnancy is the topic. However, the possibility that a single pregnant woman or a lesbian who is sexually active might be reading these magazines is not countenanced:

> When did labour start? And how did it feel to finally meet your baby? Three couples share the agony and the ecstasy. (***Our Baby***)

The three labour stories which follow this introduction are in the form of an interview, with questions and first-person answers. The use of *you* in this example, then, is odd, because the article itself is not in the second person. The explanation, it seems to me, is that the three couples are intended to 'stand for' the readership of the magazine, and their different stories represent the likely range of difference to be experienced during a delivery. This compounds the problem of there being no variation in the nuclear family/heterosexual couple, patterning, since there is an implicature that *you* (= the readers) are all in some sense like the people whose stories are being told.

Those pregnancy articles which do address the reader in the second person also assume the norm of a couple:

> Antenatal classes These are a great way of learning about everything from pain relief and labour positions to bathing a newborn. They also give you the chance to meet other expectant couples. (***Our Baby***)

The use of the iterative trigger, *other*, causes a logical presupposition that the addressee is also (part of) a couple.

The articles which detail how to have 'good' sex also regularly presuppose that the reader is a woman in a heterosexual relationship, since that is their *raison d'être*. They normally use the possessive determiner and noun structure to cause an existential presupposition. Thus *your partner* is found frequently in such articles. Similarly, there is a presupposition that *he* and *his penis* exist in the following extract from an article which promises *out-of-this-world orgasms*:

> If you can't grip *his penis* with *your vaginal muscles* during sex, then your internal vaginal muscles are too flabby! (***More***)

In addition, of course, there are presuppositions about the gender of the addressee (who has vaginal muscles), and the sexuality and sexual activeness of the addressee too.

The self-selecting nature of much of the audience for these articles is one reason why the writers will probably not give a second thought to the assumptions that they are making. This is almost definable as a genre whose linguistic norms are to address the reader, and assume she is in the target group, which happens to be the majority group in society. The teenage magazines have a particular placing in relation to the readership, however, since the target audience is probably more comprehensive, across all teenage girls, than the adult magazines. That the same assumptions are made regularly in these magazines is interesting because they reinforce the 'majority' view of normality repeatedly, not only excluding those readers who do not belong in the group, but also reinforcing the views of the majority themselves, so that all other sexualities remain marginal and thus 'other':

My breasts are big and saggy. I'm worried when I have sex with a boy he'll be put off... (***Bliss***)

The presupposition, that she will indeed have sex with a boy in due course, arises from the subordinator *when*, which functions in the same way as a verb of change to introduce a new situation which it is assumed will definitely happen.

In the pregnancy literature, it is probably not surprising to find that there are many articles which presuppose or imply not only a female reader, but also a pregnant one. It is, of course, possible that non-pregnant women and men may also read these magazines, not least if they are embarking on parenthood, or wish to do so, but these 'marginal' readers tend not to be addressed directly:

that's why it's vital you have your blood pressure and urine checked for protein levels at every antenatal visit. (***Woman***)

This extract uses pragmatic presupposition to imply that the reader is not only female, but pregnant, by addressing her using the second person pronoun, *you*, and connecting this with the existentially presupposed protein levels in urine and antenatal visits. Thus, the world knowledge of the reader comes into play here as the connector between different presuppositions in the sentence. This kind of construction of the reader is, of course, ubiquitous in the pregnancy data, but the assumptions do not stop there. Most of the assumptions about the reader also assume that the pregnancy is healthy, and therefore describe the processes which are found in successful pregnancies: *your placenta transfers antibodies.* (*Our Baby*)

Again, the presupposition is achieved by the use of *you* with the existential presupposition of the placenta and the description of the process by which the embryo is fed. The norm of the healthy pregnancy is also reinforced by the expectation in all of the articles that the pregnancy is not only wanted, but looked for:

Congratulations – you're pregnant at last! (*Our Baby*)

The iterative trigger (*at last*) in this extract indicates a change of state from an earlier state of non-pregnancy and demonstrates that the pregnancy is not only desired but also took a while to achieve. This norm of the desirability of children is confirmed and reinforced in a number of articles, as seen in the two extracts from different articles which follow:

He's filled a huge gap in our lives... (*Our Baby*)

What did prey on my mind was the thought that we were doomed not to have a family. (*Our Baby*)

The presupposition that prior to having children there was a gap in the writer's life is specific to these particular stories, and it could be argued that this is therefore not ideological in the more general normative sense. However, there are no counterbalancing stories and repeated examples of this kind of message in the absence of contrary ideologies tend to reinforce the notion that motherhood is the ultimate fulfilment of a woman's life. As we saw in the example above – *Congratulations – you're pregnant at last!* – even the introductions to otherwise quite factual and informative articles, which could theoretically be read by those who are reluctant to be pregnant or ambivalent about it, often begin with an implicature that being pregnant is a universally good thing.

Amongst the articles relating to pregnancy there are a few which deal with some of the problems or complications that can arise, but as we saw in Chapter 2 there is a tendency to use happy endings as a way of minimizing the pessimism in the text. Thus, although a text about problems of conception from *Woman* includes sections on different problems of conception and complications of pregnancy, it nevertheless gives examples reflecting the ultimately successful outcome for two readers. Even the admission that many couples have trouble in conceiving acts as an implicature to the opposite, that since so many have trouble, it is likely that most of those end up with a baby:

One in six couples will have fertility problems...

Another normalizing tendency in all of this data is the ubiquitous assumption that women (that is, the readers) are overweight, and by definition that this is a problem:

Slim from Within not only helps with your weightloss, it also brings you belief in yourself and an end to self criticism...(*Slimmer Magazine*)

The use of the second-person pronoun here, with the noun *weightloss*, causes the existential presupposition that you (the reader) do indeed have a weight problem. Logical presuppositions, that you lack self-belief and that you are self-critical are triggered in the next clause by the change of state verb *brings*, and the change of state noun *an end to*. The text that this extract is taken from is an advert for a slimming programme, so we may not be surprised at these presuppositions, though we may also note that this does not alter the potential effect for a reader, whose own perceptions may well tend to be influenced by the unerring message that she is overweight, whether or not this is really the case. The very many readers' stories in the data relating to weight, as well as being rhetorically significant by having happy endings, also use a great many superlatives to describe weight loss:

When Ros Thatcher *lost an amazing 9st* it finally gave her the courage to pursue her dream of finding the mother who gave her up for adoption. And she did! (***Diet and Fitness***)

The use of *amazing*, of course, is strictly relevant in that it represents a great deal of weight to lose. However, the use of extreme cases to demonstrate that weight loss can indeed be achieved is potentially rather alarming, as it triggers the sense that the amount of weight loss (irrespective of the starting weight) is the crucial measure of success. This extract also demonstrates the claim that weight loss also solves all other problems in life, and this is confirmed by the following extract:

And life has been looking up ever since. Amy now works in a community health centre as a pharmacy technician. She's also studying at college one day a week...(*WeightWatchers*)

In both of these cases, the weight loss is directly attributed with the power to solve difficult problems, and though it is never stated outright, the implicature, as in all these stories, is that it could do the same for the reader.

As well as assuming universal weight problems, the texts have a tendency to assume that readers have a desire to eat unhealthily, as exemplified in the following two extracts:

> Sadly, though, it doesn't give you a licence to pig out...
> (*Woman's Own*)

> Just imagine... a miracle diet that allows you to eat generous servings of all your favourite dishes: fillet steak with Béarnaise sauce, fry-ups complete with eggs, bacon and black pudding, even ice cream for dessert. (*Cosmopolitan*)

In the first example the noun *licence* causes a logical presupposition that the reader has the desire to *pig out*, and the second one that the reader wishes to eat all unhealthy food, despite it being bad for them, signalled by the verb *allow*. Since what is allowed – or licensed – is normally something that the person concerned wishes to do, the presupposition attaches to the activity following these words.

The generalized assumptions about excess weight are not confined to the slimming magazines or articles, but tend to crop up in all contexts, including post-pregnancy, exercise, and sex-related texts. The following two come from articles promoting different forms of exercise:

> Follow Lynne's example to *trim your tum and shape your bum*. (*Slimmer Magazine*)

> Stop reminding anyone who will listen *that you've got a huge arse*. One advantage of this superficial world is that everyone is too obsessed with themselves to really notice *your lumpy thighs*! (*Body Beautiful*)

The first includes an implicature that trimming the tum and shaping the bum are necessary for the reader. This arises from the pragmatic presupposition that you wouldn't *trim* or *shape* something unless it was needed. The second example is based on presuppositions triggered by the factive verb *remind* whose subordinate clause complement (italicized) is presupposed to be true and the existential effect of the definite noun phrase *your lumpy thighs*, which the reader is presupposed to have.

One of the main reasons frequently implied in the data for the importance of not being overweight is to appear sexually attractive, to men:

BEST FOR: Big hips and thighs. This is obviously because *the offending parts* are hidden from view in this position – and elongating your limbs makes saggy bits look less saggy and chunky bits less chunky. (*Body Beautiful*)

Your partner keeps pointing out how fabulous your stick thin best friend looks in her animal print skirt. Do you: a Rush out and buy *exactly the same skirt, three sizes bigger*, even though it won't suit you? b Find something similar, with a flattering silhouette which makes YOU look sensational? c Wonder if he's having an affair with her? (*More*)

These examples demonstrate that big hips and thighs, referred to as *the offending parts*, are something to disguise by using particular positions for lovemaking and, in the case of the second example, that the reader is likely to be relatively overweight – and therefore relatively unattractive – to her partner, compared with a thinner friend. These are effects of pragmatic presupposition in the first case achieved by the mechanism of rephrasing, and by implicature in the second case where the maxim of quantity is flouted, but there is an implicit link between *three sizes bigger* and being overweight.

Perfection and attraction

The connection between being slim and being sexy is part of a bigger tendency in the data to assume that the primary need is for women to appear sexy to men, and that it is also a test of success whether one enjoys a lot of good sex. The first example, below, comes from an article in **Cosmopolitan** made up of *get-beddable beauty tips*, with the built-in assumption that these are aimed at appearing sexy to men:

Want to have the most luscious lips he's ever kissed? Slough off dry flakes with a flannel while you're taking a hot, steamy shower.

This extract uses the rhetorical question to imply that no reader could fail to desire this outcome. It also hints at sexual activity by using a word with sexual connotations, *steamy*, to describe the shower. This normative message about the pursuit of sexiness begins in the teenage magazines, and even where it is not being explicitly connected to looks it is still seen as the driving ambition for girls and young women:

Confidence and charisma will never go out of fashion. In fact, the older you get, the more important they become so you might as well try to develop them now. They're such attractive qualities in anyone, especially a young woman. Trust me, I'm a guy. (*Jump*)

We have seen extracts from this article, written by a 19-year-old man, before. It aims to convince the reader that dressing beyond her years is not appropriate. However, the writer constantly undermines his message by reinforcing the very forces – the pleasing of men – that cause the problem in the first place. In this extract, the implicature that the girls are trying to please men is achieved by the final sentence, *Trust me, I'm a guy*, where what gives him the ultimate authority on attractiveness is his gender.

Whilst many articles still seem to emphasize the need to please a man sexually, (for example *Sex as a present* in **Cosmopolitan**) rather than pleasing yourself (that is, the female reader), there are some which explicitly address this issue:

How come women's mags are so obsessed with us driving the boys crazy all the time? (**Minx**)

This comes from an article in which the writer and her friends try out some of the more outlandish sex tips that they have read of elsewhere. These are not all tips aimed at male pleasure, but they do include some naturalized assumptions, such as the assumption that 'blow jobs' are normal and tight stomach muscles are to be desired:

When he starts to feel deliciously numb, switch to a normal blow job.
It made me want to squirm a bit more just like I used to when I had tight stomach muscles. Oh happy days.

The existential presupposition in the first extract is that there is such a thing as *a normal blow job*. In the second case there is an implicature arising from the comment at the end (*Oh happy days*) that the previous sentence expressed a desirable state of affairs. Perhaps the most frequent assumption, however, in the texts in relation to sexual attractiveness is that relating to the appeal of large breasts. The following extract, for example, is from an article which includes readers' stories, in this case a reader who had breast implants:

I had wanted to be a page three model from the age of 14 but wasn't blessed with the figure... I feel so much more womanly now. (*Body Beautiful*)

The change of state adverb, *now*, presupposes that the narrator hadn't felt 'womanly' before, and the pragmatic presupposition that readers are likely to draw from this is that this change of affairs came about as a result of the breast implants. This generalised celebration of the large breast starts in the teenage magazines. The text from **Mizz** is apparently a straightforward advice article about how to make sure that the reader is wearing the right bra for her shape and size and activity levels. The ostensible and responsible message is that we are all different, so we need different underwear. However, there are some messages that are not about comfort or well-being:

Padded *Are great for* girlies who have got small breasts – the padding gives you more shape than you really have. *Fantastic!*

The two evaluative comments (italicized) demonstrate that there is a desire to have large breasts, and this implicature is confirmed by other articles in the teenage magazines which advise girls how to dress to maximize their natural assets and play down their physical disadvantages:

Scoop-neck tops to show off your cleavage... (**Sugar**)

There is, however, such a thing as breasts that are too large because they unbalance the figure or are embarrassing:

A pendant or choker to take the attention away from your chest... (**Shout**)

It is the person he'll want to be with and he won't mind the size of your breasts. (**Bliss**)

The implicature in the last example is that breasts are indeed a problem, but they might be overlooked if you're interesting enough. Note, however, that there are some conflicting messages about breasts, with the padded bras being enthused about, to draw attention, and the pendant or choker to displace it. The extremes that women are supposed to go to in order to balance out their bodies is illustrated in an article from **Body Beautiful** with advice on clothing as a way of making your figure look better. The advisor gives a lot of detailed clothing advice to a questioner with a large bust. However, the caption on a photo of a woman leaning forward with her arms crossed reads:

> You can minimise a large bust by folding your arms across it, or you can take Mia's advice.

This absurd-sounding tip is given in earnest, as a way that women might arrange their bodies to avoid people (men?) focusing on their breasts. The implicature is that looking your best (that is, most balanced in body shape) is a priority, and there appears to be no recognition that women might have other, more pressing priorities such as dealing with a couple of children, or running a busy office, when folding their arms across their chest might just not be convenient.

One of the most ubiquitous messages that is carried by the data here is that there is such a thing as perfection, and that readers can – and perhaps should – try out all the advice given to work towards that goal. This is evident in all topics, whether concerned with slimming, clothing, plastic surgery or pregnancy:

> With a little help from Sweetex it's easy getting back to your pre-pregnancy shape... (*Our Baby*)

Here, we are faced with the ideology of the perfect – in this case the 'pre-pregnancy' – body which argues counter to the biological reality that women's bodies are likely to change shape fundamentally as they age, and particularly after pregnancy. It is possible, and indeed common in some cultures, to envisage an ideology of the body that celebrates the youthful shape for some women and the more mature shape in others, perhaps particularly those in the middle stages of life. But these ideas are so contrary to the pervasive ideology of our times that it seems odd even to express them here. This example works by implicature, that the pre-pregnancy shape is desired, because what we normally try to achieve is normally also desired.

The notion of ideal shape is also fostered, as we have seen in other chapters, in the teenage articles on clothing to enhance your body shape, in which the article implies some notion of 'ideal' shape, from which we all deviate but which the reader is assumed to aspire to:

> So you're tall... so you have a chest... so you're small and petite... so you don't have much of a waist... so you're smaller on top, bigger on

the bottom...so you're curvy...You'll just add extra weight where you don't need to...you don't need to add extra height...you don't need to slim any areas. (*Shout*)

This set of examples constantly implies the norm of a body which does not have any features out of balance with the rest, and which is neither too fat nor too thin, too tall or too short and so on. Rather like something in the Golidlocks story, this elusive body shape is one that is sought by many, but achieved by few, and this advice is there to minimise the bad features. The text is built on one over-arching implicature; that the reader wishes to, and can, make the best of her imperfect body. This is probably quite comforting to some teenagers who are racked with anxiety about their bodies, but it does nothing to challenge the ideologies that put them under this stress in the first place. Some of the implicatures seem to emphasise, and thus reinforce, the negatives in each body shape they consider:

Wear white skirts and trousers to even out your proportions...hide beanpole legs in baggy trousers etc. (*Sugar*)

Whilst the *beanpole legs* tag is straightforwardly critical, the suggestion of how to hide them is more implicit, and works by pragmatic presupposition, the reader being likely to conclude that what needs hiding is something shameful or embarrassing.

These messages are followed up in the adult magazines by similar assumptions about perfection in the shape of the body. In an advertisement selling a product aimed at body cleansing to beat cellulite, the process is described as resulting in:

startling cosmetic changes, reduction of puffiness and bloating, producing *slimmer, firmer body contours* (***Slimmer Magazine***)

The presuppositions created by the comparative forms (*slimmer, firmer*) are that the body is less slim and firm prior to the treatment. The implicature is that *slimmer, firmer body contours* are desirable. A similar phrase is used in reply to the question 'How many pounds can I expect to lose after liposuction?

It is difficult to assess this, as the aim of liposuction is *to improve the body's contours* rather than lose weight. (***Body Beautiful***)

Here, the change of state verb, *improve*, presupposes an earlier, less-desirable state, though it is interesting to note a slight ideological shift from weight to shape here, and this has been confirmed anecdotally by my students who say that this is the new perfection, not the actually body mass of a person. This is not a new phenomenon, and weight is still a large part of the ideological message that these texts convey. The most important part of a 'body contour', it could be argued, is the stomach, which is widely discussed in the data:

> I haul in my stomach... (*Marie Claire*)

> Though your tummy may still look depressingly big after your baby's born... (*Pregnancy and Birth*)

> You're worried about how you're going to lose all the weight you've gained... (*Women's Health*)

The first of these examples has an implicature that stomachs should be flat; a common message in many of the texts in our data. The other two are more disturbing because they transfer the standard ideas of the perfect stomach and ideal weight to one which has no hope of being perfect immediately after delivering a baby. The presupposition in the first of these examples is triggered by the iterative adverb *still* which includes the notion that the tummy looked *depressingly big* earlier, that is while the woman was pregnant. This presupposition, looked at dispassionately, is ideologically interesting since, despite the recent trend in celebrities putting their pregnancies on display, it seems that there is still a tendency to see the pregnant stomach as 'fat'. Notwithstanding the propositional content of some of these texts, the implicit message remains that pregnancy and the extra weight involved is an aberrant state, and needs to be corrected:

> Don't consider dieting until you've attended your post-natal checkup six weeks after the birth. (*Pregnancy and Birth*)

This sensible advice nevertheless accepts the likelihood that post-pregnancy mothers will wish to lose weight, and is operating in a context where re-gaining the pre-pregnancy bodily state is socially and psychologically a strong priority for mothers, possibly as a result of the overriding ideology of perfection and youth.

In addition to the very many examples relating to weight and shape, there are other minor but still significant aspects to the ideology of the female body that are conveyed by presupposition and implicature in this data. Perhaps the most interesting is the one that acknowledges that women have body hair, but also takes for granted the need to remove it:

> Upper lip hair is just caused by testosterone – the male hormone we all have in our bodies...You're in luck. There are loads of hair removal techniques... (*Bliss*)
>
> girls who prefer ecoterrorism to experiencing life and refuse to, like, shave and stuff... (*Jump*)

Rather like the conundrum of the breast implants that feel natural because you can't feel them, this position depends on the acceptance that women are 'naturally' hairy in various ways, which by the ideological context that we have already established ought to be a good thing. However, these texts also insist that the removal of this hair is vital for femininity to be established. These two examples use shock-horror tactics and exaggeration to establish female hair (anywhere but on the head) as unwanted. The first one uses the pragmatic presupposition triggered by being *in luck* combined with *hair removal techniques* which presupposes a wish to remove this offensive bodily feature. The second one pragmatically presupposes that what is refused is normally to be wished for, and that they are thus being unreasonable in not shaving (their armpits presumably).

The one aspect of the ideology of the body that we haven't discussed a great deal so far is that of the importance of youth. This is because the question of age crops up rather rarely in the data, though it is in a sense ever-present too. Apart from a few specific articles aimed at older women, these magazines tend to be aimed at the younger age groups, and though there might be, for example, older pregnant women or slimmers, there is an emphasis on the importance of being, and failing that, of *looking* young which is implicit in all the discussions of weight, body shape, clothing and so on.

> 'Good skin tone is very important for liposuction,' points out Mr Davies. 'The best candidate is someone under 30 with elastic skin. We do carry out liposuction on older people though – some people don't mind having loose skin because they are more interested in wearing a smaller size in jeans. (*Woman's Own*)
>
> At the age of 44 Cindy can, on a good day, pass herself off as a 20-something. (*Body Beautiful*)

In these extracts, the idea of being or looking young respectively is given positive evaluation. There is a pragmatic presupposition in the first example which links the statement that the *best candidate* is *under 30* with the disjunctive statement that liposuction is carried out on *older people though*. The clear message is that the adjective *older* here refers to people over 30, which from many perspectives seems rather young. The second example, similarly, expresses youth in terms of being *20-something* and there appears to be an implicature that 44 is really quite old.

With the rare exception of articles or advertisements aimed at menopausal women, there is not much recognition of the issues of the ageing body in this data, and a very great deal of assumed value for youth or apparent youthfulness. As discussed in the Introduction, the data in this project do not tend to arise in the magazines which are aimed at the older age group, where the issues of the body tend to be passed over in favour of table decorations for Christmas and knitting patterns for grandchildren.

At the other extreme, the body is, not surprisingly, a major topic for teenage magazines. The onset of menstruation is a regular topic of discussion, not least in the problem pages or pseudo-problem pages. Much of the information given in these texts is helpful and accurate, but there is a tendency to contextualize the straight information, perhaps in an effort to liven it up, but often using stereotypical concepts. Thus, an article about menstruation from *Bliss*, has a title which emphasizes the very aspect that girls are most likely to fear: *the painful truth* (*periods*).

The use of a noun phrase, with *painful* as a premodifying adjective, produces an existential presupposition not just that periods exist, but that they are intrinsically painful. There are also pressures on these teenagers towards normality in assuming that the reader will do what 'most people' do:

Most girls / usually shift over [to tampons]. (*Mizz*)

Here, though there is also a direct proposition that girls can choose their method of sanitary protection, there is also a possibly more powerful implicature that what most girls do is normal, and we have already seen that normality is a very strong normative force.

Whilst one might not be surprised – or even deeply concerned – about the texts creating 'normality' around tampons, there are other issues that create strong implicatures and presuppositions about normality which may raise greater ideological questions. One of these is the issue of teenagers' sexuality, which of course is of concern to many young people. As we saw earlier, being a lesbian is only mentioned twice in the data – both times in letters to a problem page. In both answers, the superficial message is of acceptance, but the implicatures and presuppositions give a rather different message, which amounts to the fact that being a lesbian is problematic, and anyway not very likely:

It's perfectly healthy to have questions about your sexuality. (*Bliss*)

This answer attributes to the letter-writer the implicature that she does indeed have such questions, but, more significantly, states straightforwardly that this is *perfectly healthy*, using one of the co-hyponyms of *good* that we discussed in Chapter 3. However, by emphasizing the frequency of such questions, the answer also implies that most questions are ultimately resolved in the majority direction, that of heterosexuality:

These sort of feelings happen all the time during your teens.

This works very much like the earlier example which stated that problems getting pregnant were also very frequent (*One in six couples have fertility problems* from *Woman*). Presumably, in a utilitarian fashion, it will reassure the majority who turn out not to be lesbian in due course (or manage to get pregnant for the earlier example). The assumption that not being pregnant is a problem is one that might possibly be seen as understandable in the context of a magazine on pregnancy where it may be assumed that all readers share the ideology that being pregnant is a good thing, and having babies is in some sense a vital fulfilment for a woman. In this case, however, constructing 'being lesbian' as a problem that the majority may indeed be able to avoid is not only harmful to those who do turn out to be lesbian, but is also more ideologically significant as a construct that confirms being lesbian as not just a minority sexuality but a problematic one.

The other letter and answer about this subject is if anything more negative in its construction of lesbianism. It uses a similar argument about how common it is to question one's sexuality (*looking at other girls' bods in the showers is completely natural*), but in addition, the overriding message in the answer, which we saw earlier, but is repeated here, is that this is a problem that will go away, constructing lesbianism as both unwanted and unlikely:

So chill out, you've done nothing wrong, it doesn't mean you're a lesbian and if anyone says you are, just ignore them and they'll soon forget about it, I promise (**Mizz**)

Note that the answer here intends to reassure the letter-writer that she has not done wrong in looking at her friend's body, but manages instead to provide an implicature to the opposite scenario in which both *you've done nothing wrong* and *it doesn't mean you're a lesbian* are contradicted. As we saw in Chapter 4, appositive structures may lead to the conventional implicature (Grice 1975) that their content is mutually co-referential, and the resulting implicature can also be that their negatives are also at least coincidental, if not dependent on each other. Thus, there is a strong implicature here that if the letter-writer was indeed a lesbian, then her actions would also have been wrong. The impact of these implicatures on the young readers, many of whom will have come across the use of *lesbian* as a term of abuse, may well be to reinforce the negative evaluation of a minority, but nevertheless quite common sexuality amongst young women. The actual readership of a magazine may not include many lesbians who would be directly harmed by such negative evaluations, but they will be affected indirectly by the ideology at large which is inculcated by the ideologies represented here. One interesting feature of this last extract is the use of promise as a speech act by the advisor. This speech act includes a pragmatic presupposition that what is promised is (normally) desired by the addressee. Thus, the performative use of this verb here results in the presupposition that being lesbian is not a desired outcome, which adds to the ideology already discussed.

Apart from the implicatures and presuppositions relating directly to the body, body shape and sexuality, the data also make general assumptions about the lifestyle and psychology of the reader. For example, the idea of the woman as rather silly, over-anxious and tending towards feeling embarrassed arises repeatedly, as can be seen in the following example:

Put *silly stories about super tampons being for older women* out of your head ... (**Shout**)

Here the noun phrase (italicized) causes an existential presupposition that these stories are presupposed to exist and are necessarily silly. Because the sentence is a second-person imperative, there is also an implicature that the writer of the letter is silly. Similar assumptions arise wherever the imperative occurs in relation to emotional states of mind: *Stop worrying* (**Cosmopolitan**); *So relax!* (**Mizz**)

In these cases, the change of state verbs *stop* and *relax* respectively cause presuppositions about earlier states – of worrying in the first case and not relaxing in the second. Though it is clearly to be expected that people with problems will worry, the emphasis on the anxious state of mind of many of the readers who figure in the magazines, either in problem pages or in readers' stories, inevitably contributes to the stereotyping of women as over-anxious, not to say neurotic.

The final set of assumptions that we will consider here are not directly related to the body, though being lifestyle assumptions, they do contribute to the health and fitness of the people concerned. There appears to be a general assumption that people reading these magazines will have material goods and lifestyle habits that arise from a reasonably affluent background, including the following three, which presuppose that the addressee is employed, owns a car and can afford expensive holidays respectively:

Your employer can insist that you start your maternity leave...Is your car suitable for the car seat you want? (**Our Baby**)

Now, the only thing that's standing between you and looking fabulous on that Caribbean vacation or cruise to the Bahamas is...(**Ebony**)

In contrast, there are also very many assumptions made, particularly in the pregnancy texts, that readers have the 'wrong' habits and need to inculcate better ones:

cut down on cigarettes...(**Woman**)
Stop smoking and drinking...(**Slimmer Magazine**)
You've given up junk food, taken up exercise...(**Woman's Own**)

These examples all function by the inclusion of a change of state verb (for example *stop* or *cut down*) which trigger the logical presupposition about how things were previously.

In addition to the direct exhortation to be better, there are some slightly more subtle incitements to be like the people who are discussed in the texts. These include two texts from **Pregnancy and Birth** both implying that the protagonist who is featured is setting the example that should be followed by the reader:

> Mel used to drink a glass or two of wine a week, but has now given up. Government guidelines recommend no more than one or two units of alcohol a week
>
> She's enjoying showing off her new figure and keeping herself fit with antenatal yoga, aromatherapy massage, eating healthily and getting plenty of rest between schedules.

At the risk of this comment sounding like an afterthought, it is worth noting that only one of the texts makes an assumption about readers being black, and that is only because it is in one of the two magazines I found that were explicitly for black women – both published in the USA. The remainder of the texts did not *linguistically* presuppose whiteness – nor were there textual implicatures to that effect. However, it should be noted that the models and readers photographed in virtually the whole of the rest of the data were white. The following is an extract from one of these rare magazines:

> The new scientific treatments promise to rid us of our blemishes, our wrinkles, and even our Black skin. (***Pride Magazine***)

The presupposition here, that the reader (and the author) have black skin, is made by the use of a definite noun phrase, using the possessive second-person adjective, *our*. It is striking to those readers accustomed to the mainstream, and mainly white, magazines, partly because it gives such readers a sense of the 'otherness' that might be felt each time a reader does not fit the stereotype assumed or implied by an article. It also underlines the fact that white skin is not actively assumed or implied as a norm directly in the mainstream magazines, but is so deeply naturalized as the norm that it does not have to be textually reproduced or reinforced.

Summary

The findings of this study in relation to presupposition and implicature are similar to each other. They both contribute to the creation of norms which, whilst never advocated explicitly as goals, nevertheless build up an expectation of a prototypical woman whose body is ever-youthful, slim, even after producing babies, functionally able to reproduce, and ideally has large breasts, even if these are created by artificial means. What's more, this body is expected to behave heterosexually and to have a white skin, though these norms are so deeply embedded in the ideology of these magazines that they only crop up in this implicit function of assuming and implying, where the assumption of male partners, for example, is universal.

6
The Body in Time and Space

One of the ways in which we might approach the construction of the female body in the data under scrutiny in this project is to consider its physical presence in space and time. This chapter considers the consequences of the temporal and spatial construction of the body for ideology and the potential impact upon the reader's own perceptions.

Constructing time and space in texts

There are very many ways in which the construction of time and space in a text can have an impact not only on the meaning of that text, but also on the cultural and social understanding, the ideology, of the topics that the text addresses. Thus, it seemed appropriate in the present context to consider the way in which the time frames were constructed by the texts, and also to see how the female body is located in space and as space itself.

The linguistic features that were anticipated as being potentially interesting for this part of the study included verbal tenses, adverbials, deixis and lexis connected to the topics of time and space.

Real, hypothetical, contracted and circular time

With so many of the texts in the data-set conforming to the 'readers' story' format, it is not surprising that there are a reasonably large number of texts which use a basic past-tense narrative style:

> I was 12 when I got my first bra. I was really excited because I was the first out of my friends to need one – they were still in crop tops. (*Sugar*)

I started to get frequent pains one morning and called the hospital for advice. (*Our Baby*)

At 29 weeks she woke up one morning with swollen hands and a puffy face. (*Woman*)

In the first and second cases, this past-tense narrative is combined with a first-person viewpoint. The latter, it could be argued, draws the reader into seeing the narrative through the eyes of the protagonist and could be described in deictic shift terms as inviting the reader to perceive the narrative through the narrator's eyes. The third example uses the third person, which makes it sound much more like a fictional narrative and less like a genuine reader's story. What almost all of the past-tense narratives in the data share, of course, is the rhetorical strategy of the damascene conversion or the happy ending, whereby the story being told is leading towards a satisfactory resolution, which in chronological terms is often equated with 'now':

We always expected a family to be part of our lives, but there were times when we thought we might never make it. We would have coped with that, because in those circumstances you have to get on with things, but we'd have felt that something was missing. Now everything is a bonus and we feel so lucky to have two great kids. (*Our Baby*)

What we have here is what is a relatively common pattern being played out in miniature, with the past-tense facts being followed by a hypothetical alternative outcome, and then the happy, actual outcome in last place. These time frames are those which are used repeatedly in the data, much of which is concerned with past problems, present solutions or happy outcomes and also many texts concern the hypothetical, occurrences which may happen, depending on circumstances:

if food is starting to become a big issue in your life, it is important to seek help. (*Sugar*)

I don't want to try super tampons as they're for older women, and I'd be too embarrassed to buy them. (*Shout*)

Donor eggs and sperm can be used during IVF (*Woman*)

These three examples demonstrate some of the range of triggers that create an 'alternative' timescale or 'modal' text world (see Werth 1999), in which the text projects some possibilities. These include the conditional clause introduced by *if*, the verb *want* which acts modally to suggest a desired (or in this case not desired) scenario as its clausal complement together with the modal verb *would*, and in the third case the trigger is the modal verb *can*.

Returning to the then-and-now structure of many of the texts in the data, many of these have a focal point at which the life of the protagonist changes, usually for the better:

> Newsreader Katie Derham is looking forward to the next big event in her life – the birth of her first baby in May. (***Pregnancy and Birth***)

This initial mention of the moment of change is reinforced by many phrases following in the text, including *before the baby is born* and *on the big day* all of which emphasize the life-changing moment of time which is the birth of a baby. This may be something that parents wouldn't want to argue with, though it does, of course, tap into common ideological ideas of family and parenthood which are not in fact universal, since in many cultures the birth of a baby is seen as a much more normal occurrence, with fewer implications for the life of the mother than in our society.

It is not only the birth of babies that is constructed in this data as a significant turning point, however. The moment of starting a slimming regime, reaching a slimming goal and the operation that enhances breasts or stomach contours are also seen as momentous occasions:

> Ros managed to lumber through the exercise session that night, and by the time she arrived home, a mental transformation had taken place. (***Diet and Fitness***)
>
> And it was worth it: in June 1999 she reached Goal. (***Weight-Watchers***)

Here, two readers' stories demonstrate the turning point of finding a successful slimming club and reaching a pre-set weight respectively. In a more obvious way than having a baby, these moments are clearly constructed as important by the social context of slimming clubs which use quasi-religious terminology and habits to induce intense emotions in relation to highlighted moments, such as *reaching Goal*. In some sense, of course, the goal weight of any slimmer is arbitrary, and one could conceivably decide to celebrate within a few pounds of the goal weight either way. However, the evident practice is to emphasise a precise goal, and use this as a point of celebration and inspiration to others who have yet to reach their Goal.

Surgery is another life-changing process that is usually narrated with a deictic split between the then and the now:

> She decided to have her breasts enlarged *after years of hesitating*; I had wanted to be a page three model *since I was 14*; There was no way I could go topless on the beach or anything like that. I feel wonderful *now*.

These articles tend to follow quite similar patterns of setting up a long-term problem in the form of adverbials such as *after years of hesitating* and *since I was 14*, followed by the different situation *now*, that is after surgery. The same patterning can be seen in the following extract:

> Surgery had been at the back of my mind for years but it wasn't until the accident that I decided it was time to do something. (***Woman's Own***)

Apart from the very many past narrative articles and readers' stories, there are also many articles of advice that use the present tense to give a general idea of what happens in the female body in relation to such things are menstruation, pregnancy, sexual attractiveness and eating/dieting:

> If a girl wants a guy to notice her, she needs to worry about the person underneath the façade of make up and fashion statements. (***Jump***)
>
> wear fitted shirts and tops which taper in at the waist (***Shout***)
>
> Every girl's flow is different. It varies from month to month, as well as during your period, so you should use more than one absorbency of tampon. (***Sugar***)
>
> Using a needle, a doctor removes some amniotic fluid, which contains fetal cells. (***Pregnancy and Birth***)
>
> Food is central to our lives. So there are numerous reasons why we overdose on it: eating for comfort when we're tired, angry, upset, stressed or bored... (***Woman's Own***)

These examples demonstrate the generalized advice or information that is often given in the present tense. The following examples demonstrate a different use of the present, whereby the implied time is not just a generalized present, but real time, even though the descriptions are of hypothetical narratives, rather than real ones:

> Days 8–13 ... You are definitely feeling better, if not perfect. Yippee! (***Sugar***)
>
> weeks 5–8 ... 'I'm extremely tired. I've got to look after myself, put my feet up and eat healthily. Still, Gary is taking really good care of me.' (***Our Baby***)
>
> ... I've been getting ready; my breasts are swollen; I keep thinking I can feel the baby ... (***Our Baby***)
>
> Mel's booking-in visit seems to last forever! The midwife wants details about her husband and family information on asthma, diabetes, epilepsy, heart problems, high blood pressure. (***Pregnancy and Birth***)

As is evident from these extracts, the real-time present-tense narrative of this kind causes the reader to deictic-shift into the supposed present of the narrative, particularly in those cases where the progressive aspect adds to the sense of an ongoing process. These texts are usually part of a diary-style article where the reader is invited to experience the process being described vicariously and as if it were happening at the time of reading. This technique may have the effect of drawing the reader into the text in a more intimate way, particularly if she identifies with the problem or process being described.

Perhaps as a result of the use of real-time present-tense narration, there is very little reference to future time in the data. What future references there are tend to be part of the hypothetical or alternative scenario which depends upon the reader identifying with the second-person referent in the following:

> Second trimester (weeks 13–25) ... You'll experience your greatest weight gain during this time – around 1 kg (2 lb) a week. (***Pregnancy and Birth***)

We might not be surprised to find certain indications of time as circular in these texts, given the cyclical nature of menstruation, and yet there are relatively few indications that time is anything other than linear. In one text, for example, the layout is in a circle, but the text is laid out in four quarters, of which one is clearly the 'start' as it is labelled *day 1–7*. However, there are some hints towards the repetitive nature of the menstruation process, for example:

While boobs are developing they can feel a little lumpy, and at different times of the month they'll change too, especially just before your period. But it's a good idea to get into the habit of checking your boobs now – as it's a habit you should keep for life... It's important to examine your boobs at the same time *every month*, just after your period finishes... (***Sugar***)

This text is interesting, because it combines the linear timescale of growing up with the cyclical one of being an adult female. A more straightforwardly cyclical extract is:

Every month, one of the ovaries releases an egg which travels down the Fallopian tube to the uterus (womb) (***Fresh***)

In addition to seeing time as made up of past, present and future, or as linear versus cyclical, we may also consider the difference between time conceptualized as duration and as a moment. Reflecting the lived reality of women's (and indeed men's) lives, these texts refer to many points in time and also to the duration of processes:

For weeks; little by little; that's when; at six months; first, second, third trimester; during this period; during months 7 and 8; by month 9; throughout your pregnancy; as your pregnancy progresses; near the end of your pregnancy; approaching the end of the first trimester; at around 12 weeks; before/after 20 weeks. (***Pregnancy and Birth***)

Ready to reproduce, every month; will last from three to seven days; average age to start; twelve; from any time between the ages of nine and sixteen; your breasts will have started; often; on a regular basis; every eight hours; you can start... as soon as. (***Fresh***)

13, last month, 5 days, a week, how long?, common, months, average 5 days, 23 days, just started, at first, after a few months, more regularly. (***Mizz***)

for a while; past two months; a few months ago; now; never; still; soon; until. (***Bliss***)

After 12 weeks; around 28 weeks; after that; every fortnight; four weeks early; 10 hours; four weeks before; exactly the same times. (***Our Baby***)

These extracts illustrate the sheer quantity of time references used in relation to women's bodily experiences, and perhaps this, as much as any of the detail given here, is the most important effect; that women's lives are indeed often hemmed in with measurements of time in various ways. To what extent this is either 'natural' or constructed we will have to speculate, though we may imagine societies where the counting of the days in pregnancy or menstruation will not be as obsessive as it is in rich industrial countries with a low birth-rate. Similarly, we can hypothesize that because men's bodily experience is less time-constrained than women's, their texts may be less time-oriented than these. Another study will be needed to investigate this hypothesis in detail.

Body as outer/inner space: literal and metaphorical treatments

Whilst the time zones in which women's bodily lives are lived are fairly conventional, the construction of space in these texts, particularly bodily space, appears to develop a fairly consistent ideology of the body across the data represented here. The first construction of space that we should consider is of the female body as having volume, and thus having both an outside surface and an inner space, in particular the inner space with a reproductive purpose:

> Every month, one of the ovaries releases an egg which travels down the Fallopian tube to the uterus (womb)... it is expelled from the body along with the lining from the womb... (*Fresh*)
>
> Baby moves down the birth canal... start to push her baby out into the world... entire head is out... ease out... (*Our Baby*)

In these two cases, the internal body features as a place from which things (an egg, a baby) can be expelled. This echoes the outer and inner reproductive organs division in sex education literature (see Chapter 3), and the following, possibly metaphorical, image of the inner space which is represented by the reproductive organs is also frequently found: *Deep in the reproductive system* (*Woman*).

This use of the adjective *deep* may echo a frequent conceptual metaphor where the internal organs are likened to the sea (see Jeffries 2001 and Steen 2002) and it certainly emphasizes the inaccessibility and mystery which is often associated with these specifically female organs, even in an era of medical knowledge which has largely uncovered these mysteries. It is not only the pregnancy texts which use this technique to mystify the body. Exercise regimes and advice often also use the distinction between outer and inner to distinguish those muscles that we can all feel and identify from a set of *deep postural muscles* (**Marie Claire**) which we need expert help in locating and developing. This emphasis on the unknowability of the internal body is continued by the beauty texts, even when they are essentially dealing with the outer layer of the body, the skin:

> There is some evidence that the skin has a better absorption at night so active ingredients may penetrate to deeper skin levels more easily. (**Women's Health**)
>
> This unique non-invasive treatment works in harmony with the body by improving circulation, eliminating toxins and breaking down calcified fat cells beneath the surface of the skin. (**Slimmer Magazine**)
>
> ... the cleansing capsule with the power of traditional herbs that flush fat cells from the body. (**Slimmer Magazine**)

These texts, interestingly, emphasize the possibility of changing the inner body from the outside, and there is also an emphasis on the non-invasiveness here. It is difficult to know without an equivalent study of male magazines whether this metaphor of the body as vessel applies equally to the male form. The invasion of the body space is ideologically quite an emotive subject for women though, whether it be for sex or medical reasons, and the advantage of any process that avoids the need for invasion is seen in a positive light.

In addition to the inner–outer distinction, many texts also represent the body as a conjunction of places or zones:

> we've all had a rummage around our vaginas at some point ... (**Bliss**)
>
> Turn your body into a playground (with the highly underrated art of foreplay!) (**Shine**)

As we will see in the next section, there are a wealth of metaphors used which link the body and space, these two examples being metaphorical representations of the female body as a linked set of places or areas, an ideology which appears to be quite deeply embedded in the social context in which these texts are produced and read. The body is literally treated as a set of places in many of the texts in the data:

> Lie down and draw a straight line between your genitals and your belly button. Your tanzen (a Japanese erogenous zone) is in the middle. (**Minx**)

build sexual tension by massaging the area about two and a half inches below your belly button. (*More*)

My lower body is wide, but I want my body to look in good proportion. (*Body Beautiful*)

This conceptualization of the body as a set of linked zones has similarities with the representation of the body as a set of parts, which is analogically closer to a machine than to a map or chart. The differences are, perhaps, more ideologically significant, and connect these ideological assumptions to the cyber body and the notion of intervention by technicians:

eggs are collected and fertilised in the lab, then placed back in the womb...injecting a single sperm directly into an egg and transferring the egg to the womb...a blocked fallopian tube...in one of the fallopian tubes rather than the womb...(*Woman*)

Here, the womb and fallopian tubes are treated in isolation from their context, which would have to be (at this point in history) a complete body. This conceptual separation of certain organs and parts is common, particularly where we do not like them or they are unpleasant bodily appendages:

so aware I had a bump there...(*Woman's Own*)

Bums dragging on the floor...boobs resting on our stomachs...scoop them up and go about our day...(*Body Beautiful*)

These two examples emphasize the unsatisfactory nature of ordinary bodies, but similar effects are seen where other body parts, such as breasts, are mentioned, as well as the slightly disturbing picture of a body which is no longer a whole but can have bits sucked out and bits left behind; where there are areas which can be demarcated; where the inside is as accessible as the outside; in short, where the 'perfect body' can be achieved by technological means:

To some it sounds like a miracle cure – just one night in hospital – and you walk away minus 5 litres of fat!; crude way of destroying the walls of the fat cells and then sucking out their contents; tube is inserted through a tiny cut; pumping the area to be treated (*Woman's Own*)

Upper eyelids can also benefit from a procedure capped upper blepharoplasty. This treatment (which can also be done with lasers) removes a crescent of skin and underlying fat from the upper eyelids to correct any drooping or sagging. (*Body Beautiful*)

The female body, then, is either a map of regions or made up or semi-independent parts. There are also occasions in the data when inner and outer do not correspond to bodily parts, but to mind versus body. In two texts particularly, this dichotomy has a significant potential effect. The first is the text from *Jump* written by a 19-year-old male who does not like to see young girls dressed up too sexily:

person underneath the façade;
from the inside;
clothes/make up vs. heart and soul;
girl with these qualities in a pair of jeans;
pride and esteem vs. miniskirt;
dress sexy vs. comfortable with body and sexuality.

The writer here is trying to demonstrate the importance of the psychological aspects of a young girl dealing with growing up, though it is noticeable that even here it is difficult to separate out the mind and body completely. The opposing of *dress sexy* with being *comfortable with body and sexuality* demonstrates that even when this writer is emphasizing the mind, it is the mental perception of body and sexuality that he is concerned with.

The second of these examples is from a slimmer's story where the final few lines include the following statement:

It's like I've been locked away for all these years... (*WeightWatchers*)

This identifies the narrator (the 'I') as being the mind, with the (fat) body as some kind of jail or trap. Although very many of the texts in fact link bodily problems with psychological problems, these are the only two that use spatial dimensions to explain the relationship between the inner (the mind or psyche) and the outer (the body).

What is interesting from the feminist point of view about these extracts is that whilst the mind may be construed as unavoidably linked to the body more generally, these texts represent the 'real' person as the inner being or mind, and the body is not intrinsic to this identity. Such a view is typical of first-wave, rationalist feminism which attempted to rise above bodily concerns in the same way as men were conceptualized as doing.

Other metaphors of bodily space

We have already seen that some of the outer/inner conceptualizations of the body are metaphorical in their treatment of the body as a vessel, as having depth like the sea, and so on. The work of Lakoff and Johnson (1980), Lakoff and Turner (1989) and others such as Steen (2002) has demonstrated that many of the everyday perceptions that human language reflects and constructs are in fact metaphorical and in some cases there are general metaphors which guide human thinking in particular societies to the extent that they may be termed 'conceptual metaphors'.

As one might expect, the metaphors used in connection with the body in these texts are not novel, and mostly draw on familiar structural metaphors which could be said to be so ubiquitous that they are cognitive metaphors, and structure how we perceive the body in Western society. However, this only emphasizes the embeddedness of such perceptions, and does not invalidate the analysis of them as ideologically loaded.

There are two related structuring metaphors of this kind, and many slight variations of them as we shall see. The first of these is that life experiences (pregnancy, relationships and so on) can be presented as places. Thus, we have, for example, pregnancy and its phases as places you enter:

> You've entered the first of the final 3 months... (*Our Baby*)
> We didn't go into this pregnancy lightly... (*Pregnancy and Birth*)

Similarly with menstruation and labour:

> Some girls sail through their periods (*Fresh*)
> I was in early labour; going into labour... I reached a plateau at 6 cm dilated;

And we have already seen that the body itself can be seen as a place:

> Turn your body into a playground... (*Shine*)
> Pile on the weight... (*Best Diet Now*)
> pile on extra weight... (*Woman's Own*)

We also find that sex and relationships are places that you can be on or in:

Move onto sex. (*Minx*)
You are in a relationship... (*Cosmopolitan*)

Quite closely related to the place or space metaphor for life experiences is the structural metaphor of life (and thus of parts of life) as a journey. There are very many ways in which this underlying metaphor is delivered in these texts, including the following, where finding a good diet is likened to changing direction and in the same text the journey of trying to lose weight is slowed down by *emotional baggage: My life has turned around* (*Slimmer Magazine*).

The conceptual metaphor of DIET AS A JOURNEY is commonly used, and could be viewed as a sub-type of the LIFE IS A JOURNEY metaphor. It is clearly present in the following example which requires some kind of cognitive mapping from the domain of travel to the domain of dieting in order to understand it (see Steen 2002: 25 for more on the identification of metaphors):

Following a low fat diet... go back to the beginning... one can follow basic healthy eating guidelines... as the goal weight comes into sight... the fast track to weight regain... (*Slimmer Magazine*)
Reach my goal weight... (*Best Diet Now*)

Notice that the journey metaphor is useful for many of the life experiences discussed in the data, having the destination or end of the journey as a focal point that can represent success, which in the case of diets is the goal-weight and in the case of pregnancy is the safe delivery of a healthy baby. These link to the rhetorical strategy of the happy ending, whereby the metaphor of a journey provides a clear end-point; *now I'm nearly there* (*Pregnancy and Birth*).

Though in many cases the traveller on these life journeys is the woman herself, the perspective changes from time to time, and the life process or its culmination will instead be seen as the traveller:

Hopefully the birth will be here soon... (*Our Baby*)
ground to a halt; the way your labour was going... (*Our Baby*)

In these examples, then, the woman appears to be the place, or at the place of arrival, and the expected traveller is the birth or the labour. This deictic change from the woman as traveller to being the place where things (birth and so on) happen is potentially important in seeing the ideological construction of birth and labour as being things that happen to women, rather than something they do. We will consider this issue again in Chapter 7.

A similar effect is achieved in a number of texts where it is not the woman that is moving or travelling, but the fat that attaches itself to her:

> Lingering roll of fat ... (***Woman's Own***)
> Before it takes up residence on your hips ... (***Body Beautiful***)

In these examples, we have the personification of *fat* by the collocation of the word (or a pronoun in the second case) with *lingering* in the first example and *takes up residence* in the second. In each case, these verbs normally occur with a human or at least animate subject, and this usage thus gives the fat a will of its own and the woman none.

Though this happens particularly at those points in the narrative where the protagonist is least able to take control of the situation, there is also the opposite effect in some extracts, whereby the woman is given the role of the traveller and the body shape, body weight, healthy baby or breast measurement is the destination of this particular journey:

> Getting back to your shape; a trimmer, slimmer you is just around the corner. (***Our Baby***)
>
> the search for the perfect body (***Woman's Own***)
>
> We always expected a family to be part of our lives, but there were times when we thought we might never make it; no reason why you can't get there in the end (***Our Baby***)
>
> I went from a 32B to a 32D (***Body Beautiful***)

In all of these cases, the verbs and adverbials indicate some form of movement, with the aim or life goal as the destination of this movement. The journey for the woman in some cases has a particularly mountainous feel to it, as in the following extract where the physical body throughout its life is seen as being like a climbing expedition, with one main high point, and the rest of life leading either towards or away from this: *At my physical peak* (**Marie Claire**).

The problem with some structural metaphors of this kind is that they are so common that they are not generally interpreted as metaphors and this can mean that the user or the reader may become trapped by the limitations of the metaphor, and, for example, not envisage physical fitness as a fluctuating state, and thus see the peak as unattainable and progress or its opposite as irreversible.

Apart from the life-as-journey metaphor, the other main metaphorical underpinning of the body in this data is the body (or body-parts) as container, which links to the outer/inner distinction made earlier:

I had silicone put in... I'd never ever go back and ask to have them taken out. (*Body Beautiful*)

Breast implants removed... having the plastic out... (*Body Beautiful*)

Inserting your finger... as he penetrates you... (*More*)

inserted into your vagina... inside me/you... withdrawing etc. (*More*)

they'd removed a couple of litres of fat... (*Woman's Own*)

A particular realization of this metaphor is implicitly part of a larger structural metaphor which sees the body as a machine, and the storage of fat therefore as storage of fuel:

This in turn sends the excess into the muscles for fuel... Your body stores it as fat... Clog the heart with fats... (*Cosmopolitan*)

Draw the fat out of storage and burn it off... (*Diet and Fitness*)

Burn fat. (*Slimmer Magazine*)

Here, we see the fuel storage and the breakdown of parts (the heart) due to inefficient use of fuel. These metaphors may indeed be useful ways for us to comprehend our bodies, though one of the questions that arises when a metaphor is so pervasive is to what extent it may be limiting our thinking. Thus, the extent to which people rely on the body-as-machine metaphor or even the body-as-parts metaphor to reassure themselves that if one part goes wrong, it can be fixed by a technician arises from this data.

Summary

The dimensions of time and space through deixis structure our understanding of the corporeal experience of girls and women, and the analysis has shown that the basic division into inner and outer body is fundamental to this perception. It is less clear from this data that these magazines reflect the full range of the female life in temporal terms, and the 'final' bodily development (menopause) is hardly mentioned, though certain bodily processes (for example menstruation and pregnancy) are excessively, if not obsessively, time-constrained and measured.

Strangely, given the lack of later life references, the metaphorical representation of bodily experience in this data favours the LIFE IS A JOURNEY metaphor and produces a large range of variations on this theme. The arrival point in each case is usually perfection, rather than anything approaching the 'end' of life. To be fair, this is probably true of many LIFE IS A JOURNEY metaphors, in our culture, death being the strong taboo that it is. Other metaphors include those that separate the body into a number of zones, like a map, or parts, like a machine. Both metaphors tend to see the body as 'managed' (including improvements and repairs) in parts. This twenty-first century take on the Enlightenment view of the body leads us towards the science-fiction cyber-body and the notion that bodies are ultimately just the places where we live (even if they're a jail), confirms the separation of body and mind at the same time as women's ultimately physical destiny is reinforced by other aspects of the texts investigated.

'expressed' through the grammar of the clause, in fact not all of the different transitivity categories, are reflected straightforwardly in syntax and they are also only partly captured in the semantics of some English verbs. Thus, although the subject and object syntactic functions can each carry a range of possible participant roles, precisely which role is indicated may require analysis of both the syntax and the semantics of that particular example. The picture is further complicated by passive and ergative structures, which combine syntactic and participant roles in still different ways. Also, the creativity of language is such that the likely participant frames of verbs cannot be fixed by dictionary makers, since they can be – and often are – used in many frames which are not their 'usual' one – giving rise to metaphorical usage in some cases. Thus, for example, the verbs *vomit* or *throw up* might normally be seen as unintentional actions, called 'supervention' in this model. However, the increase in levels of bulimia in recent years means that these verbs have begun to appear more frequently as intentional actions.

A further problem with the model is that its use in critical-discourse analysis suggests that the writer may choose a verb with one kind of transitivity precisely to avoid making an ideology explicit, because s/he wishes to naturalize that ideology, or because the ideology is already naturalized to the extent of being seen as common sense. However, the presentation of processes in metaphorical or other ways may be so common that the reader is likely to 'read' the meaning as literal (that is, translate it) anyway, thus undermining any sense that there is an ideological purpose at work in the particular choice of lexical verb. The use of euphemistic ways of talking about death, for example, such as *pass away* or *lose* (*I lost my mother last year*) do not resonate with their non-metaphorical transitivity (material action intention and supervention, with the speaker as Actor, respectively). Rather, they both seem to carry the 'new' metaphorical force of supervention, with the mother as Actor, despite the surface form. Nevertheless, in certain cases, we may wish to argue that the most natural metaphors are those that are indeed most naturalized – and thus most ideologically manipulative. In relation to dying, then, we might wish to argue that the avoidance of matters relating to death and dying is a deeply embedded ideology in our culture (see Holt 1993).

I am not attempting to develop or challenge any particular model of transitivity here, but to use one version to look at the transitivity choices, and potential ideological effects, of the data. I will therefore use the model as described in Simpson (1993), though as it turns out, not all of the categories of transitivity are equally relevant to this data:

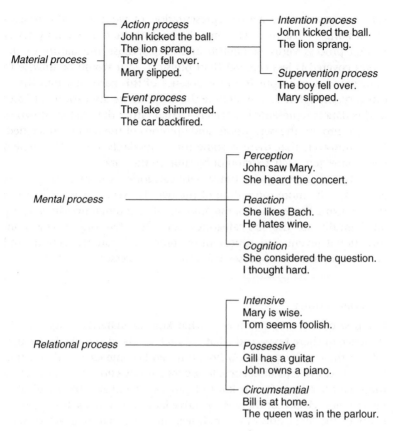

Figure 7.1 Transitivity model
Source: Adapted from Simpson (1993: 89–92).

Whilst there are some verbalization processes in the data, many of them are concerned with the information passed between, for example, professional (for example doctor) and patient, or between partners. Since many of these are not concerned with the body, there is relatively little to comment upon in relation to this type of transitivity. However, relevant cases of reporting of speech and thought which uses this type of transitivity are considered later in the chapter.

The other major type of transitivity which is not given any space here is mental processes. Though as we saw in Chapter 3 there are a small number of cases of women being described in terms of their mental state, these usually involve intensive verbs (*I am worried*), and very few involve the active representation of women in the process of thinking or reacting. This may be because there are simply fewer mental process verbs in English and also because the nature of the topics covered is less cerebral than physical, so it would be unwise to draw grand conclusions from the absence of this particular transitivity category, though it does underline the fact that the discussion of bodies in this data is represented as largely factual rather than being shown as filtered through the perceptions and opinions of the people concerned. Note, however, that there is some use of modality (pp. *182f*), which contributes just such a strand of opinion to the data.

Of the other two major transitivity categories, the material process is perhaps the more interesting of the two. However, as we will see in the following three sections, the most significant differences in category ideologically are the sub-categories, such as intentional versus non-intentional (event and supervention processes) material actions and between intensive and possessive relational processes.

Material actions

The first question to consider is what kind of material actions are in evidence in these texts, and what they tell us about the ideologies that inform these publications. Although it had become clear early on that the context was crucial in considering transitivity choices, and therefore the quantification of each kind of process would not be useful, it is nevertheless clear that there is a relative lack of material action verbs in many of the texts, and as we shall see, there is certainly a lack of such verbs with the reader (*you*), the reader as character (*she*) or the implied reader in the Actor role.

However, the sheer number of instances of any particular process type is not necessarily the most significant question here, where the context can make all the difference to the effect. For example, there may be a significant number of material action intentional verbs in the data as a whole, but if very many of these are in the imperative form, and thus effectively instructing the reader how to behave or move, then any interpretation of the results as showing a readership that is actively in control of their own actions would be misleading.

The texts where there is indeed a great deal of imperative use of intentional material action verbs is in the instructions for exercises, as in *sit upright; lift one arm* from **Bliss**, and *shed extra pounds; follow these; start with* from **Our Baby**. The imperative form also crops up in other texts, as we can see below, where the pregnancy advice text from

Our Baby burdens the reader with advice in the form of imperative structures:

> *take* folic acid; *discuss* your options at your booking-in appointment; *ask* about different hospitals; *call* the NCT.

This text is a diary-style article which purports to tell the pregnant woman what will happen at every stage of her pregnancy, and is divided into 4-week blocks with each block having a 'what to do now' and 'what to think about' section. In the 'what to do now' section, one might expect the most material actions to be performed by the pregnant woman. However, what we find is a single sentence in the imperative mood, and then a number of actions performed by others. Here is an example, from weeks 12–16:

> *Go to* your booking-in appointment. *A midwife will gather* family medical histories of you and your partner. *She'll measure* your height, weight and blood pressure, and *take* urine and blood samples. *She may do* a physical examination. *You may be asked* where you want to have your baby.

This sets the scene for many of the pregnancy texts, as we shall see, with minimal apparently volitional action on the part of the pregnant woman. Other imperative material actions on the part of the reader are found throughout the data, the ones in articles about sex often being more about what the female may do to the male body than about her own:

> *Position* your lubricated hand above the head of his penis like an open umbrella. (*Minx*)
> *Squat* over your partner's torso, you on top. *Raise* yourself up and down, balancing above him. (*Body Beautiful*)

The articles aimed at older women, too, are full of instructions:

> *Keep having* regular checks for breast cancer ... *Be alert* to changes in your bowel habits ... *Look out for* warning signs of heart disease ... (*Woman*)

Interestingly, there is somewhat more of material action intention processes in the dieting texts (44–53), though this is partly because these are often readers' stories and therefore have the before-and-after format of the damascene conversion story. Whilst there is some concession to lack of control in the more general texts on dieting, there is also lots of exhortation to do things as in this extract from *Slimmer Magazine*:

> *Don't be* tempted to keep trying different methods – *keep to* what works for you and good luck.

In the readers' stories on slimming, there is, as mentioned earlier, a higher proportion of material action processes than found in the other texts. This is because the slimmer is portrayed as active both in the self-harming and over-eating part of the story, but also, significantly, after the moment of revelation (attending the first WeightWatchers meeting or Rosemary Conley class, etc.) The following examples are from *Diet and Fitness*:

> At home, Diane *would snack* her way through afternoons with a packet of biscuits, crisps and chocolate bars.
>
> With her confidence boosted, Diane *joined* a gym and *started* weight training. She also *started going swimming* once a week.

In the context of such a dearth of material actions, these are foregrounded as strikingly active, both in the negative sense of self-harm and then in a positive way as the success takes off. The slimming stories, then, appear to show the protagonists as actively out of control in the early stages and actively in control in the later ones, but always with a significant turning-point at the centre of the story. Transitivity choices have their place in this format. An extreme version occurs in *Woman's Own* where there is apparently no intentional material action by the subject of this article ('you'), except right at the beginning in the introductory sentence:

> you've given up junk food, taken up exercise and STILL you can't manage to shift that lingering roll of fat.

The rest of the article details the process of liposuction, and includes discussion of the advantages and disadvantages of this procedure. There is little further addressing of the reader, who nevertheless is implicitly asked to consider whether this might be a solution to the problem set out at the beginning of the article. There are two interpretations of this opening sentence: that people cannot succeed in slimming on their own and that it's impossible anyway. Both interpretations lead to the need for a third party to intervene, and the article suggests one possible kind of intervention.

The only other occasions when there is material action on the part of the reader is in subordinate or heavily modal clauses such as the following from *Sugar*:

It's a good idea to get into the habit of *checking your boobs* now – as it's a habit *you should keep* for life ...

It's important *to examine your boobs* at the same time every month, just after your period finishes ...

These are probably no more than alternatives to the more baldly directive imperative constructions we saw earlier, and their slightly less aggressive effect is one of the reasons that we might expect to find them in the teenage magazines, as here, more than in the adult ones.

The relative inactivity by the reader and/or protagonists of these articles represented by their limited number of material actions contrasts quite strikingly with the actions of others. In the photojournal of a home birth, for example, from *Our Baby*, the midwife (Marlene) is the most active until the point of delivery, when the mother (Claudia) becomes the actor:

Marlene gently manipulates Claudia's tummy (right). *She can tell* how effective the contractions are by *feeling* how the baby moves down the birth canal during each one ... Claudia has now reached the second stage of labour, when *she can start to push* her baby out into the world.

Articles on sexual technique tend to either advise women how to please men, which makes them the Actors in material action as we saw earlier, or they are the receiver of activities with the male as Actor, as in:

Mike had to rub quite hard, but I was surprised how good it felt ... When *I started sucking* Rachel's toe, she stopped relaxing. (*Shine*)

Neither of these tendencies is particularly surprising, though our lack of surprise may simply show us how ingrained the ideologies concerned are. The transitivity pattern seems to indicate that what you do to others gives pleasure to them, but the contrary – that what you do might also give the Actor pleasure – is not normally embedded in these texts.

The other main type of Actor in material action processes is the expert, often a surgeon, who intervenes in the woman's body:

some surgeons do try to improve the appearance of cellulite by removing fat. (**Woman's Own**)

Here, the surgeon is not specific (*some surgeons*) and the action (*removing*) is very deeply embedded in the structure, as a subordinate clause, attached to a higher-level action (*improve*), which is also subordinate to a catenative verb (*try*). To what extent this embedded representation of surgical intervention undermines confidence in its efficacy, it is hard to tell without psychological testing of readers. However, we can certainly say that the action of removing fat has not been foregrounded here, and this could either have the effect of limiting the reader's focus on the (unpleasant?) reality of liposuction, or of focusing the reader on the hoped-for outcome (improvement), or both.

Those texts which concern celebrities also seem to link these protagonists with material actions more often, and more positively than where the articles concern the 'ordinary' reader. For example, an article about Katie Derham's pregnancy has her as the Actor (grammatical subject) in many material action verbs:

chasing news stories; selected her maternity wear with care; keeping herself fit; eating healthily. (**Women's Health**)

Most of this article is concerned with external issues, and not the bodily detail of labour or delivery, which is one reason for the levels of active verbs. However, there can be a contrast between celebrity and ordinary 'coping', even when the process itself is represented as a material action:

For most of us mere mortals, having our bums dragging on the floor or our boobs resting on our stomachs as we get older doesn't mean we won't work again. *We can pretty much scoop them up* and go about our day...If you were in their shoes, wouldn't you want to try to turn the clock back to recapture your youth so you could keep on doing what you did in your early 20s? (**Body Beautiful**)

Here, the ordinary 'mortal' is portrayed as active in keeping going despite her bodily handicaps, whereas the celebrities are trying to *turn the clock back* with plastic surgery. There is also quite a lot of material action in the celebrity fitness article where they are portrayed as self-made women who are not only successful but slim:

I got my weight down to;
I got my act together, etc.
(*Diet and Fitness*)

This is a noticeable departure from the slimming articles featuring readers, where they are not presented as being in control until, and unless, they pass through that 'turning point', or damascene moment, which is often also an indirect advertisement. This article, instead, emphasizes the fact that the celebrities have the answers worked out:

I swim every day;
In London, I go to a gym, where I've been getting on very well with the running machine;
Once I got on a roll with recording I was able to exercise right up until the day before I gave birth, although at that point I was only power walking.
(*Diet and Fitness*)

Although the material actions performed by individual women are in relatively short supply in our data, and often associated with celebrity or self-harm (e, g. over-eating) in any case, there are an interesting sub-set of material actions which are carried out by the parts of the body. This is particularly prevalent in pregnancy texts where the body appears to have a will of its own, and there are numerous cases like the following:

The pelvis sags backwards, the spine curves excessively and the back becomes vulnerable to damage and low-back pain (**Women's Health**)
Your waist is thickening gradually;
Your uterus... pushes out above your pelvic bone;
you may find that your navel has flattened and popped inside;
your placenta transfers antibodies from your body to the baby.
(**Our Baby**)

It may indeed be difficult to envisage the processes of pregnancy in any other way than this, where body parts work in concert to achieve a particular end, seemingly without the will of the person concerned being involved. This 'functioning machine' view of the body, however, is metaphorical, and inevitably delivers a particular ideology of the body which has served medical progress to a large extent since the eighteenth century at least, and is therefore relatively little questioned in such contexts.

It starts to be more unusual, though still largely unchallenged, when it is used in relation to bodily processes over which women in fact have more control, and where the dividing of the body into component parts is less naturalized an ideology. This is true, for example, of the dieting texts in this data, where we have a lot of events with body part actors and diet /food actors:

> Some weight did creep on; it went straight onto my stomach; that bump wouldn't shift... (***Woman's Own***)

It is common, of course, for the unsuccessful dieter to avoid taking responsibility for weight gain by putting the extra weight into Actor role, in effect personifying the stored fat by using verbs (for example, *creep*) which are normally restricted to human Actors. Similarly, though not so clearly personifying, there are many occasions when the body part is the Actor in an event process, which is very similar to the material action intention, but appears not to be presented as animate in itself:

> Our muscles tend to slacken; the skin of the breasts loses its tone. (***Body Beautiful***)
>
> Waistlines tend to expand. (***Diet and Fitness***)
>
> the weight came off. (***Diet and Fitness***)
>
> While boobs are developing they can feel a little lumpy. (***Sugar***)

These examples all demonstrate body parts (muscles, boobs and so on) apparently acting in isolation, though they are not presented as having free will or being animate. The loss of control, then, for the 'owner' of these body parts is implicit, though over time and repetition, the ideological effect may be fairly strong.

Intensive relations

Despite the findings of the previous section, these magazines tread a fine line between convincing readers that they are not in control, and convincing them that they can be in control, with the right help. One of the ways that the magazines attempt to appeal to their readers is by showing that they recognize that not all women are the same. This is mainly achieved, as we have seen, through the use of articles divided by category of women, usually by body shape, with different advice in each section. These sections rely on intensive verbs (usually the verb *be*) which mostly make assumptions about the readers' category, normally to introduce the different sections:

> you're spiritual;
> you're a strong character;
> being such a perfectionist. (***Bliss***)

The same kind of effect occurs where women (or young girls) are categorized according to breast size, as in ***Mizz***:

> you are an A cup;
> you're a 32C;
> you're a sporty type.

As we saw in Chapter 3, there is also some use of possessives, *girlies who have got small breasts*, which draws attention to the relative permanence of features appended to intensive verbs, in contrast to the possible impermanence – and thus the changeable nature – of features that are merely owned. In *Shout*, for example, the problem-letter-writer uses a possessive, and the response uses the same possessive structure:

> My problem is *I have* huge boobs;
> don't be embarrassed about your
> breasts – *we've all got* them!

The use of possessive verbs may not directly imply separation or changeability, but it does make breasts sound like a part of the body which can be considered separately from the body itself. This appears to contradict the other tendency, for the person to be wholly identified with their breasts. However, these contradictory messages seem to coexist in the data, and both have potential consequences for the way that women see themselves, including the obsession with sexual body parts, such as breasts, to the extent that large or small breasts are seen as a problem which technology can fix.

Another example of the choice of intensive over possessive verb is seen in the problem-page letter about bulimia which we saw in Chapter 3,

where the use of the intensive verb in *are we bulimic?* identifies the letter-writer and her friend more closely with the condition than if she had asked *do we have bulimia?* The result is that the condition and the girls concerned seem to be more inherently connected, meaning that it is harder to envisage one without the other, though less so than if a noun were used (*am I a bulimic?*). Note that this letter also uses a normally superventive verb, *throw up*, as a material action intentional verb, emphasizing the abnormal nature of this condition where young people choose to do something normally seen as involuntary.

The use of intensive processes is prevalent in some of the texts here, often coinciding with quite conventional ideas or stereotypes of women's sexuality or identity. Take, for example, the 'myth-busting' section, entitled 'Bloody lies' in a text about periods from **Bliss**. Whilst attempting to put the teenage readership straight on questions of tampon use and when you can get pregnant, it nevertheless uses the term *virgin*, with an intensive verb, confirming ideas about virginity being an identifying and in some sense intrinsic characteristic:

> You can't use a tampon if *you're a virgin*. Busted: Inserting a tampon can be a bit tricky at first, but if *you're a virgin* the only difference is your hymen will have to stretch to let the tampon in.

Here, we have not only the notion that girls either are, or are not, virgins, but that this is a condition defined physically by the presence of the hymen. There would have been a choice, of course, of using a possessive verb instead, such as *if you haven't yet had sex*, and this would reduce the distance between those on one side of this over-emphasized dividing line and the other.

Another potential effect of intensive verbs is as part of the wider effect of establishing norms in relation to the female form. In a section of text from **Slimmer Magazine**, entitled 'Feminine Foods', there are a great many examples of such normative tendencies using intensive verbs:

> Women reported that salads, vegetarian dishes and soups *were* their favourite dishes; drinking [lots of] beer *is seen as* macho, whereas sipping modest amounts of wine *is* more acceptable for a woman.

Note that although this is reporting on a survey, the slippage from *is seen as* where perception is being reported, to *is*, which sounds more categorical, subtly changes the potential impact of the text which as a result fluctuates between reporting opinions and apparently stating facts.

As we saw in Chapter 3, the use of adjectives such as *normal* and *natural* is common, particularly in the teenage texts, and these usually co-occur with intensive verbs, so that the question *Am I normal?* and its response *you're normal* typify the process that is going on in the data as a whole, the defining of normality, and encompassing of the readership within this definition.

One of the main reasons why there is a high proportion of intensive verbs in these texts is that many of them purport to have a semi-pedagogical role, as discussed in Chapter 4, and the intensive process is useful for definitions and explanations:

This *is* vaginal discharge... Beneath *are* the inner lips, labia minora. They*'re* hairless and thinner and *can* be any shape, size and even colour... Normal discharge *is* wet, clear-to-milky in colour and not itchy. (*Bliss*)

There is, however, a difference between 'teaching' facts, as in the above example, and teaching habits and good practices:

periods *are* a physical sign that your body *is* ready to reproduce... Exercise *is* good for period pain... It *is* important to keep clean during your period. (*Fresh*)

The first example, here, has a pedagogical aim in making sure that readers know the significance of periods. The second and third extracts, however, use intensive verbs (*is*) to give value judgements (*good, important*) about certain kinds of behaviour (*exercise, keep clean*). This is similar to the distinction between epistemic and deontic modality, which often make use of the same set of modal verbs, thus blurring the distinction between what is factual and what is personally approved of or culturally agreed. This is not to say that the advice given here is wrong or misleading, but just that it is presented by the same means as facts, and yet is in a sense a constructed view of what is good for a menstruating woman.

The final common use of intensive verbs in this material, particularly where it concerns sexual problems or taboo areas of the body, is in describing the emotions of the women concerned. The following examples are from a problem page on sexual issues, though they are typical of many, including readers' stories where problems are discussed:

We're both really worried...; I'm really afraid...; I'm too embarrassed...(*Body Beautiful*)

As mentioned in the introduction to the investigation of transitivity,
such structures appear to be used more frequently than, for example,
mental process structures, which are more active, and may represent
the efforts of the person concerned to deal with bodily concerns in an
active, albeit mental, process. The intensive process is intrinsically more
passive than these, and represents a reactive state more than a mental
process.

Events, supervention and agentless passives

Although, as we have seen, there are some material actions attributed to third parties involved in women's bodily issues, including
surgeons, midwives and the like, the data also contains a large number
of processes that are not assigned either an intentional actor or an agent.
These include passive structures with no specified agent, supervention
processes, where the subject of the verb is nevertheless not in control of
the process, and event processes, where the Actor is an inanimate object
or force. In many of these cases, the process being described does in
fact have an intentional Actor, though s/he is not mentioned, and the
choice of transitivity is therefore significant in downplaying the role of
this Actor.

I've seen some very poor results – you could actually see the tracks
where the tubes had passed through the fat...(*Woman's Own*)

The final subordinate clause here is concerned with bad liposuction
practices, but the event structure, with the inanimate *tubes* as Actor,
glosses over the practitioner him/herself and focuses on the technical
process. A similar effect is found in the following:

Cosmetic surgery can correct an inverted nipple. (*Woman*)

The traditional herbs in this formula work synergetically...(*Slimmer
Magazine*)

It is not obvious in the latter case that there would be an alternative
involving a direct Actor, nor in the former case that mentioning the
Actor (the surgeon) would change the emphasis greatly. However, this
information certainly adds to the larger patterning of reliance on technological fixes, and blame-free effects.

Similarly, the supervention processes represented in the data are not necessarily 'hiding' an actor or agent, but nevertheless indicate the various bodily processes that a woman may be subject to:

> *women who've undergone* operations like hysterectomies or Caesareans... (***Woman's Own***)
>
> you may experience extreme tiredness because of hormonal changes, and *you may go completely off* tea and coffee. (***Our Baby***)
>
> If I had one day a week without food *would I lose weight?* (***Slimmer Magazine***)
>
> *As we age*, our eyelids stretch... (***Body Beautiful***)

More common than superventions and events is the agentless passive, which regularly puts body parts in subject position, and foregrounds the process which is done to them without identifying the Agent:

> a tummy tuck *can be carried out*;
> stretch marks *may be cut out*;
> loose muscles *can be tightened up*;
> further liposuction *can then be carried out*;
> a narrow tube *is inserted*;
> so much fat *has been removed* (***Woman's Own***)

These examples from a text about liposuction demonstrate the almost complete absence of the woman herself from these descriptions, and the absence also of the human being who is to perform the actions. An even stranger effect occurs in an agentless passive from an article about periods:

> Tampons are inserted into your vagina... (***Bliss***)

The reason for the absence of the actor here is difficult to establish, though it may be that the writer is responding to the horror that she imagines young girls experiencing if they were told directly that it was they themselves who would be inserting the tampon. Whether or not this squeamishness is indeed the reason for such an odd sentence, the result of the agentless passive form is, contrarily, the implication that there may be some unspecified agent who is separate from the addressee.

The same mechanism operates in the following extract, but with a different potential effect:

Girls have an orgasm by *having their clitoris stimulated*... when boys *get stimulated* to orgasm they also ejaculate. (***Bliss***)

The implied separate agency in the agentless passive is much stronger here for the girls where self-administered stimulation (that is, masturbation) is not apparently included, because of the use of *having* as the auxiliary here. The version used for boys, with the alternative auxiliary, *get*, is more open to the masturbation interpretation. This is not, of course, conclusive proof that girls are still discouraged from masturbating, whilst boys are 'permitted' to see this as acceptable behaviour. It may, nevertheless, be part of a larger ideological emphasis.

In addition to the question of how processes are presented in this data, the question of whose 'voice' we are receiving the texts in may also tell us something about the point-of-view that is being presented in these texts. Whilst the reader may be vaguely aware that there is a host of writing and editorial staff behind such a production, the resulting texts are normally more single-author-voiced than this would imply. Nevertheless, there are opinions, doubts and other voices which complicate this picture, and which may play a part in constructing the reader's perceptions of the female body, by creating the authority and/or influence that enables the ideologies of the text to be easily assimilated.

Modality

In much Critical Discourse Analysis, the analysis of modality has been seen as an integral part of the uncovering of the 'real' message behind the text, and it is mostly through modality that we can access the view of the writer or narrator on the issues s/he is discussing. Simpson puts it as follows:

> modality refers broadly to a speaker's attitude towards, or opinion about, the truth of a proposition expressed by a sentence. It also extends to their attitude towards the situation or event described by a sentence. (Simpson 1993: 47)

The broad concept of modality is a good model from which to understand all of the textual processes that I am proposing here. It is formally based on a grammatical category, modal verbs, which do much of the work of this function – undermining certainty, demonstrating obligation and so on, but there are also many other ways of delivering the modality beyond this grammatical category. Thus, in face-to-face inter-action one can shrug one's shoulders to indicate uncertainty as well as – or instead of – using *might*. More linguistically, there are main verbs (such as *think*) and modal adverbs (for example *possibly*) which can have the same meaning and effect. Once the analyst is searching after particular functional effects, the structural delivery of those effects is a secondary, though important, consideration. This functional priority is, of course, one of the reasons why it is very difficult to be entirely sure that the methods being used are not circular – any analysis is always reliant on the recognition of a variety of ways of delivering that category, and these structural indicators may be an open-ended list.

Though some models of modality have been developed by stylisti-cians (see, for example, Simpson 1993: 75) aiming to characterize the different kinds of narration to be found in literary texts, the question for the Critical Discourse Analyst may be asked more simply, and it is whether the certainty or desirability (expressive or relational modality) of the issues being raised is founded upon some inexplicit authority of the writer or producer. Fairclough (1989: 127) explains it in the following terms:

> Notice that the authority and power relations on the basis of which the producers of this text withhold permission from, or impose oblig-ations upon, the people it is sent to, are not made explicit. It is precisely implicit authority claims and implicit power relations of the sort illustrated here that make relational modality a matter of ideological interest.

Here, Fairclough focuses on the ideological impact of unstated authority (in his example, in a communication from a library over late books), and it is this unstated authority that is behind the deontic modality to be found in the texts in this study. The idea that a published magazine will, naturally, have a better understanding of issues relating to the experience of living in a female body than, for example, one's friends, relations or other advisors is, in itself, an ideological viewpoint. This is not to say that all readers accept all that they read, but it is likely that they will take much of what is printed to have the authority that comes with publication.

Though Fairclough is less interested in what he calls 'expressive modality' (epistemic and perception modality here), we may consider its effect in the texts being investigated here. Epistemic modality with low levels of certainty in particular, enables writers to give information without being accused of overstating their case. These texts, particularly the more pedagogical ones, use epistemic modality a great deal to hedge, so that those readers with different experiences will not feel that they have been misled:

> It doesn't mean you'll; you might feel freaky; it may turn; you may have an infection; discharge may seem yucky; it may seem weird. (*Bliss*)
>
> It can take months; it varies loads; if you're still worried; most girls usually remember; may not be as effective. (*Mizz*)
>
> It will last from three to seven days; the average age to start having your periods is about twelve; it can be from any time; you can't tell when you are going to start; although your breasts will usually have started to develop. (*Fresh*)

Note that in the last example there is a combination of the future use of *will* with other more obviously epistemic modals such as *about, can* and *usually*. In English, references to future time being necessarily modal, the simple use of *will* is almost categorical, since there is no alternative way of discussing the future. Fairclough (1995: 147) notes that in some texts 'the authority of the institution is marked through high-affinity epistemic modalities' of this kind. However, the certainty of this usage is undermined, in this case by the vagueness of from *five to seven* and *any time*. The young reader whose first periods last for over seven days and who has read this article may be justified in feeling herself to be abnormal. The vagueness somehow implies that the whole extent of possibilities has been covered, and that experiences outside of this range are abnormal.

In the pregnancy texts, the use of epistemic modality to ensure that this doesn't happen is ubiquitous, and at times the hedging is so highly emphasised that the writer sounds very unsure of herself indeed:

> It's possible that you could...; if you're expecting twins; you could go into labour early; you can't have; you won't have to share; yoga etc will help; it can be hard if. (*Our Baby*)

Note that one of the common structures in this data, particularly where the text is trying to cover different eventualities, is the combination of a conditional subordinate clause (If it's fertilised...) and an epistemic modal (will) referring to the future in the main clause:

If it's fertilised you'll get pregnant, if not it'll flow out;
can help ease;
your GP can prescribe;
can also help;
usually occur;
you can't get pregnant;
you can't use a tampon;
it's possible to lose;
it may still be alive. (*Bliss*)

Most of the epistemic modality in these texts has the function of covering the writer for eventualities other than the ones being described and is therefore toward the uncertain end of the range. However, there are some uses of a more emphatic or definite epistemic modality which seem to serve a slightly different function, as a reassurance to the readers, and an assertion of the writer's authority to make such definite statements: *Definitely; it WILL happen* (*WeightWatchers*).

In some cases, this use of the emphatic type of epistemic modality can undermine the strength of the message, by being modal at all, where a simple categorical statement might have sounded more convincing. However, in the spirit of this kind of text, it reflects the very common spoken style of language where speakers often mistakenly overstate their convictions in this way:

They'll soon forget, *I promise*. (*Mizz*)

It's definitely an exciting prospect...; certainly a little alarming. (*Body Beautiful*)

Just pop a few drops into a bowl of boiling water to create an instant facial sauna which will leave your skin glowing and your mind feeling invigorated. *Honestly!* (*Pregnancy and Birth*)

so pleased; *so* natural; *so* well; I *always* wanted; *really* want perfection. (*Body Beautiful*)

There is something odd about the intensifiers in the last example here and it almost seems as if the speaker doesn't really believe what she is saying. Note that there is almost no modality in the verbs, as one might expect perhaps in a narrative in past tense. However, the emphatic use of intensifiers seems to cast a little doubt on this version of history.

The other uses of modality in this data to reflect different points of view include the uncertainties of the first person narrators:

I believe that if anyone wants a breast enlargement, they should have it done. It *really does* make you happy. (***Body Beautiful***)

Perhaps even more than the articles written in the voice of a journalist or expert, this sounds like protesting too much. A categorical version, *It makes you happy*, may, ironically, sound more convincing since, as Simpson (1993: 49) points out:

This distinction is crucial, yet it may strike some as counter-intuitive to argue that *You are right* is actually epistemically stronger than the modalized *You must be right*.

Simpson bases this comment on Lyons (1977: 763), who maintains that 'categorical assertions express the strongest possible degree of speaker commitment'. Thus, the more that a text insists, the more it undermines its case.

However, the writers of the texts in this study, and the people that they quote, often make the understandable and very human assumption that strongly certain epistemic modality as well as hedging with weaker epistemic modality, can give an impression of authority. Such effects can be seen in quotations from the 'experts', such as plastic surgeons, who wish to emphasize their sense of responsibility by distancing themselves from what they might see as bad practice as in these extracts from ***Woman's Own***:

We would *never* remove more than three litres of fat
This *may* help for a while
Irregularities *can* start showing through
you *could actually* see the tracks

The emphatic use of *never* in the first example shows the surgeon protesting his sense of responsibility and the doubt introduced by *may* about some techniques seems calculated to impress upon the reader his own credentials as a reliable and knowledgeable practitioner who won't cut corners. Similar effects are achieved by the use of epistemic modality in the two final examples, using *can* and *actually*, where the reliability of someone so honest can hardly be doubted by the reader.

Modality does, however, supply other means of the writer or other 'voice' asserting her (or occasionally his) authority. The deontic system, using some of the same modal verbs, but a different set of adverbs and adjectives, sets out the writer's view of what should happen or what the addressee ought to do:

Don't worry; it's good. (*Bliss*)
You need to; got to. (*Sugar*)
It's a good idea; should keep; should visit; it's important. (*Sugar*)

In *Sugar*, the letter-writer asks for advice and gets the precise advice she doesn't want; to see the doctor:

> I'm too embarrassed to see a doctor or talk to anyone about it. What should I do?
> I know you might find it embarrassing, but you *should* still get it checked out.

This imperative is delivered by deontic modality (*you should, it's better*), though there is some epistemic modality to soften the blow (*It's more likely to be due to the breast bud developing; she'll be quite used to doing breast examinations*).

The use of deontic modality in teenage magazines will not surprise the reader, since she will be used to adults telling her what she should do, and this is part of the ideology of childhood; that adults know better than children what is good for them. Again, though this reflects the experience of those of us who are parents, it should still be recognized as a naturalized ideology, in just the same way as the privileging of the experts' opinions over those of friends and family.

The latter is the norm for many of the adult texts, where the assumption that the writer has the authority to tell the reader what to do is not only found in the imperative verb forms that we saw earlier (*Discuss your options; tell your GP; take folic acid*), but also occurs in more subtle ways in the deontic modality:

> Mel *should* tell the midwife; she *should* see her GP; Mel *needs to* avoid contact. (*Pregnancy and Birth*)
> you *should* not smoke; your diet *should* consist of; milk *should be* avoided. (*Slimmer Magazine*)
> You *must* take care; no diet sheet *should be*. (*Slimmer Magazine*)

By contrast with the authority of the writers, the anxiety and lack of confidence of the readers as represented in the letters to problem pages, readers' stories and so on may also be delivered by modality. This insecurity of the readers manifests itself as a combination of lack of certainty (epistemic modality) and expressions of desire or hope (boulomaic modality):

I don't want to have sex in case there's something wrong with me. (***Bliss***)

This example combines boulomaic lack of desire (*I don't want*) with epistemic uncertainty (*in case*) about the writer's body, which results in an impression of a letter-writer that is insecure and plagued by self-doubt.

Though modal in the sense that they express an opinion, value judgements, because they are very much like categorical statements, have an authority that is missing from the earlier modal examples:

A neat arm workout *is the best* exercise for you (***Bliss***)

Speech and thought

The final aspect of the data that will be investigated here is that concerning the speech and thought presentation in those articles where this representation of others' words is of relevance to the ideology of the body. The terms used here will be those introduced in Leech and Short (1981). Whereas they might have simply been interested in how a particular novel constructed the ideas of its characters, and to what extent they differ from the author's and/or narrator's ideas, this approach sees the interweaving of different people's ideas and words as part of the overall ideology-construction of texts. The tracing of free indirect style, in particular, is crucial to understanding the range of opinions and outlooks which are being set out in a text, and the possible hidden viewpoints which arise from this merging of voices.

The presentation of speech and thought has a particular role in this data which may differ in some ways from its role in other texts, such as news reporting or fictional writing. Here, it allows different voices to enter what is often presented as a straightforward narrative or factual report, and this can have a range of effects as shall see from the examples in this section. For example, an apparently neutral article will suddenly include a statement that is clearly in the writer's 'voice':

You may have a rush of energy at this stage and start cleaning and preparing your baby's room and clothes – this is called 'nesting' , and is normal, *but try not to overdo it as it's really important to conserve energy now.* (***Our Baby***)

This diary-style article about pregnancy is fairly informal in tone, but mostly factual, until the imperative (*try not to*), followed by the modal (*it's important*) brings the writer's own authority and voice into the article. A similar effect is seen in **Pregnancy and Birth** where, despite the byline *Words Elizabeth Lismore*, the tone is mostly neutral, with small exceptions in the form of imperatives:

> You'll experience your greatest weight gain during this time – around 1 kg (2lb) a week. *Remember that* you don't need to eat vast amounts of food on top of your normal daily diet –

This imperative is entirely interpersonal in function, as it introduces the writer's voice and reminds the reader of her authority without adding any ideational material at all. The same passage without the imperative would not be substantially different in content, but would lack the intervention of the writer in this personal way. Similarly, one of the extracts quoted earlier as using epistemic modality to assert the writer's authority also has the effect of a factual article interrupted by purely interpersonal functions:

> Just pop a few drops into a bowl of boiling water to create an instant facial sauna which will leave your skin glowing and your mind feeling invigorated. *Honestly!* (**Pregnancy and Birth**)

This cross-over article, which is framed as advice but actually also advertises products, is introduced as *Jo Hansford answers your haircare questions*. However, although we know who is writing the text, and although the style is fairly informal (*pop a few drops*), the use of a direct appeal to the reader such as *Honestly!* stands out as a reminder of the voice behind the remainder of the 'facts' on offer.

The other way in which the voice of an expert may come through is in the choice of vocabulary used. In some problem pages, the vocabulary of the letter-writer is reflected back by the advisor, but in other cases, there is a distinct difference in the choice of words:

> My problem is I have huge *boobs*...
> don't be embarrassed about your *breasts*... (**Shout**)

This change of word is relatively unusual in the data here, where quite often the voice of the advisor takes on the 'jokey' or informal word of the question (such as *boobs*) rather than choosing to distance herself from the letter-writer and using a more neutral word. Here, the effect of what might be seen as 'correcting' the language of the letter-writer may be the one that such advisors possibly fear – of seeming distant from their concerns, but there is also the possibility that the answer to this question will be seen as treating this part of the body with respect, rather than joining in with the ridicule that the letter-writer suffers. In both cases, the authority of the advisor is asserted by this vocabulary change.

In the standard terminology of speech and thought presentation, 'direct speech' refers to quoted language which is normally contextualized within a report or narrative, though this is relatively rare in the current data. In a text, for example, which deals with problems like body hair and vaginal discharge, there are quotations from 'typical' girls:

> Carrie was 14 when she had her first moustache scare: 'I pretended to be ill for a week. I didn't want to see anyone or go anywhere. Then I noticed just how many beauty products there were in the shops for facial hair bleaching and removal. I realised it wasn't just me. Now I bleach my upper lip and nobody's any the wiser.' (*Bliss*)

Note that this is semi-free direct speech, since there is no reporting clause, though there are quotation marks and the extract is in the first person and present tense. The damascene conversion storyline is acted out in miniature here, though it has all the same features as those we saw earlier. The suspicion that, if not invented, Carrie at least has words put into her mouth arises from the slight inconsistency in the story – how do you notice things in shops if you don't go out? It can be explained as it provides the necessary turning point in Carrie's life and indirectly suggests the solution for all readers who have this problem. This gives the writer two possible authorities to help influence her readers; her own and the authority of the peer group.

The more straightforward use of direct speech tends to be from experts who are brought in as additional authority in some texts:

> It's an exciting thought, but surgery is not a substitute for weight loss, warns Mr Dai Davies, consultant plastic surgeon and Medical Director of the Stamford Hospital in west London. 'The only real treatment is to eat less and exercise more', he stresses. (*Woman's Own*)

The merging of free direct and direct speech here echoes the development in the speech and thought presentation model made recently by

Semino and Short (2004) where these are no longer treated as separate categories because there is no difference in the claim to faithfulness between them. In other words, the attribution of direct speech to a third party is perceived as being as faithful to the original utterance whether it is signalled as direct speech or whether it is presented in a freer way. The example here shows both free direct speech (*but surgery is not a substitute for weight loss*) and direct speech (*'The only real treatment is to eat less and exercise more,' he stresses*) as having similar functions, in persuading the reader of the sense of these words. The free direct speech is attributed to the doctor, but faithfulness does not seem to be important and one might easily suspect that these are not his exact words. Equally, with the direct speech the question of how accurate they are is almost irrelevant, as their task is to make the reader take in a particular message, and the attribution – to either writer or expert – is simply that of giving the words more authority.

The texts in the data which are in a sense more like faithful direct speech are those which are wholly 'in' the voice of a reader or advisor. These include problem page letters and readers' stories, though here again the issue of faithfulness is less significant than the advisory function:

> During my teens there were times when I spotted dresses I really liked, but didn't buy. (***Bliss***)
>
> During my period I get tired, depressed and my body aches. (***Sugar***)

In these cases, the suspicion that they are either invented or 'ghostwritten' by a journalist arises from the formality of the language, including the use of *during* to introduce a time adverbial, and the list in the second example, where the comma between the first and second items indicates a relatively formal style. If these letters are indeed written by someone other than the apparent writer, this only serves to highlight the overriding function of the text, which is to inform and advise according to the current received wisdom of those producing the publication and their advisors. Any sense that this is a forum where 'real' women share their anxieties and concerns is undermined by the control that is clearly exercised over all the language in the magazines, including language which is presented as others' verbatim speech or writing.

The use of indirect speech and free indirect speech is more patchy than the direct speech in this data, and does not have a clear relation to the construction of the female body, except in that much indirect speech is reporting the words of experts, friends and acquaintances, and normally not the woman or women at the centre of the text's concerns. This is not surprising in a first-person narrative, where other people's ideas are being reported, but the content of the indirect speech at times clearly reflects some of the ideologies that we have been examining in this book. The following, from **Bliss**, illustrate this reporting of male speech:

> I've told him to leave them alone, and to be less rough, but *he says all girls enjoy this and there must be something wrong with me.*
>
> *A (boy)friend told me last night that he and his friends like 'big, big, big' breasts.*
>
> I'm worried when I have sex with a boy he'll be put off, *tell his mates* and I'll be a laughing stock.

These extracts come from three different problem-page letters, but each exhibits the problem as being with the viewpoint of a boy or boys, and in particular what they are reported as saying – or what the writer is afraid that they will say. It may be that here the faithfulness of what is reported is more significant, even though the presentation is indirect. Notice that the second example uses a small amount of direct speech (*'big, big, big'*) which seems to confirm the fact that the actual words used are important, and can be very hurtful.

Summary

The analysis of transitivity processes in these texts indicates a tendency for women not to have agency in relation to their bodies, except when they overeat or, conversely, when they have been inducted into the regime that will save them from themselves. Though the female protagonists appear as actors in material action processes relatively rarely, their body parts have a life of their own and are frequently to be found 'doing things'. The nightmare quality of bodies that do things like *sag* or *curve* of their own volition feeds the impetus to 'get back into shape', particularly after a pregnancy, with the emphasis on returning to a shape that preceded this life-changing event. Supervention and event processes, as well as agentless passives also contribute to this sense of the woman being out of control, with the main material action intention processes occurring in the instructions for exercises to give her back this control.

The other aspect of transitivity that relates to the bodily experience of women is the important difference between being and having (intensive and relational processes). Where there is a choice of expression, the significance of using the intensive (*you are a virgin*) rather than the possessive (*you haven't had sex*) is to make the characteristic more intrinsic to the person, and thus more defining of her as a whole. This may have different effects, depending on the views of the reader, though I imagine the pressure on young girls to have sex at an early age is made greater by the creation of this enormous dividing line between those who have, and those who haven't been initiated. The same mechanism is at work where we see the possession of certain kinds of breast contrasted with being *small-chested* or *large-breasted*. The effect may be different, with the possession version leading towards the more technological view of breasts which can be fixed.

The function of modality and speech and thought presentation in these texts seems to be to create and sustain the authority of the writer in informing the reader and telling her what she should do. Epistemic modality allows the writer to make generalizations whilst covering other possibilities, with the illusion of more information content than is sometimes really the case. Deontic modality asserts the right of the writer to tell the reader what is the right thing to do, and this is supported by the quotation of experts, including self-appointed experts, whose words may be semi-integrated into the text by the use of free direct speech, so that the voices of authority merge into one.

8
Conclusion

This study provides evidence from the early twenty-first century that what magazines published for the mass market are presenting to us and our daughters is an ideology of the body which emphasizes the stable, youthful and clean (unleaky) body over the real lived experience of women. The division of their bodies into parts that can be fixed by medical technologies and the normative pressures towards being heterosexual, maternal and slim face the women and girl readers of these magazines. Perhaps, ironically, it is easier for those who read these magazines who know they are not reflecting their own bodies – lesbians, black women and the old (certainly anyone over 50) will not feel the pressure in quite the same way as young, pale skinned and heterosexual readers.

This concluding chapter aims to draw together some of the main insights arising from this study of women's magazines' construction of the female body at the turn of the twenty-first century. Though I suspected at the outset that the enlightened view of the body that I thought prevailed in the wake of the second-wave feminism of my own generation might not be fully represented here, I was nevertheless surprised at the extent to which the naturalization of certain attitudes towards perfection and constructed naturalness – often, but not only through surgery – had taken hold.

Teaching feminist linguistics to young female students in recent years has been a wearying activity, where repeatedly confronting attitudes to the body that appear to me part of a frightening backlash are presented by the confident young women I see before me as a step forward, as 'girl power'; the power to take control. This (as I see it) skewing of the feminist ideology of equality by re-constructing femininity as an attainable ideal body is one that is hard to counter, since women are apparently choosing freely to starve themselves, go under the knife, squeeze into uncomfortable clothes and generally spend ever more time and money in the pursuit of perfection.[1]

Critical discourse analysis: an evolution

Critical Discourse Analysis (CDA) appealed as a general approach to the work I wanted to do in this area, as it legitimized the inclination to use one's expertise in linguistics to investigate socio-political issues such as the one I perceived as being at the root of the problem in relation to women's bodies. However, as Walsh (2001: 27) points out, 'a number of approaches to CDA, including that of Fairclough, marginalize the importance of specifically gendered identities and the social inequalities to which these contribute'.

The hypothesis, then, was simple, the expected findings very vague. I thought that magazines may be at the centre of the reproduction of ideologies about the body that seemed to me the opposite of freedom and equality. I did not know quite what to expect in detailed ideological construction of the female form. This, then, was a largely inductive project working within a deductive framework in that it was testing the larger hypothesis by exploring any patterning in the language of magazines which would support the general view that women's bodies were being naturalized in oppressive ways.

CDA began as a left-wing reaction to the hands-off objectivity of early linguistics, when there was clearly so much wrong with the world that was based in texts, and so much information about manipulation and political dishonesty that could be revealed by a few judicious uses of some fairly accessible tools of analysis:

> Language is therefore important enough to merit the attention of all citizens. In particular, so far as this book is concerned, nobody who has an interest in modern society, and certainly nobody who has an interest in relationships of power in modern society, can afford to ignore language. (Fairclough 1989: 3)

Fairclough's laudable aim, then, was to educate the masses about one of the causes of their own oppression. The direction that CDA took following his and others' early forays into a more socially engaged linguistic practice was an inevitably more and more contexualized and thus more sociological direction. Perhaps because of the political focus of those concerned, the details of analytical techniques, particularly those concerned with the texts themselves, have not been thoroughly debated. The discussion initiated by Widdowson (1996, 1998) and reviewed in Chapter 1 did focus on the methodological circularity of CDA and to that extent was more textually-focused. What has not happened is the same kind of focus on methodology that, say, sociolinguistics itself, or stylstics, have had, with the result that there is still not even a provisionally agreed set of tools or procedures for practising CDA.

I hope that this study will in a small way contribute to the evolution of CDA as a text-based practice, particularly in the kinds of situation where there is a relatively stable assumed audience for the text concerned, as in the current case. The questions about hegemony and reader response remain, of course, and there is no doubt that some readers can and sometimes will resist the ideological force of these magazines. These issues remain to be investigated.

The female body in women's magazines

This book began life as a reaction to the naming conventions relating to parts, particularly sexually significant parts, of the woman's body. The result, however, is very much more than a commentary on the naming of parts in women's magazines. Cameron (1998) comments that:

> sexist language is not best thought of as the naming of reality from a single, male, perspective. It is a multifaceted pheonomenon, taking different forms in different representational practices, which have their own particular histories and characteristics. (Cameron, 1998: 11)

This view is upheld by the findings of this study to the extent that even when I tried to concentrate on the naming of parts in the data, I found that the more interesting features of language were in the modification of names, not the choice of names themselves on the whole.

Summarizing the findings of this study, then, is more than a list of names. It involves commenting on the rhetorical strategies used to persuade readers that they ought to be like the exemplary women in the data. It requires a reminder of the almost religious flavour to some of the advice on slimming. It needs a reprise of the comparative lack of material actions performed by women in the data, unless they have passed through their damascene turning point or are giving sexual pleasure to their (male) partner.

These summaries, however, belie the complexity of the data. Much of it is surely intended to – and probably does – help women deal with their everyday embodied experiences. The findings here do, however, confirm the kinds of pressure that are culturally loaded upon women which necessitate support in their physical lived experience. Thus, there is pressure to maintain a low body weight and ideal shape, even shortly after giving birth. There is pressure to 'balance up' the body visually by clothing choices. There is pressure to undergo surgery or other interventionist techniques to preserve youthful features or improve one's body shape or looks.

Despite the many pedagogical-style definitions, explanations and information, there is not a great deal of real educational potential arising from these magazines whose first aim is presumably to entertain and thus to sell widely. I have argued that some of the information content is only apparent, and that the use of technical vocabulary is of value to the magazines in being indicative of authority rather than full of insight. Likewise, the value of readers' stories appears to be in their feel-good happy endings as much as in any vicarious learning that readers may do.

Whilst the pleasure gained from reading women's magazines cannot be denied, given their popularity and ubiquity, the question also arises in the light of the findings in this study to what extent they reinforce the insecurity that women feel about their physical form, and thus perpetuate the need for their own existence. Finding out the answer to that question will require a different kind of research project.

Studying the female form: future directions

As already indicated, there is more that could be done to follow up the research presented here, and just a few of these directions are indicated in this final section as a pointer to the work still to do.

In order to try and get at the effect of these texts on readers, we might take one or two possible directions. The most empirical route would be to work on reader-responses in a psychological framework such as the one used by Emmott (1999) or Gibbs (1994). In both cases, these researchers use the techniques of psychology to obtain information about cognitive processes involved in reading (narrative structures and metaphors respectively). The same kinds of technique could be used to try and access the cognitive effects of the data considered here, including the testing of perceptions of female bodies after reading certain items from magazines. Similar studies have been undertaken in the past, and Grogan (1999) reports on these and on some of the theories of self-perception that have informed such studies as well as her own study

(Grogan *et al.* 1996) where she looked at 'the effects on both men and women of viewing same-gender, slim, conventionally attractive models' and the results suggested that 'these men and women felt significantly less satisfied with their bodies after viewing attractive same-gender models' (Grogan 1999: 104). This study could be usefully replicated but using controlled texts with different linguistic indicators of bodily ideology as demonstrated in the current study.

A less-empirical direction to turn would be to start to apply all of the cognitive stylistic developments of the last few years to the question of how readers respond to texts like these. Stockwell (2002) introduces the range of approaches that have grown up in recent years from the basic premise that it is legitimate to consider the likely cognitive effects of reading text. Obvious applications, which have not yet been taken up in by many researchers, are to investigate the possibilities for building of text worlds (Werth 1999), adopting a text's point of view (Simpson 1993), being affected by deictic shifting in texts (McIntyre 2006) and the potential of blending as a process of assimilation (Dancygier 2005). In other words, the same processes that are at work when we laugh or cry with the characters of a novel are also in play when we read a problem page or a reader's slimming narrative. What is different is the context and our assumption that there is a difference between reading fiction and reading non-fiction.

At the other extreme from reader response studies, we can see a flourishing of corpus-based studies in the wake of the development of ever more powerful computers. Baker (2006) is just the latest in a number of recent corpus-focused works in which questions of discourse context as well as the minutiae of searchable textual features is considered. A number of the findings of this study could usefully be followed up by a corpus study using magazine data. These include the use of definite articles versus possessive determiners in the premodification of nouns referring to internal/external body parts; tracing the use of superordinate opposites such as *natural/unnatural, normal/abnormal* and *healthy/unhealthy* in women's magazines; investigating opposition triggers, such as *but*, to establish patterns of opposite use and creation in these texts. A tagged corpus could also investigate structures like apposition and listing to see where there are equivalences being created and where the ambiguity between these structures may be ideologically interesting. Naming conventions for body parts would also be easy to trace by computer, and confirmation of the apparent link between large size and terms like *boobs*[2] would be relatively accessible.

Perhaps the biggest challenge facing feminist linguistics in the near future is to make itself relevant again in the context of a general cultural acceptance that 'political correctness' has indeed gone mad, and in the face of young women – some of them our daughters – to whom a nose job is the most natural thing in the world.

The picture of what women and girls were reading around the turn of the millennium is not a simple one, and from a feminist perspective we may conclude that this post-structuralist confusion of messages is entirely in keeping with the post-feminist spirit of the times. The analysis presented here, however, undermines such a notion of conflicting messages to the extent that the patriarchal, clean (that is, masculine) body is still held up as superior to our own, leaky ones, and the destiny of women still tied intrinsically to childbirth and other bodily functions is not celebrated in a second-wave feminist manner, so much as managed and coped with in an increasingly technological manner. The illusion of the ever-youthful perfect body is repeatedly held up here as achievable, though only through the most extreme of means. What's most striking of all, perhaps, is that one of the bundle of 'readers' that makes up our individual identity can usually be found to agree.

Notes

1 Studying the Language of the Female Body

1 Some large-scale corpus studies informed by CDA have been undertaken, most notably Baker (2006).

2 The arguments of this section are discussed in more detail in Jeffries (2000). The idiom of 'throwing out the baby with the bathwater' was first used by me in relation to the rejection of code-based theories of language in that article.

3 Note that implicatures, first proposed by Grice (1975) are more technically defined than the vague 'implications' of everyday life and depend on the flouting of conversational maxims. See Chapter 5, and in particular page 131, for more information.

4 There may be some mileage in using some of the more recent developments in cognitive stylistics, including Text World Theory, Deictic Shift Theory and Blending Theory to explore the extent of ideological influence that texts may have and the mechanisms by which this influence is exerted. Work in literary stylistics on empathy and affect may be of great interest to such an endeavour.

5 Though, admittedly, some of the force of his attack is that counter-evidence is very clearly ignored in favour of the preferred interpretation.

6 A southern British English intonation system is assumed here, whereby the fall-rise in each case indicates the 'proclaiming tone' of David Brazil's (1997) discourse intonation system of notation.

7 Which is not to deny that men have to do so too, but to emphasize the fact that women's bodies present a particular range of challenges to certain kinds of public activity which are perhaps not as severe for men.

8 Notice, however, that the problematic body is not left as the only outcome, as we shall see in reference to the 'happy ending' rhetorical strategy in Chapter 2.

2 Genre, Text Type and Rhetorical Strategy

1 This research was carried out with girls in a youth organization of about 10–11 years old and with sixth formers aged 17–18 years. They were given a questionnaire on their reading habits and amongst other things they were asked whether they would only read sections of articles that were relevant to them. They overwhelmingly answered 'no' – they read everything, in case it might be relevant in the future.

2 Though I am calling these text types 'quizzes', they are in fact more like questionnaires. However, the magazines themselves tend to use the term 'quiz' for this text type and they are distinct from the kind of questionnaire used by researchers where the results are cumulative, rather than individual as in these cases.

3 Naming and Describing

1 In one case here the man is also referred to as his penis, though whether this is common or spreads more widely to other body parts as it does for women, it is hard to know.

4 Equating, Contrasting, Enumerating and Exemplifying

1 A book on this topic is currently being produced by the author, and the PhD thesis of Matt Davies (Huddersfield) will also be an investigation of the textual construction of opposites.

2 Some grammatical models may well hypothesize that such structures are reduced relative clauses, with ellipses accounting for the missing words. This example would thus be derived from *Mr Bun, who is the baker.* However, this point does not distinguish between the list and the co-referential apposition at surface structure level, and the reader is thus obliged to draw some conclusions which are relevant for him/herself.

5 Assuming and Implying

1 It is generally the case that definite noun phrases do trigger existential presuppositions and indefinite ones do not. However, the context can alter this general rule, as in the current case.

8 Conclusion

1 It is no comfort to realize that men are travelling down a similar road, albeit at a slower pace, and not in such numbers. A casual glance at the many male magazines on display in W.H.Smith would confirm that male looks are also beginning to be a major drain on their finances, and male anorexia and plastic surgery are on the increase.

2 One interesting observation is the complete lack of the use of the word *tits* in this data. It would, presumably, occur frequently in 'lads' magazines' and the differences could easily be studied in a corpus project. It is also interestingly different in its sound symbolism, having a close front vowel and sharp (unvoiced) plosive consonants, in contrast to the open back vowel and voiced consonants of *boobs.* Thanks to Dan McIntyre for this latter point.

Bibliography

Abelove, H., Barale, M.A. and Halperin, D.M. (eds) (1993) *The Lesbian and Gay Studies Reader*. New York and London: Routledge.

Atkinson, J.M. (1984) *Our Masters' Voices: The Language and Body Language of Politics*. London: Methuen.

Baker, P. (2006) *Using Corpora in Discourse Analysis*. London: Continuum.

Bakare-Yusuf, B. (1999) 'The Economy of Violence: Black Bodies and the Unspeakable Terror' in Price and Shildnick: 311–23.

Battersby, C. (1999) 'Her Body/Her Boundaries', in Price and Shildrick: 341–58.

Berlin, B. and Kay, P. (1969) *Basic Color Terms: Their Universality and Evolution*. Berkeley, Los Angeles: University of California Press.

Brazil, P. (1997) *The Communicative Value of Internalia*. Cambridge: Cambridge University Press.

Butler, J. (1999) 'Bodies that Matter' in Price and Shildrick: 235–45.

Cameron, D. (ed.) (1990) *The Feminist Critique of Language: A Reader*, 1st edn. London: Routledge.

Cameron, D. (ed.) (1998) *The Feminist Critique of Language: A Reader*, 2nd edn. London: Routledge.

Clancy-Smith, J. (2006) *Exemplary Women and Sacred Journeys: Women and Gender in Judaism, Christianity, and Islam from Late Antiquity to the Eve of Modernity*. Bloomington, Indiana: American Historical Association.

Cook, G. (1992) *The Discourse of Advertising*. London: Routledge.

Croft, W. and Cruse, D.A. (2004) *Cognitive Linguistics*. Cambridge: Cambridge University Press.

Cruse, D.A. (1986) *Lexical Semantics*. Cambridge: Cambridge University Press.

Cruse, D.A. (2004) *Meaning in Language: An Introduction to Semantics and Pragmatics*, 2nd edn. Oxford: Oxford University Press.

Culler, J. (1975) *Structuralist Poetics: Structuralism, Linguistics and the Study of Literature*. London: Routledge & Kegan Paul.

Dancygier, B. (2005) 'Blending and Narrative Viewpoint: Jonathan Raban's Travels through Mental Spaces', *Language and Literature*, 14(2): 99–127.

Davies, M. (2007) 'Construction of Out-Groups: A Study in Opposition-Creation', unpublished PhD thesis, University of Huddersfield.

Edwards, D. and Potter, J. (1992) *Discursive Psychology*. London: Sage.

Emmott, C. (1999) *Narrative Comprehension*. Oxford: Oxford University Press.

Fairclough, N. (1989) *Language and Power*. London: Longman.

Fairclough, N. (1995) *Critical Discourse Analysis*. London: Longman

Ferguson, M. (1985) *Forever Feminine: Women's Magazines and the Cult of Femininity*. London: Gower.

Fowler, R. (1991) *Language in the News. Discourse and Ideology in the Press*. London: Routledge.

Gatens, M. (1999) 'Power, Bodies and Difference' in Price and Shildrick: 227–34.

Gibbs, R. (1994) *The Poetics of Mind: Figurative Thought, Language, and Understanding*. New York: Cambridge University Press.

Grice, H.P. (1975) 'Logic and Conversation', in P. Cole and J.L. Morgan (eds), *Syntax and Semantics* Vol 3: *Speech Acts*. New York: Academic Press, pp. 41–58.

Grogan, S. (1999) *Body Image: Understanding Body Dissatisfaction in Men, Women and Children*. London: Routledge.

Grogan, S., Williams, Z. and Corner, M. (1996) 'The Effects of Viewing Same Gender Photographic Models on body Satisfaction.' *Women and Psychology Quarterly*, 20: 569–75.

Halliday, M. (1985) *An Introduction to Functional Grammar*. London: Arnold.

Halmari, H. (ed.) (2004) *Persuasion Across Genres. A Linguistic Approach*. Philadelphia: John Benjamins.

Henry, A. (2004) *Not My Mother's Sister: Generational Conflict and Third-Wave Feminism*. Bloomington, Indiana: Indiana University Press.

Hepburn, A. (2002) 'Figuring Gender in Teachers' Talk about School Bullying', in P. McIlvenny (ed.), *Talking Gender and Sexuality*. Philadelphia: John Benjamins, pp. 273–97.

Holt, L. (1993) 'The Structure of Death Announcements: Looking on the Bright Side of Death', *Text*, 13(2): 189–217.

Jäger, S. (2002) 'Discourse and Knowledge: Theoretical and Methodological Aspects of a Critical Discourse and Dispositive Analysis', in Wodak *op.cit.*: 32–62.

Jefferson, G. (1980) 'On "Trouble-Premonitory" Response to Inquiry', *Sociological Inquiry*, 50: 153–85.

Jefferson, G. (1990) 'List Construction as a Task and Resource', in G. Psathas (ed.), *Interaction Competence*. Lanham, MD: University Press of America.

Jeffries, L. (1994) 'Language in Common: Apposition in Contemporary Poetry by Women', in K. Wales (ed.), *Feminist Linguistics in Literary Criticism*. London: Boydell & Brewer, pp. 21–50.

Jeffries, L. (2000) 'Don't Throw out the Baby with the Bathwater: In Defence of Theoretical Eclecticism in Stylistics', PALA Occasional Papers no. 12.

Jeffries, L. (2001) 'Schema Theory and White Asparagus: Readers of Literature as Culturally Multilingual', *Language and Literature*, 10(4): 325–44.

Jeffries, L. (forthcoming) *Opposites We Die By: The Textual Construction of Semantic Opposition*. Cambridge: Cambridge University Press.

Jones, S. (2002) *Antonymy: A Corpus-based Perspective*. London and New York: Routledge.

Jones, V. (1990) *Women in the Eighteenth Century: Constructions of Femininity*. London and New York: Routledge.

Katz, J.J. and Postal, P. (1964) *An Integrated Theory of Linguistic Descriptions*. Cambridge, Mass. The MIT Press.

Kress, G. (1993) 'Cultural Considerations in Linguistic Description', in D. Graddol *et al.* (eds), *Language and Culture*. Clevedon, UK: Multilingual Matters.

Labov, W. (2006) *The Social Stratification of English in New York City*, 2nd edn. Cambridge: Cambridge University Press.

Lakoff, G. and Johnson, M. (1980) *Metaphors We Live By*. Chicago: University of Chicago Press.

Lakoff, G. and Turner, M. (1989) *More than Cool Reason: A Field Guide to Poetic Metaphor*. Chicago: University of Chicago Press.

Lanis, K. (1995) 'Images of Women in Advertisements – Effects on Attitudes Related to Sexual Aggression', *Sex Roles*, 32 (9–10): 639–49.

Leech, G. and Short, M. (1981) *Style in Fiction*. London: Longman.
Levinson, S. (1983) *Pragmatics*. Cambridge: Cambridge University Press.
Lucy, J. (1997) 'Linguistic Relativity' *Annual Review of Anthropology*, 26: 291–312.
Lyons, J. (1997) *Semantics, Vol. I*. Cambridge: Cambridge University Press.
Mackay, R. (1996) 'Mything the Point: A Critique of Objective Stylistics', *Language and Communication*, 16(1): 81–93.
Mackay, R. (1999) 'There Goes the Other Foot – a Reply to Short *et al.*', *Language and Literature*, 8(1): 59–66.
MacLaury, R. (1991) 'Prototypes Revisited', *Annual Review of Anthropology*, 20: 55–74.
McIntyre, D. (2006) *Point of View in Plays*. Amsterdam: John Benjamins.
Meredith, S. (1985) *Usborne Facts of Life: Growing Up*. London: Usborne.
Mettinger, A. (1994) *Aspects of Semantic Opposition in English*. Oxford: Clarendon Press.
Milroy, L. (1980) *Language and Social Networks*, 2nd edn. Oxford: Blackwell.
Morrish, E. (2002) 'The Case of the Indefinite Pronoun. Discourse and the Concealment of Lesbian Identity in Class', in Sunderland: 177–92.
Pope, R. (1995) *Textual Intervention*. London: Routledge.
Potter, J. (1996) *Representing Reality: Discourse, Rhetoric and Social Construction*. London: Sage.
Price, J. and Shildrick, M. (eds) (1999) *Feminist Theory and the Body: A Reader*. Edinburgh: Edinburgh University Press.
Rich, A. (1993) 'Compulsory Heterosexuality and Lesbian Existence' (orig. pub. 1982), in Abelove *et al.*, *The Lesbian and Gay Studies Reader*: 227–54.
Rosch, E. (1973) 'Natural Categories', *Cognitive Psychology*, 4: 328–50.
Rosch, E. (1978) 'Principles of Categorisation', in E. Rosch and B. Lloyd (eds), *Cognition and Categorisation*. Hillsdale, New Jersey: Lawrence Erlbaum Associates.
Schulz, M. (1990) 'The Semantic Derogation of Woman', in Cameron *op.cit.*: (134–47).
Semino, E. and Short, M. (2004) *Corpus Stylistics: The Presentation of Speech, Writing and Thought in a Corpus of English Writing*. London: Routledge.
Short, M., Freeman, D., van Peer, W. and Simpson, P. (1998) 'Stylistics, Criticism and Mythrepresentation Again: Squaring the Circle with Ray Mackay's Subjective Solution for All Problems', in *Language and Literature*, 7(1): 39–50.
Simpson, P. (1993) *Language, Ideology and Point of View*. London: Routledge.
Steen, G. (2002) 'Towards a Procedure for Metaphor Identification', *Language and Literature*, 11(1): 17–33.
Stockwell, P. (2002) *Cognitive Poetics: An Introduction*. London: Routledge.
Sunderland, J. (2002) *Gender Identity and Discourse Analysis*. Philadelphia, PA: John Benjamins.
Swales, J.M. (1990) *Genre Analysis: English in Academic and Research Settings*. Cambridge: Cambridge University Press.
Terry V.S. and Schiappa E. (1999) 'Disclosing Antifeminism in Michael Crichton's Postfeminist Disclosure', *Journal of Communication Inquiry*, 23(1): 68–9.
Thomas, J. (1986) 'The Dynamics of Discourse. A Pragmatic Analysis of Confrontational Interaction', unpublished Doctoral dissertation, Lancaster University.
Toolan, M. (1997) 'What is Critical Discourse Analysis and Why are People Saying such Terrible Things about it?', *Language and Literature*, 6(2): 83–103.

Toolan, M. (1996) *Total Speech: An Integrational Linguistic Approach to Language.* Durham, USA: Duke University Press.

Trask, R.L. (1998) *Key Concepts in Language and Linguistics.* Florence, KY, USA: Routledge.

Trudgill, P. (1974) *Sociolinguistics: An Introduction.* Harmondsworth: Pelican.

Tuffin, K. (2002) 'Attitudes, Culture and Emotion in Police Talk', in H. Giles (ed.), *Law Enforcement, Communication, and Community.* Philadelphia, PA, USA: John Benjamins, pp. 67–83.

van Dijk, T. (2002) 'Multidisciplinary CDA: A Plea for Diversity', in Wodak *op.cit.*: 95–120.

van Leeuwen, T. (1996) 'The Representation of Social Actors', in C. Caldas-Coulthard and M. Coulthard (eds), *Texts and Practices.* London: Routledge.

Walsh, C. (2001) *Gender and Discourse: Language and Power in Politics, the Church and Organisations.* London: Longman.

Werth, P. (1999) *Text Worlds: Representing Conceptual Space in Discourse.* London: Longman.

Widdowson, H.G. (1996) 'Notes and Discussion: Reply to Fairclough: Discourse and Intepretation: Conjectures and Refutations', *Language and Literature*, 5(1): 57–69.

Widdowson, H.G. (1998) 'The Theory and Practice of Critical Discourse Analysis', *Applied Linguistics*, 19(1): 136–151.

Wodak, R. ed. (2002) *Methods of Critical Discourse Analysis.* London: Sage.

Wolf Thompson, E. (1947) *Education for Ladies, 1830–1860.* Morningside Heights, New York: King's Crown Press.

Zuckerman, M. (1991) *Sources on the History of Women's Magazines, 1792–1960.* Westport, Conn.: Greenwood Press.

Zuckerman, M. (1998) *A History of Popular Women's Magazines in the United States, 1792–1995.* Westport, Conn.: Greenwood Press.

Index